PEOPLE OF THE

EARTH

AMERICAN INDIANS OF COLORADO

Sally Crum

ANCIENT CITY PRESS
SANTA FE, NEW MEXICO

▲

Book designed by Shadow Canyon Graphics

Front cover illustration and design by Faith DeLong

International Standard Book Number
0-941270-88-2 clothbound
0-941270-89-0 paperback

Library of Congress Cataloging-in-Publication Data

Crum, Sally.
    People of the red earth: American Indians of Colorado / by Sally Crum
       1st ed.
       p. cm.
    Includes bibliographical references and index.
    ISBN 0-941270-88-2 (clothbound: acid-free paper).
    ISBN 0-941270-89-0 (pbk: acid-free paper)
       1. Indians of North America — Colorado — Antiquities.
       2. Indians of North America — Colorado — History.
       3. Indians of North America — Colorado — Social life and customs.
       4. Colorado — Antiquities.
       I. Title.
    E78.C6C78 1996
    978.8'01—dc20   95-32115
                                                    CIP

10 9 8 7 6 5 4 3 2 1

▲

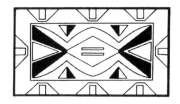

Contents

▲ ▲

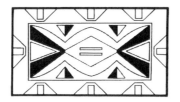

Preface

▲ ▲

*C*OLORADO'S HUMAN HISTORY DATES BACK at least twelve thousand years when Paleo-Indians, armed only with spears, hunted woolly mammoths and huge species of bison. When the giant mammals became extinct, people increased their hunting of smaller animals and gathering of a wide variety of wild plants—a somewhat dependable lifestyle that survived until the nineteenth century in some parts of the state.

Agricultural civilizations that flourished along the great rivers of the Midwest and in Mexico had some effect on the people of Colorado. By a.d. 500, a lifestyle based on agriculture had become dominant in the Four Corners region (where the states of Utah, Colorado, Arizona, and New Mexico join), and some hunters on the eastern plains pursued farming part-time. Although the farmers abandoned the southwestern part of Colorado by a.d. 1300, Indian tribes still hunted and some farmed part-time in the eastern part of the state until the arrival of Spanish horses altered their lifestyle in the 1600s. At that time a new culture centered around horses and their use for raiding and buffalo hunting was adopted by all Colorado peoples, including the Utes, who are considered the first historic tribe in the state. These cultures based on buffalo hunting were unrivaled in their glory—until their calculated and thorough destruction by non-Indians.

It took only a little over two decades for Euro-Americans to decimate the millions of buffalo which had been the economic base of Colorado tribes for nearly twelve thousand years. The Indians, who had ranged over 35 million acres, were confined to small reservations. Of the dozen or so tribes that had lived or hunted in Colorado, most were moved by force to Oklahoma, Montana, Wyoming, or Utah; only two bands of Utes remained in the southwestern part of Colorado. Today, nearly twenty-one thousand Indians live in Colorado, many of them in large cities, particularly Denver. Although many are from tribes that did not originally inhabit the state, they share a universal pride in their heritage.

This book presents an overview for the general public as well as for advanced high school and undergraduate college students who want information about Colorado's first inhabitants. Because an integral part of understanding these early people is a knowledge of their descendants, the book also includes accounts of the cultures of contemporary Indians living in Colorado and tribes now located elsewhere that once lived in the state. In addition, each historical chapter includes a list of sites and places to visit to obtain further information about the tribes. Indians are not symbols of a romantic past but people whose varied lives unfold not only on reservations but in cities and towns across the nation.

The terms "American Indian" and "Indian" are used in this book because they seem to be the most accepted by those whose ancestors lived on this continent before it was settled by people from other countries. Although technically incorrect (because they derive from Christopher Columbus's mistaken notion that he had landed in India rather than North America), the terms have been in use so long that most Indians feel that the words are no longer offensive and that the name "Native American" is inaccurate because it applies to anyone born here. Whenever possible, however, it is preferable to call someone by the name of the specific tribe, or nation, to which he or she belongs, such as Ute, Cheyenne, Arapahoe, and so forth.

It has been the practice of Indians to pass down legends, history, traditions, morals, and standards through oral tradition—a method of memorization and communication much more difficult than reading books. Although some books and articles have been written by Indians, as well as by people who have lived with various tribes, most information about the historic Indians of Colorado is available to non-Indians only through the writings of other non-Indians—by people such as early explorers, fur traders, emigrants, army officers, historians, and anthropologists, who gathered knowledge through observation and enquiry. Several books are available on prehistoric cultures and historic Indian tribes of Colorado, notably Steve Cassells's *The Archaeology of Colorado* (a revised edition is being published that contains new information about recent excavations and other studies) and J. Donald Hughes's *American Indians in Colorado*. Sally J. Cole's *Legacy on Stone: Rock Art of the Colorado Plateau and Four Corners Region* is an excellent overview of the rock art of the Colorado Plateau. This book, *People of the Red Earth: American Indians of Colorado,* draws from the scholarly research of these and other references, including recent archaeological reports, to provide general background information on the history of Indians in Colorado. Although I have attempted to be objective in writing this book, it is nevertheless a work by a non-Indian. I hope that future books on this topic will be written by Indian people so that their perspectives can be shared.

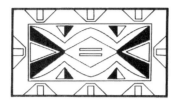

Acknowledgements

MANY OF THE PEOPLE WHO REVIEWED my manuscript at various stages are descendants of Colorado's original inhabitants, and I am grateful for their input. These include Deborah Ahtone, Kiowa, editor of the *Feather Review* and *Kiowa Indian News*; Jacob Ahtone, elder and former Kiowa tribal chairman and administrator; Jesse Botone, Cheyenne-Arapahoe; the late Geraldine Botone, Cheyenne-Arapahoe; Annabelle Eagle, elder, Southern Ute; Alden Naranjo, historian, Southern Ute; Clifford Duncan, historian, Northern Ute; Betsy Chapoose, director of the Ute Cultural Rights and Protection Department, Northern Ute; Merle Haas, storyteller and Arapahoe language and culture curriculum specialist, Wyoming Indian School, Northern Arapahoe; Alonzo Moss, Sr., elder, Northern Arapahoe; Richard Moss, Northern Arapahoe; Ira Sinkey, Southern Arapahoe; Virgil Franklin, Sr., Southern Arapahoe; Ozzie Red Elk, director, Comanche Education Department, Lawton, Oklahoma, Comanche; Abraham Spotted Elk, elder, Northern Cheyenne; Jennie Parker, Northern Cheyenne Tribal Council member and Cheyenne culture studies coordinator, Dull Knife Memorial College, Lame Deer, Montana; and Steve Small, tribal planner, Northern Cheyenne, Lame Deer, Montana.

Many thanks also to the following people who reviewed the book, or portions pertaining to their expertise: Judith Davis, Acting Academic Dean, Dull Knife Memorial College; Lynn Hartmann, public relations coordinator for the Ute Mountain Utes; Tom Rome, historian; Susan Collins, Colorado State Archaeologist; Sally J. Cole, Steve Cassells, Laurie Reiser, Deb Angulski, Susan Chandler, Kevin Black, and O D Hand, archaeologists; Richard Sims, director, Museum of Western Colorado; Marlise Reed, student; Herm Hoops, interpreter, Dinosaur National Monument; and Mary Tarleton, teacher.

▲

I am indebted as well to the following people who provided books or articles, or information over the phone: Sue Judis, interpreter, Great Sand Dunes National Monument; Deb Dandridge, archaeologist, Comanche National Grasslands, U.S. Forest Service; Mike Selle, archaeologist, Bureau of Land Management, White River Resource Area; Frank Rupp, archaeologist, Bureau of Land Management, Kremmling Resource Area; Michael Piontkowski, archaeologist, Bureau of Land Management, Grand Junction Resource Area; Susan Collins, Colorado State Archaeologist; and Karen Brockman and Carl Conner, private contracting archaeologists. I owe thanks to Bill Schroer for the use of his computer during the initial stages of the project. Hail to Danni Langdon and Carl Jacobson for putting up with my total abuse of their computer as well as providing meals and laughter every weekend during the last summer of the book's completion—and to Danni for her voluntary editorial contributions. Three cheers to Camelia Berry for her patience and talent in completing the illustrations! Ninety-four-year-young Harriet Walck prompted me with enthusiastic moral support throughout the entire project. Thanks to Mom, Dad, and brother Pete for sharing with me their interest in the land and the history of its people. And to Ann Mason, editor, and Mary Powell, publisher, for their patience in working with someone with rare access to a telephone.

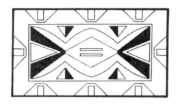

1

The Paleo-Indians

▲ ▲

PEOPLE HUNTED AND GATHERED FOOD in Colorado at least as early as twelve thousand years ago. Although an archaeological site in Texas may date to thirty-seven thousand years ago, this date is disputed, and the earliest known sites in Colorado have been radiocarbon dated at no more than 12,000 B.P. (before present). Archaeologists call the first humans to occupy the New World Paleo-Indians, the word *paleo* meaning ancient in Greek.

Many American Indian legends, such as that of the Hopi of Arizona, describe people's emergence from three underworlds to the one where they now live. Creation stories of Colorado tribes often describe animals helping to bring humans into the world (the coyote in the case of the Utes). Despite differences in creation stories, according to most traditional beliefs Indian tribes have always been in North America.

Some researchers, such as Thor Hyerdal, think that people may have arrived in the Americas on boats, drifting from the Old World on ocean currents. The most popular theory among archaeologists, however, is that people crossed a great land bridge from Siberia, which today is the island-dotted passage called the Bering Strait. During the Ice Age, ocean water was taken up by glaciers, huge masses of ice that slowly moved down the northern portions of what we know as the United States. The lowered sea level exposed a land mass so large that it is often referred to as the continent of Beringia. It is likely that small groups of hunters followed herds of caribou, mammoths (large elephantlike mammals that became extinct after the Ice Age), and other large beasts east from Asia towards Alaska. Although some may have followed the coast, probably most traveled inland, unaware that they were crossing a land bridge because the land all looked the same to them—vast tundra.

After generations of slow migration south, descendants of these first hunters probably made their way down the east side of the Rocky Mountains through an ice-free corridor. As they entered the new territory of the Great Plains, they saw huge species of wild animals, including giant ground sloths and seven-foot-long beavers. The first Americans continued to hunt and migrate, some eventually reaching the southern tip of South America.

Gradually, the land bridge connecting Asia to North America disappeared under the water of the melted glaciers, but people still continued to come to the New World. The last ones to cross from Asia to America were Eskimos and Aleuts, who paddled from island to island in boats until they reached the Alaskan shore. Today, Eskimos and Aleuts speak languages similar to those of their relatives in Siberia. Modern transportation has enabled the groups to participate in shared religious ceremonies, which have remained similar despite geographical and temporal separation.

However, the first people who migrated farther, into South America, have less in common with Asians. Their languages have no similarity, and, aside from likenesses in their teeth (particularly molars), they are very different physically. This suggests that South American Indians must have separated from their motherland many thousands of years ago.

What was Colorado like twelve thousand years ago? The climate was cooler because of the glaciers. Although the continental ice sheet did not reach as far south as Colorado, smaller alpine glaciers hollowed out huge valleys in the Rocky Mountains. Large lakes and marshes were connected by gushing streams. Along with giant sloths and beavers as large as bears, the water and lush grasslands supported herds of mammoths, mastodons, giant bison (much larger than today's buffalo), camels, and horses, as well as elk, deer, antelope, and other species still known today. Except for a small, curly-haired variety that persisted in the northern part of the continent, the horse became extinct in North America after the Ice Age and did not reappear in the New World until it was brought by the Spaniards in the mid-1500s.

Colorado's first hunters artfully fashioned sharp points of stone called projectile points by archaeologists. These they attached to long spears by slipping them into notches at the ends of the spears, which were made from straightened shafts of willow or other long-branched trees. The term "projectile point" applies to both spear points and arrowheads, but true arrowheads were not made until the bow and arrow were introduced less than two thousand years ago. A projectile point was tied to a spear with sinew, the stringy muscle attachments or tendons from a hoofed animal's back or leg. The spear was hooked to a spear thrower, called an *atlatl,* an Aztec word (Figure 4, page 11). A hunter would raise the atlatl over his shoulder and throw the spear forward. Acting as an extension of the hunter's arm, the atlatl allowed a spear to be thrown farther and with greater force.

THE CLOVIS PEOPLE—HUNTERS OF MAMMOTHS

Although future excavation may unearth evidence of an older tradition, the Clovis is presently considered the first culture in the New World, flourishing roughly twelve thousand years ago. The points used by the early mammoth hunters of this culture are called Clovis points, named after a site near Clovis, New Mexico, where such points were originally found.

Clovis points are four to five inches long and have a groove, or "flute," running partway up the center of the point from the base. This groove probably allowed the point to be more securely attached to the spear shaft. Because fluting requires much skill, it is likely that Clovis hunters tried to retrieve the finely made points from the bodies of the animals they killed so the points could be reused.

In his excellent book *The Archaeology of Colorado*, Steve Cassells gives detailed information on excavations that provides the basis for much of the material on Paleo-Indian and Archaic sites.

Several sites in Colorado have yielded mammoth bones in probable association with man-made tools. One, the Lamb Springs site, is located near the town of Littleton, just outside of Denver. Another, the Dent site, in the region of the South Platte River near Greeley, yielded the remains of twelve mammoths speared by Clovis points, found eroding out of a stream bank. A mystery surrounds these dead mammoths; they were not cut up after they died. No butcher marks were present on the bones. This indicates that they were perhaps wounded by hunters, escaped, and died sometime later. Other animal bones found at Clovis sites suggest that the human diet of the time was diverse and included small game as well as mammoths. In fact, because of the great effort required to kill even a few mammoths a year, the Clovis people probably survived on plants and small game much of the time.

Hunters of mammoths risked injury and death because they had to get very close to the animals to thrust their spears hard enough to penetrate the thick skin. Isolating a mammoth from the rest of the herd would have been a challenge since the herd was probably protective of individual members, particularly the young ones. Once isolated, a mammoth, which had tusks over eight feet long and weighed up to ten tons, was probably too strong to be killed outright and instead had to be wounded and followed, perhaps for days, until it was weak enough to be finished off. Some hunters might have torn leg tendons with stone knives to cripple the animal while others perhaps thrust spears through the inch-thick skin to pierce the lungs and heart.

It has been proposed that Clovis hunters speared mammoths in water holes, where they would have bogged down and had trouble escaping. However, George Frison, noted archaeologist of the Great Plains (including eastern Colorado), believes that strong mammoths would have had no trouble extricating themselves from mud, and that, had one been killed in a bog, removal of the meat from the huge submerged body would have been difficult.

The ancient Clovis mammoth hunters inspire visions of bravery and daring. Although current archaeological evidence indicates the culture lasted only a thousand years, it is possible that future work may produce artifacts and features that push back the dates of Colorado's first people several millennia prior to 12,000 B.P.

Figure 1:
Although younger mammoths were easier to kill, Clovis hunters probably had to deal with
enraged mothers if the hunters were detected.

THE FOLSOM PEOPLE—HUNTERS OF BISON

Roughly eleven thousand years ago, the climate became warmer. The massive ice sheet that covered much of the northern United States melted, and water flowed back to the oceans, covering the land bridge connecting Asia and Alaska. Many Ice Age mammals—the camel, ground sloth, dire wolf, saber-toothed tiger, short-faced bear, horse, and mammoth—became extinct at this time, the cause of which is disputed.

Although there was still much more water than there is now and lush grasses abounded, it is possible that mammoths, which required up to fifty gallons of water per day, may have died of lack of water or may have had difficulty digesting the new grasses, which were much shorter and tougher. In addition, extreme seasonal changes—freezing winters, hot summers—may have affected their reproductive cycles. It also may be possible that the Clovis people overhunted some species of animals. Prairie fires set by man could have driven the animals over cliffs or concentrated them in dead-end arroyos, where, over the years, they were slaughtered by the thousands. But were there enough Clovis hunters to cause the extinction of so many animal species? An estimate cited in the Time-Life book *The First Americans* suggests that within only three hundred years, the population of an original band of one hundred could have skyrocketed to half a million because of the massive amounts of protein being consumed by the big game hunters. At this rate, if only 25 percent of the people hunted, obtaining two tons of meat per month, they could have caused the extinction of the species within a thousand years. This estimate, however, does not address the many natural hazards faced by humans, which probably kept the population lower than it could have been; it is also questionable whether the Clovis hunters' protein-rich diets would have resulted in such an increased population.

Regardless of cause, with many of the large Ice Age mammals gone, the long lancelike Clovis point was no longer needed. A shorter projectile point with a longer groove in the center now appeared. Named for Folsom, New Mexico, where similar spear points were found imbedded between the ribs of bison, these shorter points are called Folsom points and are present, sometimes in great numbers, at sites all over the United States, including Colorado.

During this time the early bison, which were much larger than their modern relatives the buffalo, roamed much of the continent. (In

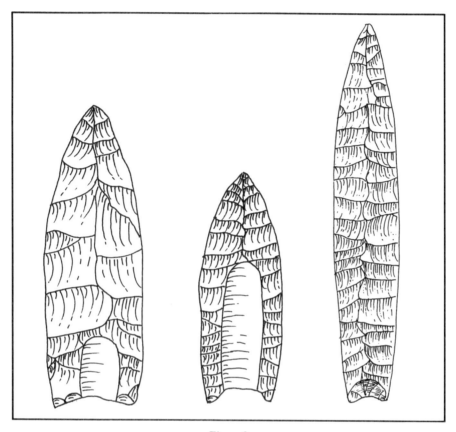

Figure 2:
Clovis points (left) hafted to spears were used to hunt mammoths. Folsom points (center) were shorter, fluted, and were thrown at the ancestors of today's smaller bison. Long, unfluted Plano spear points (right) were hurled at bison during communal game drives.

this book the term "bison," the correct name for buffalo, is used when referring to prehistoric hunting practices and the term "buffalo" when discussing historic Plains hunters.)

Even though they hunted bison, the Folsom people may not have wandered as much as their predecessors, the Clovis people, did. An indication of this is a site near Albuquerque, New Mexico, that contained circular depressions which probably served as foundations for brush- and mud-covered houses. Among the remains were over eight thousand Folsom points. Possibly the oldest village yet found in the New World, this site suggests that Folsom people sometimes had a "home base" from which they made hunting trips. The women could collect nuts, berries, and other wild foods from the surrounding area and carry them back, perhaps using the bladders of bison or other animals, just as historic Plains groups did. Perishable items such as these deteriorate over time and leave no remains. Most Folsom people probably did not live in permanent houses; no Folsom houses have been found in Colorado. Rock overhangs and tents of bison hide placed over wooden poles or brush structures called wickiups would have been more logical shelters for people following animal herds.

One of the most important Folsom sites in the New World was discovered in 1924 on the Lindenmeier ranch in the Colorado foothills northeast of Fort Collins (Figure 5, pages 12–13). Much information was obtained from the Lindenmeier site because it was a campsite not a kill site. Numerous bones of animals were found there (bison, antelope, rabbit, fox, wolf, coyote, and turtle). Small animals had been carried to the camp whole, but large animals had been butchered elsewhere with sharp stone knives and brought back to camp in smaller pieces. Hundreds of stone knives and scrapers were also found. The thin knives were probably used to cut through tough tendons and muscles, while scrapers were used to shave hair from animal skins before they were processed to make tents and clothing.

Many of the tools found at the Lindenmeier site were made of obsidian, a hard, glassy volcanic rock much more desirable than the local Colorado cherts. Archaeologists traced the obsidian to two areas— one now known as Yellowstone National Park, over 350 miles away, and the other a quarry in New Mexico. Either the Folsom hunters ranged for hundreds of miles, or trading was already a profitable business for some individuals who could carry heavy loads of rock.

The most exciting discovery at the Lindenmeier site was a series of unfinished Folsom points, which gave archaeologists insight into the process by which these beautiful points were made. Even today's best "flintnappers," those who make stone tools as a hobby or for educational purposes, find it difficult to copy Folsom points. Other artifacts of interest included bone gaming pieces, used in gambling much like cards or dice, and bone knives and needles. No doubt the needles were threaded with sinew and used to sew clothing and tents of bison or antelope hide.

Folsom sites have also been discovered near Great Sand Dunes National Monument in the San Luis Valley of south-central Colorado (Figure 5, pages 12–13). There water and lush grasses attracted thousands of bison and other animals and, in turn, Folsom hunters. At Stewart's Cattle Guard site, at least eight bison apparently had been killed at one time or in a series of closely timed events. The front and hindquarters and rib slabs had been carried to a nearby camp, where meat was removed from the bones and marrow was extracted. (Historic groups froze bones and ate the fatty marrow in the spring. After pounding the marrow, they boiled it in water and skimmed off the fat to add to meat to make pemmican, a process Folsom people may have used.) Folsom butchering tools found at the site are of a rock type known only in Texas, further evidence that trading occurred in the days of the Folsom people.

The Folsom tradition was not confined exclusively to lower elevations. Archaeological investigations of the last decade have shown that Paleo-Indians traveled to the alpine tundra of the Colorado Rockies for trade and hunting. The Black Mountain Folsom site, near the headwaters of the Rio Grande, produced evidence of a Folsom hunters' campsite at an elevation over ten thousand feet. West of Mount Achonee, a Paleo-Indian tool-making site was excavated on the shore of Caribou Lake (Figure 5, pages 12–13). Archaeologists believe that travelers camped by the lake en route from the Plains to Middle Park, via Arapaho Pass. Trade between Plains and Great Basin groups also may have occurred at the site. The fact that Caribou Lake may have been sacred to the travelers is suggested by some Folsom artifacts found there that are thought to be offerings. Artifacts at the Lower Twin Mountain site in Middle Park indicate occupation by a bison-hunting group that made Folsom points out of local materials. Artifacts below the Folsom layer may be evidence that the site was occupied by Clovis (or earlier) people.

Much is yet to be learned about the Folsom people, whose culture persisted for about a thousand years after that of the Clovis mammoth hunters. Excavations reveal they hunted giant bison on the Colorado Plains, traded with western peoples at campsites high in the Rocky Mountains, bartered for obsidian from the Yellowstone area, and found time for leisure activities such as the universally popular sport of gambling.

THE PLANO PEOPLE—COMMUNAL GAME HUNTERS

Beginning roughly 10,000 B.P. the Folsom-style point was no longer widely used. The new style of point, the Plano point, was long and narrow and as finely worked as a Folsom point but had no center groove.

Perhaps a new method of attaching a point to a spear shaft was invented, and the point's center groove was no longer needed (Figure 2, page 7). The people who produced the new points are called Plano.

Plano sites are numerous in Colorado. Most are located on the Plains, some of them places where hundreds of bison were killed. Such mass slaughter required social organization: many people had to work together to herd the animals into game drives, corridors of rocks or branches leading into traps or over cliffs. If the bison didn't die from trauma, from the fall, or from being crushed by the animals falling on top of them, they were speared to death. Because families had to assemble in larger groups for these hunts, no doubt such hunts were also times of courtship, marriage, ceremonies, and feasting.

If tasks were assigned among the Plano people as they are in hunter-gatherer societies today, women not only butchered and prepared the meat, hides, and clothing, but spent much of their time gathering wild fruits, roots, nuts, and seeds. They dried the fruit, cooked the roots, and shelled the nuts; the seeds were used to make mush, breads, and cakes. They may have been ground into flour with stones; however, no grinding stone artifacts have yet been found at Plano sites.

One intriguing Plano find, called the Jones-Miller site, was discovered near Wray in eastern Colorado (Figure 5, pages 12–13). Here in 1972 a rancher found bison bones washing out of the ground. Excavation revealed that over three hundred bison had been killed with long, narrow Plano spear points and butchered at the site. In addition, a post hole, a tiny spear point too small to use for hunting, the bones of a dog, and a bone flute were discovered, causing speculation about why such objects were at a butchering site.

In his book *The Archaeology of Colorado* Steve Cassells includes an account of a recent tribe that may provide a clue. During the winter, the Cree Indians of the eastern Plains placed a tall pole in the ground in a snowy basin near a bison herd. Offerings were attached to the pole, and a medicine man climbed the pole and played a flute to call the bison to him. All tribal members, including women and children, surrounded the herd, screaming wildly and waving blankets. The frightened bison ran into the basin, crashing into the wavering pole as the medicine man on top held on and played his flute. As the bison floundered in the deep snow, the men moved in for the kill.

Cassells speculates that a similar event may have occurred at the Jones-Miller site. Perhaps the artifacts found were tied to a pole as an

Figure 3:
A Plano shaman encourages bison into an arroyo trap
while snowshoed hunters throw spears propelled by atlatls.

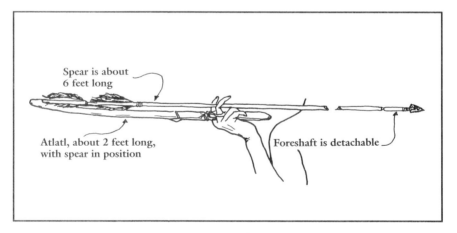

Figure 4:
With an atlatl a hunter was able to increase the distance
that a spear could be thrown.
The hunter threw the spear by hurling his arm forward,
causing the spear to fly at the target while the atlatl remained in his hand.
After LeFranc, Indians of the Four Corners.

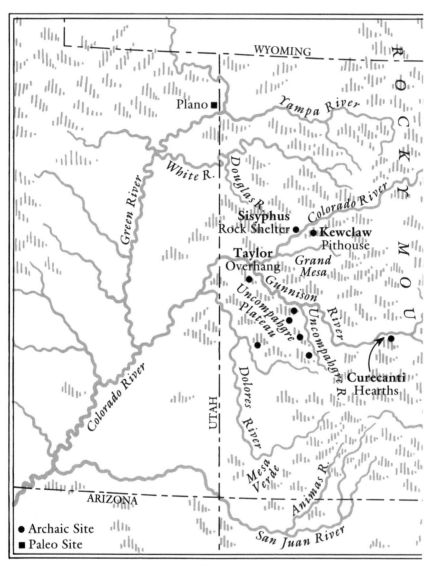

Figure 5: (This page and page 13)
Locations of some excavated Paleo-Indian and Archaic sites in Colorado.

offering. After the kill, maybe the medicine man was startled as a huge
wounded beast rolled towards him and dropped his flute, which was
crushed under the bison's shaggy body. Whatever the case, part of the
challenge of archaeology is attempting to put pieces of information
together to obtain a general knowledge of a culture using what is
known about similar historic cultures (Cassells 1983).

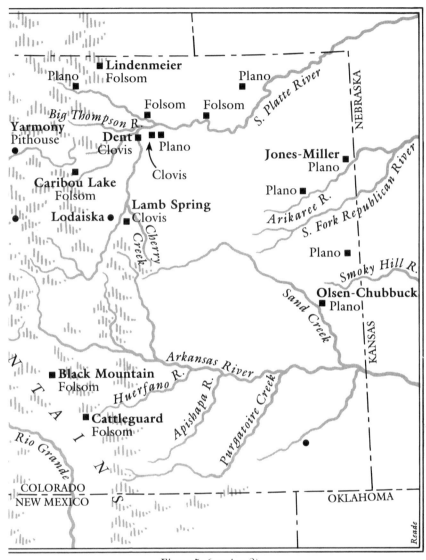

Figure 5: (continued)
Locations of some excavated Paleo-Indian and Archaic sites in Colorado.

Another Plano kill site on the eastern Colorado Plains is the Olsen-Chubbuck site north of Big Sandy Wash near the small town of Kit Carson (Figure 5, pages 12–13). Excavation revealed that over two hundred bison were herded over a bank into an arroyo. Archaeologists estimated that at least one hundred and fifty people were required to frighten and chase that many bison. They also determined that the kill occurred in the spring, around eighty-five hundred years ago. Many of the animals died from the fall, breaking legs and being smothered by those falling on top of them; others, stuck between the arroyo walls, were speared by the hunters. On many of the bones, knife cuts showed where the meat had been sliced off.

The Plano culture lasted from about ten thousand to seven thousand years ago. Although Plano subsistence was centered around the hunting of big game, wild roots, nuts, and berries were also gathered and eaten. This more varied diet laid the groundwork for the culture that followed.

PLACES TO VISIT

Colorado

Most Paleo-Indian sites which have been excavated have been covered up and are not open to the public. However, traveling east towards Kansas on Interstate 70 between Bennet and Strasburg in Adams County you can visit an old tower from which five states can be viewed. In the museum next to the tower, owned by Mr. Chubbuck, is a large collection of Paleo projectile points, some of which were found near the Olsen-Chubbuck site.

Suggestions for Further Reading

Cassells, E. Steve. *The Archaeology of Colorado*. Boulder, Colo.: Johnson Books, 1983.

Cordell, Linda S. *Prehistory of the Southwest.*Orlando, San Diego, New York, Austin, Boston, London, Sydney, Tokyo, Toronto: Academic Press/Harcourt, Brace, Jovanovich, 1984.

Frison, George C. "Experimental Use of Clovis Weaponry and Tools on African Elephants." *American Antiquity* 54, no. 4 (1989): 766–84.

———. *Prehistoric Hunters of the High Plains*. Laramie, Wyo.: Academic Press/Harcourt, Brace, Jovanovich, 1978.

Hughes, J. Donald. *American Indians in Colorado*. Boulder, Colo.: Pruett Publishing Company, 1987.

Stanford, Dennis J., and Jane S. Day, eds. *Ice Age Hunters of the Rockies*. Denver, Colo.: Denver Museum of Natural History and University Press of Colorado, 1992.

Wormington, H. M. *Ancient Man in North America*. Denver, Colo.: Denver Museum of Natural History, 1957.

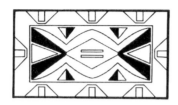

2

The Archaic
Hunters and Gatherers

▲ ▲

APPROXIMATELY SEVEN THOUSAND YEARS AGO American Indians began to hunt smaller game and gather wild plants more intensely than in Paleo times. The giant bison had become extinct, as had the earlier Ice Age mammals. Hunters now speared or trapped smaller bison, deer, antelope, bighorn sheep, wolves, rabbits, squirrels, mice, and birds, as well as snakes and lizards. This culture, with its emphasis on hunting a great variety of game and gathering numerous edible plants, is called the Archaic, which means "old." The wider variety of nutritious foods may have been responsible for an even larger population than in Paleo times. A typical band of hunters and gatherers probably consisted of several nuclear families and numbered as many as fifty.

Figure 6:
Women and children spent much of the summer gathering wild seeds and
berries in huge baskets. A tumpline across the forehead supported
the heavy basket, which rested on the carrier's back.

As did their Folsom and Clovis predecessors, Archaic people moved seasonally, following herds of deer, elk, bighorn or mountain sheep, antelope, and bison. When berry bushes or yampa and other roots ripened, small bands packed up baskets, tents, and children and followed well-known routes to the available wild food. Here they stayed for days, collecting berries and roots. Then a herd of antelope might be sighted, and the band would break camp to follow the herd in pursuit of meat. Or the bands might move to a known migration route or summer grazing range for antelope, elk, deer, or bison. Thus, each band moved within its own territory according to the availability of natural resources. Studies of historic tribes and archaeological evidence suggest that Archaic people established base camps if sufficient resources were within roughly six miles in any direction. From these large base camps, small groups would venture forth daily on gathering or hunting expeditions. If a vital plant or animal food was not within a six-mile radius, the people moved their camp closer to where that resource was located. Territory size changed according to the needs of the band.

As in Paleo times, Archaic people probably gathered together for game drives, ceremonies, feasting, and courting. But they must have split up into small bands again afterwards and returned to individual territories since otherwise a given area would be too populated to be sustained by available resources. Although spring, summer, and fall were seasons of plenty, during winter plant foods were not available, and snow made it difficult to follow animal herds. Consequently, the people constantly dried wild foods and meat and made pemmican for times when fresh food was scarce.

NATURAL RESOURCES OF THE ARCHAIC PEOPLE

Archaic groups usually camped near springs, streams, or rivers, choosing locations according to the availability of game and edible plants. Occasionally, they built houses consisting of wide shallow pits dug in the ground and covered with walls and roofs of poles, beams, branches, and mud. These pithouses (until recently thought to have been constructed only further south and much later in time) may have sheltered a nuclear family for a few weeks or several months while they collected resources.

A three-thousand-year-old Archaic pithouse excavated on the north flank of Battlement Mesa, south of Parachute, provided valuable information concerning Archaic diet and plant use. A flat, worked metate and several manos were found on the hard-packed dirt floor of the pithouse. When dirt from the metate and manos was examined by a palynologist (one who studies pollen), it was discovered that the pollen types which had adhered to the stone artifacts for the last few thousand years included Indian rice grass, hackberry, chokecherry, wild buckwheat, and prickly pear cactus. With the exception of hackberry, all of these plants grow near the site today. It is assumed that either the Archaic gatherers had to forage in a more distant location for the hackberry or that it grew along the Colorado River bottom three thousand years ago. Another interesting fact was that the seeds of the Indian rice grass were larger than the variety growing in the area today. According to the project director, Carl Conner, the foragers of Battlement Mesa may have practiced limited horticulture, planting the largest rice grass seeds nearby so the plants would be closer to home next season (Conner 1994, personal communication).

Analysis of hearth stones and soil from the pithouse's firepit yielded pollen of goosefoot and purslane and the burnt seeds of groundsel, milkweed, and amaranth. Purslane is sold in European markets today, and nutritious amaranth seeds can be purchased in domestic health food and grocery stores. Because fiber from milkweed stems was often used to make cordage, archaeologists do not know whether the seed fell in the firepit during the processing of the plant stem or whether it was being cooked for food.

Archaic people also ate a variety of roots. Gatherers probably made treks to the moist meadows and valleys of the Yampa River drainage in north-central Colorado to dig up roots of yampa plants. Yampa roots have a sweet, nutty flavor when eaten raw and taste like carrots when cooked. They were ground into flour or dried and stored for future use. Out on the Plains, wild mustard, prairie turnips, onions, service-berries, buffaloberries, and plums were available to Archaic gatherers. A prairie turnip is a root that looks similar to a large peanut with a smooth shell. Archaic people probably moved their camps to thick pinyon forests in the fall, where meaty pinyon nuts were collected. If the gatherers arrived before the nuts had fallen from the cones, the cones may have been roasted to pop the nuts out.

Supplementing the plant diet were probably birds' eggs, water fowl, and meat from bison, elk, deer, prairie dogs, and other animals. In the Rocky Mountains and the rugged plateau country to the west, hunters stalked nimble-footed desert bighorn and mountain sheep. Evidence of this are the thousands of sheep figures carved into sandstone cliffs by Indians throughout western Colorado, perhaps to depict hunting exploits or to ensure good fortune in hunting. (Because wild sheep have a low tolerance for disease, they virtually disappeared after the introduction of virus-carrying domestic animals of the Spanish.)

Berries and roots were gathered in large "burden baskets" made of willow branches, yucca leaves, or juniper bark cordage. The women, helped by their children, gathered berries with the baskets hanging in front of them but transported the filled baskets back to camp on their backs. Smooth, supporting headbands, called tumplines, extended from the baskets up to their foreheads.

Figure 7:
Prior to the introduction of horses, dogs carried camp provisions on small travois.

Having no pottery, Archaic women cooked food in hide bags, stomachs of animals, or in tightly woven baskets coated with sap (often of pinyon trees), which made the baskets watertight. Because bags and baskets would burn if placed over fire, rocks were heated and put in the stomachs, hide bags, or baskets full of water. After the hot rocks boiled the water, they were removed, and vegetables, meat, and other raw foods were added to make a nutritious stew. Rice, amaranth, and other seeds were often parched on hot rocks.

It was probably during the Archaic period that pemmican, perhaps the most useful food of prehistoric times, was first made. This food is so practical it is still eaten today, especially by backpackers. To make it women first pounded and ground dried meat and berries on their metates. Next, they combined the powdered meat and berries in baskets and poured on hot animal fat. This very nutritious, high-energy mixture was then dried in the sun and cut into strips. While the berries contained essential vitamins, the meat provided protein. Pemmican was a very practical food. It lasted for months, and a small amount could sustain a person for a long time. With a handful of pemmican in his leather pouch and an antelope bladder full of water, a hunter could survive for days.

Bark, grass, and leaves provided the materials for making products to meet many human needs. Shredded bark of juniper trees was braided into sandals, ropes, clothing, and sleeping mats. Indian rice grass was likely used as bedding; a site south of the Colorado River, although dating a bit later than the Archaic period, revealed a human "nest" of rice grass (Conner 1994, personal communication). Leaves of yucca plants were scraped with sharp stone knives or scrapers to expose the threadlike fibers underneath, which were then twisted into cordage to make ropes, fishing lines, nets, and snares. In addition, willow stems were carefully split in two and woven into versatile baskets.

Archaic people set snares and traps to catch smaller animals such as rabbits, squirrels, mice, and other rodents. Nets made of yucca fiber and human hair have been found at sites throughout the Southwest and were presumably also used by Archaic peoples of Colorado. Dozens of screaming men, women, and children would close in on hundreds of frightened rabbits, herding them toward a large net stretched between two points. The entangled rabbits were then killed with curved wooden rabbit sticks. Archaic people ate the meat of rabbits and used the fur for clothing and blankets. Rabbits comprised a significant part of the Archaic diet, especially during the winter months when other game was farther away and more difficult to hunt. The large number of rabbit bones excavated in the pithouses at the Archaic Yarmony site in north-central Colorado (probably occupied during the winter) helps to confirm the popularity of rabbits as a source of food and clothing.

Spears and atlatls were used to kill larger mammals such as elk, bison, deer, antelope, and bighorn sheep. Various types of ambushes were also used. For example, a hole was dug next to a deer trail where a hunter would wait for a deer to walk by. Or when deer migrated down from the mountains in the fall, piles of brush or stone were placed in converging wings along a trail. A deer would be funneled towards a waiting hunter or towards a brush-covered pit from which it could not escape. According to archaeologist Brian O'Neil, several examples of the ambush method have been recorded on the western slope of Colorado (O'Neil 1993).

Antelope and bighorn sheep were also generally hunted in the fall, when fattened by a summer's grazing. The animals were often ambushed from hunting blinds or individually stalked. In a cave in western Colorado, an antelope head with its ears tied up was found, perhaps worn by a hunter to arouse an antelope's curiosity, luring it closer (Sally J. Cole 1994, personal communication).

Winter was a good season for elk hunting. Men wearing snowshoes of bent twigs and rawhide chased small herds towards snowdrifts and speared elk as they struggled in the deep snow. Individual elk were also stalked by small hunting groups during other times of the year.

Several cliff-lined drainages extending towards the Gunnison River near Grand Junction have V-shaped drivelines of rocks terminating at the cliff edges. In these drainages antelope and sheep were probably driven towards the point of the V, where they fell over the cliff (Jonathan Horn, personal communication). In the canyon bottoms the dazed or crippled animals were killed. (Use of a slightly different bighorn sheep driveline located on the Continental Divide is described in the "Plains Woodland" section of Chapter 5.)

The pithouses of the Yarmony site (named after nearby Yarmony Mountain and a well-known Ute Indian of early Steamboat Springs)

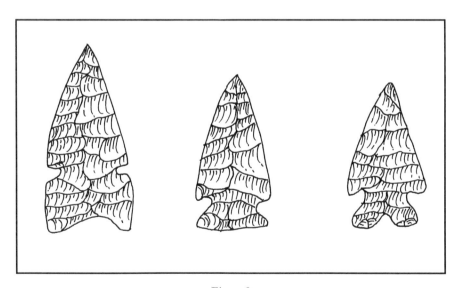

Figure 8:
Spear points of Archaic hunters were shorter, wider, and generally not as finely worked as Paleo points. Spear points from left: San Rafael side-notched, Elko side-notched, Elko eared.

yielded bones of deer, elk, bison, sucker fish, porcupine, and domesticated dog, illustrating the variety of animals eaten by Archaic people. Porcupines provided not only meat but quills, which, when flattened, could be used to decorate hide shirts and dresses (historic Plains tribes commonly utilized quills for decoration). Dogs were probably invaluable as camp guards, scavengers of spoiled meat, hunting companions, pets, and, when times were tough, a food source. The dog bones found at the Yarmony site had been broken to extract the marrow. The family living in a pithouse at the site had eaten dog meat, which is high in protein and calories.

According to archaeologists Michael Metcalf and Kevin Black, the majority of bones excavated at the Yarmony site had been "smashed practically beyond recognition," and most jaw bones of the larger animals had been cracked. This is further evidence that the site was occupied in winter; bones cracked and bashed to this extent show that people were desperate to get to the marrow and grease inside the bones, to either eat it raw or cooked in soup broth (Metcalf and Black 1991).

Buffalo were hunted throughout Colorado; bones of the large creatures have been found both west and east of the Rockies. It was difficult to hunt buffalo on foot. Although there were millions of buffalo on the Plains during Archaic times, a herd might be grazing next to a group of hunters one day and be forty miles away the next. If the hunters caught up with a herd, some might have disguised themselves by putting on wolf or coyote skins and mingling with the buffalo to get close enough for a few shots with spears. This sort of disguise would work, since a few wolves were not a threat to the buffalo. It is likely that occasionally groups gathered together to drive buffalo over cliffs, as in Paleo times; the importance of buffalo (and other animals) as a resource probably encouraged cooperation.

The buffalo provided much more than just food. When one was brought back to camp, no part of it was wasted. The thick hides with fur were made into warm robes and beds. Hides with fur removed were tanned and used to make tents, clothing, and pouches. In order to tan hides, they were first stretched and pegged to the ground. Then the hair, flesh, and muscles were scraped off them, and brains were rubbed into them (folklore has it that every animal has enough brains to tan its own hide). The hardest part was making the stiff hides soft enough to work with; they had to be rubbed over sticks, pulled, stretched, and rubbed some more until they were flexible.

Bones, sharpened to points, and deer antlers were used to punch holes in tanned animal skins in order to sew them together with sinew. These sharp tools are called awls. Bones were also used as scrapers to remove the hair from hides. An antler tip was held tightly in a person's hand while it was pressed on the edges of flaked stone to make tools and projectile points (Figure 8, page 21). Stone tools were more durable than bone, and the edges could be resharpened when they became dull.

Not everyone was good at making stone tools, although most men, women, and children could make a simple scraper or crude knife. The spear points and fine drills used to make holes in rocks and shells (used for beads) were made by experts. These people may have spent much of their time making tools, trading them for tanned hides, clothing, or jewelry made by other craftspeople. Similarly, among traditional Indian groups today there are certain individuals who have specific knowledge about plants, medicine, foods, hide preparation, hunting, birth, various types of ceremonies, dances, and songs (Jennie Parker 1994, personal communication).

Figure 9:
Although some bison died from the fall during a game drive, others were slaughtered at the base of the cliff, where most of the butchering subsequently occurred.

ARCHAIC HOUSES AND ROCK SHELTERS

Archaic people used light, portable tents made of animal hides that were carried by dogs from camp to camp. Brush shelters (wickiups) were also practical houses for these people on the move. In addition, natural protection was offered by caves, overhangs, or rock shelters.

Recent archaeological excavations, such as the pithouse at the Battlement Mesa site south of Parachute, have revealed that some Archaic people may have stayed in one area longer than just a few days. Some sites offer additional evidence of longer residency in a shelter. Before Interstate 70 was widened near DeBeque in northwestern Colorado, an Archaic rock shelter in the path of construction, called the Sisyphus (SIS-a-fis) Shelter, was excavated. During the excavation, typical Archaic artifacts were found, such as stone tools and projectile points, along with a unique rectangular floor made of flat-lying slabs of rock, indicating that the dwelling may have been semi-permanent. Perhaps the occupants sealed off the opening to the rock shelter to make a cozy room that could be lived in for several weeks or months.

Another site that offers evidence of longer occupancy is located several miles east of the Sisyphus Shelter and called the Kewclaw site (designated by a name combining syllables from the names of two of the archaeologists associated with it). Here is the pithouse where the pollen analysis provided information concerning the Archaic diet. On the surface the site revealed flakes of stone from tool making, a few spear points, and scattered manos and metates. As the archaeologists dug deeper in the ground, they discovered a layer of dirt so hard they could not easily dig through it. They had uncovered the floor of the pithouse. The pithouse was constructed partly underground; the floor was dug about two feet deep. It was circular and about fourteen feet wide. Several holes near the edge of the circle indicated that wooden posts had been placed around the pit to hold up the roof of branches and mud.

The Kewclaw site was in a perfect location for a base camp. To the south of the pithouse, dense shrubs grew where berries were found. High-altitude berries grew farther up on the mesatop. Surrounding the site were sagebrush grasslands where grass seeds were picked and rabbits burrowed. To the north the Colorado River attracted many kinds of birds as well as herds of deer, bison, elk, antelope, and other animals, which used its canyon floors as a natural roadway. Archaic people also traveled on these animal paths along canyon and valley floors. Today, most highways, such as Interstate 70, follow these ancient paths first made by animals then deepened by thousands of ancient human feet.

There may have been similar pithouses scattered all along the Colorado River from DeBeque to New Castle and along the Eagle River as well. A few years after the excavation of the Battlement Mesa site, the Yarmony pithouses were excavated on a terrace above the Colorado River, north of Wolcott and State Bridge (Figure 5, pages 12–13).

Although the archaeologists were surprised to find another pithouse this far north in Colorado, the biggest surprise was the radiocarbon date—the house foundation was dug over six thousand years ago, almost three thousand years earlier than the pithouse at Battlement Mesa. The Yarmony pithouse, which measured over eighteen feet in diameter, was large enough to have housed children, parents, and grandparents. A smaller room had been attached to it—with floor features identical to those of the main room—perhaps a work area. Recently, another pithouse at the Yarmony site was excavated next to the original one, a house occupied almost three hundred years later than the one first excavated. Judging from the artifacts found in the original one, archaeologists think that the family living in the more recent pithouse dumped garbage in the older one, which by then was a convenient hole in the ground.

There is ample evidence to suggest that the Yarmony pithouses were occupied in winter—despite the theory that Archaic hunters and gatherers usually moved to lower elevations during the winter months. In the Yarmony pithouses storage bins (rock-lined holes in the ground) were located inside the houses, making them accessible on cold days. Cooking hearths were also located inside, although people would not normally have a smoky fire in the house if not necessary. Similarly, while tool making would normally occur outside, the waste flakes from chipping stone tools lay all over the floor. In addition, the rocks had been chipped down to very tiny flakes; no part was unused, even though material was available locally, indicating that perhaps it was too cold to extract tool stone from the frozen ground, since the sources were at higher elevations. Finally, bones tentatively identified as a fetal bison approximately seven months of age suggest the mother was killed sometime in the early spring, much earlier than people would normally be in the area if they were camped in the lowlands. Since local ranchers say that despite the high elevation of the valley that is the site of the

Yarmony pithouses it has a low level of snowpack much of the winter. This means that herds of deer, elk, antelope, mountain sheep, or perhaps even bison may have grazed there throughout the winter instead of migrating to lower elevations. This might explain why Archaic hunters would remain during the winter—to hunt animals that would have been more numerous there due to deep snow elsewhere.

The apparent winter occupation of the Yarmony pithouses has forced archaeologists to reevaluate former theories that Archaic people abandoned mountainous areas during the winter—at least in the early Archaic period. Although the Archaic people did not stay on the high ridges and peaks, highly adapted family groups may have remained in Colorado mountain parks, such as North and South parks, throughout the winters so they could take advantage of the clustered game.

During the summer of 1994, several more Archaic pithouses were excavated in northwestern Colorado—two near the town of Maybell and four south of Rangely in East Four Mile Draw. In addition, several sites were previously excavated along the shoreline at Blue Mesa Reservoir (located west of Gunnison in western Colorado) before it filled to its highest level. There archaeologists found numerous circular firepits, the floors and sides lined with large flat rocks. When the firepits were radiocarbon dated, it was proven that people had cooked in them more than six thousand years ago. Near the stone hearths was a large circular stain of charcoal that dated to about 4500 B.P., indicating that the Archaic house had been occupied again twenty-five hundred years after the hearths had been originally used for cooking. These sites are now underwater, and motorboats roar across Blue Mesa Reservoir where Archaic families lived in their modest pithouses by the Gunnison River several thousand years ago.

The apparent presence of semi-permanent houses in mountain areas during the Archaic period also supports a theory of many archaeologists that between seventy-five hundred and forty-five hundred years ago people left the Great Basin west of Colorado and the Plains east of the Rockies and moved to the mountains. There have been very few sites found at these lower elevations that date to this period.

Scientists have discovered that during the years 7000 to 4500 B.P. the climate was much drier and warmer than the years before or since—a period called the Altithermal. Perhaps the Archaic people flocked to the cooler and wetter mountains during the few thousand years when the Great Basin and Plains areas were scorched—along with the bison, elk, and deer that would have moved up higher where the grass was greener.

A pithouse excavated on the Plains in southeastern Colorado on the McEndree Ranch indicates that following the Altithermal period the Archaic people once again occupied the lower elevations. The McEndree pithouse is about two thousand years old, dating well past the end of the Altithermal period. The presence of the pithouse in this area and at this time period is evidence that the climate was cooler and wetter by then and that the Archaic people had moved down from the mountains again and were gathering and hunting the natural resources of the Plains. (Some archaeologists do not accept the Altithermal theory and believe the lack of evidence that the Archaic people occupied the lower elevations is simply due to limited excavation of sites of this era at lower elevations.)

Groups of Archaic people may have occupied favorite campsites year after year during various seasons. Perhaps they discovered that seeds of the wild plants they had dropped or eaten would grow in the garbage and human waste of camps where they stayed for a long time, and that it was convenient to have these plants growing close to camp. Or maybe they purposely planted some wild seeds near camp. Although it is possible Archaic peoples practiced limited gardening, the origins of true agriculture were in Mexico, and the incredible impact of plant domestication on a large scale would not be felt until the end of the Archaic period.

Archaic sites with houses provide fascinating evidence about the lifestyle of these people. Much information about the Archaic culture also has been obtained from large open campsites and from overhangs and rock shelters. Overhangs are recessed areas in cliff faces, often formed by springs seeping through the different rock layers; rock shelters are large boulders which lean in such a way that they form slanted roofs.

Archaeologists call the edge of a rock shelter or overhang a dripline because that is where rain drips down. Inside the dripline, the rock ceiling protected an Archaic family. A small fire warmed the shelter, and the smoke blackened the ceiling (ancient smoke stains are still visible in many Colorado rock shelters and overhangs). On warm days, people would work in front of the overhang in the sun, making tools, tanning hides, and playing with their children. Garbage and the waste flakes from tool making washed downslope from the shelter, years after the people had left.

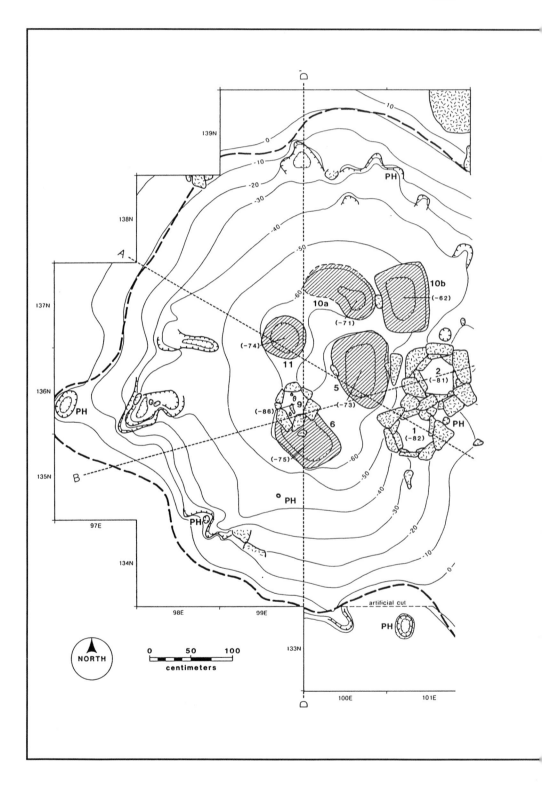

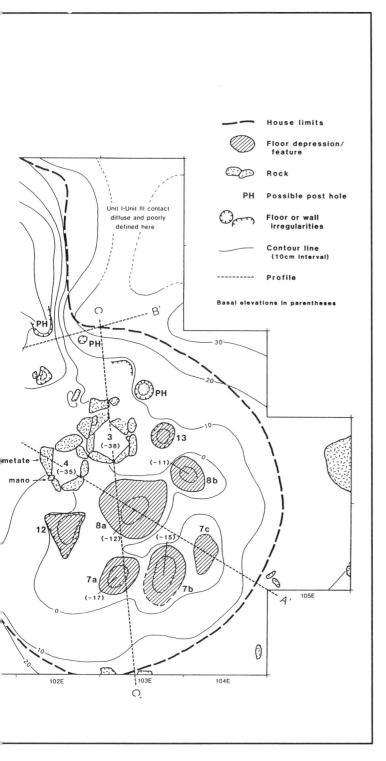

Figure 10:
Archaeologists' map of the Yarmony pithouse first excavated shows the locations of roof support post holes, stone-lined storage areas, and cooking hearths. Courtesy of Michael D. Metcalf and Kevin D. Black, Metcalf Archaeological Consultants, Inc., and the Bureau of Land Management.

Large, south-facing rock shelters and overhangs were used off and on for centuries by hundreds of hunters and gatherers. Each group stayed different lengths of time, some one night, others perhaps for weeks, depending on the availability of local natural resources.

THE UNCOMPAHGRE COMPLEX—
A LOCALIZED ARCHAIC LIFESTYLE

Many of the excavated Archaic rock shelters are located on the Uncompahgre (Un-cum-PAH-gray) Plateau. Uncompahgre comes from a Ute word meaning "red water source," describing the source of the Uncompahgre River. This pinyon-covered land mass cut with hundreds of red rock canyons rises south of Grand Junction and west of Montrose.

From the late 1930s to the early 1950s Marie Wormington, a famous Colorado archaeologist, excavated four rock shelters on the Uncompahgre Plateau, assisted by Al Look, who was well known in Grand Junction for his historical and archaeological work as well as his interest in dinosaurs. Both Wormington and Look are fondly remembered by Coloradans because of their tireless enthusiasm for their respective sciences.

The shelter excavated by this team containing the most layers of garbage and soil deposits is the Taylor site. Over seventeen feet of soil buildup had been deposited by the different people who had lived there throughout the centuries. Many projectile points were found, so many that Wormington was able to put together a point sequence that told which types of Archaic points were made first and how they changed through time. Today, this point sequence is useful for dating points that are found on the ground surface.

The Uncompahgre Plateau encompasses a variety of environments, from the valley of the Gunnison River and adjacent ridges and mesas covered with sagebrush, pinyon, and juniper, to the ponderosa pine and aspen forests at the top of the plateau. Archaeologist Bill Buckles observes that the culture that adapted to this varied landscape represents a convergence of traits from surrounding peoples. He calls the amalgamated lifestyle the Uncompahgre Complex and proposes that it survived for thousands of years, possibly continuing through the Ute occupation (Buckles 1971).

Kevin Black believes the culture that thrived on the Uncompahgre Plateau for so long belonged to what he terms the Mountain Tradition.

He proposes that over nine thousand years ago groups from the Great Basin to the west migrated to the mountainous areas of Colorado. By 6500 B.C. they had established a unique culture adapted to the mountains and competed for resources with their lowland neighbors, people of the Uncompahgre Plateau foraging to the west, perhaps as far as the rich wetlands surrounding the Great Salt Lake in Utah. The Archaic mountain dwellers of the Rocky Mountains probably made trips to the Great Plains to hunt antelope and bison.

Accounts of the division of labor of historic tribes suggests that Archaic men hunted constantly and spent hours making and reworking their hunting tools. Women collected plants and prepared meals as well as processing the food for winter storage, tanning hides, making clothing, and raising children. Colder months were hard on old people; and broken bones, infected wounds, snake bites, and difficulties with childbirth were some of the other problems Archaic people had to face.

Around two thousand years ago the Archaic way of life began to change in southwestern Colorado, although it continued in other parts of the state, particularly among the Utes in western Colorado. At this time people living in the Four Corners area started to farm. Although farming led to great cultural advances, in time these "advances" were partly to blame for the total abandonment of large areas by these people.

PLACES TO VISIT

Colorado

The Hanging Hearths site south of Rangely could provide a rare educational opportunity to the public. As of 1994 four Archaic pithouses are being excavated by a field school sponsored by Colorado Northwestern Community College and the Bureau of Land Management, White River Resource Area. College students from throughout the state may enroll in the school to receive credit, and the materials and information being obtained from the twenty-five to thirty feet of fill at the site could provide several topics for graduate projects. Contact the BLM White River Resource Area in Meeker for more information.

Plans are in the works to interpret the Yarmony Pithouse site along U.S. 40 between Kremmling and Granby. Contact the Kremmling District Office of the BLM for the most recent update.

Suggestions for Further Reading

Benedict, James B. "Footprints in the Snow: High-Altitude Cultural Ecology of the Colorado Front Range, USA." *Arctic and Alpine Research* 24, no. 1 (1992): 1–16.

Cordell, Linda S. *Prehistory of the Southwest*. Orlando, San Diego, New York, Austin, Boston, London, Sydney, Tokyo, Toronto: Academic Press/Harcourt, Brace, Jovanovich, 1984.

Ebeling, Walter. *Handbook of Indian Foods and Fibers in Arid America*. Berkeley and Los Angeles: University of California Press, 1986.

Irk, Donald R. *Wild Edible Plants of the Western United States*. Happy Camp, Calif.: Naturegraph Publishers, 1975.

Metcalf, Michael D., and Kevin D. Black. *Archaeological Excavations at the Yarmony Pit House Site, Eagle County, Colorado*. Colorado Bureau of Land Management Resource Series No. 31. Denver, Colo.: Bureau of Land Management, 1991.

Reed, Alan. *West Central Colorado Prehistoric Context*. Denver, Colo.: State Historical Society of Colorado, 1984.

Wormington, H. M., and Robert H. Lister. *Archaeological Investigations on the Uncompahgre Plateau in West Central Colorado*. Denver, Colo.: Denver Museum of Natural History, 1956.

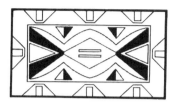

3

The Anasazi Farmers

▲ ▲

T HE IDEA OF PUTTING SEEDS IN THE GROUND to produce food was not new to the people of the Four Corners area. People to the south, in New Mexico and Arizona, learned how to grow corn from farmers in Mexico (corn was grown in the Valley of Mexico, where Mexico City is today, over five thousand years ago). On the plateaus and in the mountains of southwestern New Mexico, a culture known as the Mogollon (Mo-go-YOWN or, locally, Muggy-own) developed, which relied increasingly on crops of corn, squash, and eventually beans. The Mogollon culture is best known for the Mimbreno people, who farmed along the Mimbres River and produced beautiful pottery with fanciful human and animal designs known worldwide.

Some Arizona farmers called the Hohokam (Ho-ho-KAM) dug miles of irrigation ditches to water their fields, portions of which can still be seen near Phoenix and Tucson. Consequently, hundreds of towns thrived near the Salt and Gila rivers and the canals that drained them.

EARLY AGRICULTURE AND ARCHITECTURE IN COLORADO

Gradually, farming practices, and probably certain ceremonies that accompanied them, were introduced by these people to the inhabitants of southwestern Colorado and the areas nearby. It took some time for farming to take hold in this region, since hunting and gathering had been a more reliable lifestyle for thousands of years. Perhaps groups of migrant farmers from southern Arizona were forced north, already equipped with farming tools and techniques. Another theory proposes that some Archaic groups, beginning around 1000 B.C., planted small corn plots in spring before traveling their summer hunting and gathering circuits, and returned to harvest in the fall. The delicious, large-seed grain made it tempting to cultivate all season long. By 500 B.C. people in the Four Corners region were almost totally reliant on corn production. These farmers are most often called the *Anasazi*—a Navajo word meaning "Ancient Ones," or "Ancient Enemies." The term "ancestral Pueblo" is being used now and may eventually replace the Navajo word. Hopi descendants of the ancient Pueblo people prefer their term, *Hisatsinom*. The first Anasazi are called Basketmakers because of the beautiful, tightly woven baskets they made. Soon squash as well as corn was planted by the Anasazi, since it was not only good to eat, but good water carriers could be made from the dried shells.

When the former hunters and gatherers found they could grow enough food that they did not have to gather many wild plants, they built pithouses near their fields. An Anasazi mesatop pithouse on the Loop Drive at Mesa Verde National Park has been excavated and is open to the public (see "Places to Visit"). Another pithouse has been re-created inside the Anasazi Heritage Center near Dolores, Colorado. This impressive reconstruction has been furnished with all the tools and utensils that were used by a typical Anasazi family. Sometimes pithouses were built in large overhangs, such as Step House located on

Figure 11:
Large overhangs beneath canyon rims provided shelter for the Basketmaker people in
southwestern Colorado. Pithouses often were constructed in the overhangs, providing
further protection. Diorama photo courtesy of Mesa Verde National Park.

Wetherill Mesa at Mesa Verde (also open to the public). This structure was rebuilt on the original pithouse foundation to illustrate how the log and brush walls and roof were originally constructed.

Basketmaker pithouses were large and often comfortable, although they could probably be very cold and damp if the roof and walls needed repair. They often had covered entryways. Holes in the roof over the center fire hearth allowed smoke to escape while ventilator shafts opposite the entryways let in fresh air.

Archaeological evidence suggests that several useful tools were acquired through trade with the Mogollon people. Sharp stone axes hafted to wooden handles made tree felling a lot faster than burning the trunks. Grooved hammers made driving posts and breaking up slabs of sandstone easier. However, the most important new tool of this period, although the source is unknown, was the bow and arrow, which was considerably more efficient and accurate in hunting than the atlatl and spear.

Figure 12:
Semi-subterranean pithouses provided well-insulated abodes for Basketmaker people and for
some Archaic dwellers as well. Roof support poles were placed in holes dug around the
pithouse foundation, and the earthen walls were occasionally lined with sandstone slabs.

Clothing of the period has been found at some sites in the Four Corners area, giving some indication of what was worn. Small women's aprons have been found which were made of strings of yucca fiber, cotton, or shredded juniper bark that hung down from a cord tied around the waist. Cotton aprons had tightly woven panels in the front with woven or painted designs in yellow, pink, blue, brown, black, and red.

There is little evidence of what the men's clothing of this period was like except for a collection of long sashes found in two Basketmaker cave villages in northeastern Arizona. Fine examples of workmanship, the sashes were tightly woven and braided with white and brown dog hair. These sashes, along with hundreds of other artifacts, are on display in the museum at Mesa Verde National Park.

Numerous finely woven scallop-toed sandals have also been found in Basketmaker caves in the Four Corners region. They were made with Indian hemp or fine yucca cord, and many had intricate raised designs on the soles. Although the Basketmaker people took pride in craftsmanship, it is unusual to decorate the soles of shoes. Perhaps such soles served a more utilitarian purpose such as providing better traction on slippery surfaces or identifying the wearer by individualized treads. Larger, undecorated and roughly woven sandals padded with juniper bark and cornhusks were also found and may have served as overshoes. Evidence that seems to suggest this is the fact that some were found with mud on the soles, indicating use in wet weather.

Blankets woven with cords wrapped with turkey feathers replaced heavier ones made of rabbit fur. Later, wild turkeys were penned, making blanket material more available. Analysis of turkey bones found in refuse areas has indicated that most birds were not eaten.

The Basketmaker people often wore their hair in side bobs, but frequently both men and women cut it short, probably for use as cordage. Jewelry was popular with both sexes. Turquoise was mined throughout the Southwest to make thousands of beads, which were traded for necklace

Figure 13:
Features of Basketmaker pithouse design that were incorporated
into later kiva construction included good ventilation, roof entry, and a sunken floor.

making. Shell necklaces and bracelets of olivella, clam, and abalone indicate heavy trade with the Mogollon, Hohokam, and other cultures closer to shell sources on the Pacific Ocean and Gulf of California.

Medicine bags, prayer sticks, feather bundles, and other ceremonial objects which have been found indicate that the Anasazi had an elaborate ceremonial and religious life. Basketmaker pipes made of clay or stone may have been smoked during certain rituals; tobacco, which was sacred to American Indians, had been introduced from Mexico.

Around A.D. 450 the art of making pottery was introduced by the Mogollon people, and pots replaced baskets for many uses. Although baskets were still made, pots were preferable for carrying water and cooking since they could be put directly in the fire. Also, corn, beans, and squash survived better when stored in rodentproof pottery jars. Although bowls and jars were the most widely made ceramics, ollas, pitchers, ladles, seed jars, and, later, mugs, were also crafted.

The first step in making a pottery bowl was to mix clay with water and temper (crushed sand or potsherds added to inhibit shrinkage). Next, the clay was shaped into a long rope and coiled around a disk-shaped clay base until the desired height was attained. Coils were then smoothed out on all pottery except cooking pots with a piece of wood or broken pot. After drying, pots to be decorated were coated with a wash of clay, called a slip, then polished with a smooth rock. Designs, which became more elaborate through time, were painted on with brushes of yucca fiber; colored minerals and plants such as bee weed served as paint. Finally, the pots were fired under a dome-shaped pile of burning wood.

Pots which broke and were tossed into garbage heaps in front of villages provide archaeologists with excellent clues as to the time such sites were occupied. A chronology of design patterns has been developed which allows researchers to assign even small fragments of pots to a specific period.

The increasing popularity of beans, which were later introduced indirectly from Mexico, added more protein to the Anasazi diet and may have been linked to the appearance of pottery; beans take a long time to cook, and this is difficult to do with only hot stones and baskets. Today, you can buy Anasazi Beans, a trademark of Adobe Milling Company, in many food stores; they are purple and white and more nutritious than pinto beans. It is uncertain whether these beans originated from beans found in Anasazi storage rooms, were growing wild

Figure 14:
Towards the end of the Basketmaker era, women began to make pots
to replace their cooking baskets. Long coils of clay were rolled out
and coiled upwards to form the shape of the vessel.
After they were smoothed, the ceramics were often painted,
then fired to harden the clay and make them waterproof.
The introduction of beans to the Anasazi diet may have encouraged
cooking in pots rather than baskets because beans
took a lot longer to cook than corn or squash.

Figure 15:
Erecting common walls saved Anasazi builders construction materials.
Occasionally, pithouses were built next to the early pueblo room blocks.
Diorama photo courtesy of Mesa Verde National Park.

in Anasazi farm fields, or were obtained from modern Pueblos who still grow them. Although most botanists believe that a bean over fifty years old could not grow, corn kernels found in Anasazi ruins have grown when planted after being stored for seven hundred years.

By A.D. 700 the Basketmaker people were moving out of their pit-houses and constructing the first American apartment houses. Series of rooms of coursed rock were connected horizontally and vertically— sometimes two to three stories high. The small pueblos (Spanish for towns) were always oriented towards the sunny south.

In Colorado the majority of the population of this area, which exceeded today's population, was eventually concentrated in the broad farmland north and west of Mesa Verde. Hundreds of small Anasazi villages dotted the ridges and low hills that rose slightly above vast fields of beans, squash, and corn. Today's fields closely resemble those of the Anasazi, and beans are still a vital local crop.

During this period the pithouse design was still used, but the round structures were dug deeper into the ground and mostly used for ceremonies. These structures are called kivas, which according to some authorities means "old house" in Hopi, the language of Anasazi descendants; they were built in front of the multiroomed complexes, always to the south or southeast.

For decades researchers thought that the people who built the mesatop villages were a totally different race from the Basketmaker people because they had broad, flat skulls that were very unlike those people. However, careful study of skeletal remains revealed that use of a new type of cradleboard was responsible for the difference in the skull shape. Originally, Basketmaker women placed their babies in soft, padded cradles, but then suddenly they began to use hard boards with no pillows, causing the babies' skulls to permanently flatten in back and bulge out at the sides. Within a couple of generations this new fashion had spread throughout the Southwest with the result that it was a rare Anasazi who had a natural long, narrow skull.

For almost four hundred years the Anasazi flourished in their pueblos on the mesatops. According to the practices of their Pueblo descendants, their religion focused on bringing rain to water the crops because the Anasazi did not have ditch irrigation systems like the Hohokam farmers to the south. This method of farming—without irrigation—is called dry-farming. Although their crops were watered by rainwater, the Anasazi did build reservoirs (a possible reservoir that could contain a half-million gallons can be seen at Mesa Verde National Park). Rock dams called check dams were built across intermittent drainages, and small gardens were planted behind the dams so they received extra water during rainstorms.

Ceremonies probably were held in kivas, which were primarily religious and social centers for males of the same clan. A clan traced its heritage back to a common ancestor. A baby inherited his or her mother's clan; so, for example, if a boy's mother belonged to the Spider Clan, the boy would spend time in the Spider Clan's kiva. It was forbidden to marry within one's own clan.

In the winter men and boys in the kivas were far more comfortable than women and girls above ground. The females probably stayed in the tiny, smoky rooms or, to breathe fresh air, worked on the chilly rooftops (modern Pueblos allow females in the kivas for certain ceremonies, and this may have also been the case in Anasazi times). When the weather was unusually cold, however, entire families may have huddled in the kivas, cooking their meals, and perhaps playing games and listening to stories until the cold snap was over.

With a fire of juniper and pinyon crackling in the center, a kiva was warm. A ventilator allowed fresh air in through the side, but the air rushing into the room was stopped from blowing the fire by one stone or mud wall called a deflector. As the fresh air circulated around the room, smoke rose through the smoke hole in the ceiling. The ladder was placed through the smoke hole, perhaps providing a ritual purification from the smoke when climbing into the kiva. A small, shallow hole dug into the floor near the firepit represented the *sipapu* (SEE-pah-pooh), the place where humans emerged from the underworld. Some modern Pueblos believe the *sipapu* is located in the deep canyon of the Little Colorado River.

When ceremonies were not taking place in the kiva, clan members may have practiced ceremonial songs, talked about their crops and other happenings in the village, and fixed tools and bows and arrows. Historic Pueblo men, who were good weavers, also wove sashes of cotton thread and blankets of turkey feathers in the kivas, an activity that has been documented by the remains of looms often found on Anasazi kiva floors. Cotton, though not grown in the higher elevations of Anasazi country such as Mesa Verde, was provided by the Hohokam people, who grew it in the lowlands of the Salt and Gila river valleys and traded it throughout the Southwest.

Ceremonies including more than one clan were often held in outdoor plazas, and people from other pueblos might attend. To get a better view of the dancers, who were dressed up to represent various gods, people might climb to the high rooftops. From there they could see the drummers beating a constant rhythm as the lines of colorful dancers moved in unison. Off to the west, they might see black clouds rolling towards the dry farm fields and believe that the gods were listening.

THE ABANDONMENT OF ANASAZI VILLAGES

After hundreds of years of living in the mesatop villages, around A.D. 1100 some of the Anasazi abandoned these villages and built apartments in overhangs located in steep-sided canyon walls. Massive apartment buildings, often four stories high, were jammed into the overhangs. We may never know exactly why some of the Anasazi moved into these cliff dwellings while the majority of the population remained in their mesatop villages. Some speculate that this adaptation was a result of decreasing resources amidst an increasing population. By this time the land had been farmed for over seven hundred years; consequently, soils lacked nutrients, and crops often failed. Also, wood was already scarce. At the same time, the population had increased; sedentary farmers had more children than wandering hunters. Although the people who lived in the cliff dwellings had to tolerate the discomforts of climbing up and down the perilous, often icy cliff faces and living in the stench of confined quarters, resources in the cliff dwellings could be more easily defended from aggressive neighbors who might be hungry and thirsty. Spring water flowed from the back of many overhangs, and storage rooms were tucked high above. However, the hoarding of resources is not the way of modern Pueblo people so this theory may not be correct.

Whatever the reasons for construction of the cliff dwellings, the Anasazi reached their cultural peak during the short time these cliff dwellings were occupied (A.D. 1100 to 1300). Pottery designs were elaborate and beautiful. Traders from the south walked hundreds of miles to trade with the Anasazi, exchanging turquoise from Arizona, macaw feathers and copper bells from Mexico, and shells from the Pacific Ocean for ceramic pottery and smooth deer hides tanned by Anasazi women.

The cliff dwellings had been lived in less than two hundred years, however, when the Anasazi began to leave, presumably due to depletion of resources and climatic changes. Pueblos on the mesatops were also abandoned. Tree rings show us that during the years between 1275 and 1300 the summer rains all but stopped. Fields were abandoned that could no longer sustain crops, and the rootless soil then washed away during the few remaining summer storms, leaving gaping arroyos where rows of corn used to grow. Although the Anasazi had survived serious droughts in the past, the drought combined with depleted resources probably made habitation of the area too difficult. Wood gatherers may have had to travel over seventy miles to find trees for construction and firewood, and game was probably scarce since there was little vegetation for animals to eat.

In addition, it is possible that the ancestors of today's Navajos and Apaches (the Athabascans) or the Utes had migrated into the area this early and were raiding the peaceful farmers, although there is no con-

Figure 16:
One of the first discovered and the second largest cliff dwelling at Mesa Verde National Park,
Cliff Palace was excavated and stabilized for public visitation.
Today, the structures differ little from the time the Anasazi abandoned them
in the late 1200s to join their Pueblo neighbors to the south.
Photo by Jesse L. Nusbaum, 1907, courtesy of the Museum of New Mexico.

crete evidence of warfare. Whatever the reasons, clan by clan, the Anasazi began migrating to a more prosperous area. They probably headed east, and south, following the Rio Grande as it left Colorado and headed towards the villages of the Pueblo people, who had a similar farming culture and social organization. Ceremonies held in the kivas and plazas of these pueblos (Zuni, Acoma, Laguna, those along the Rio Grande, and the Hopi villages) today may have changed little from the days when the Anasazi migrants arrived.

PLACES TO VISIT

Colorado

Mesa Verde National Park

On a crisp winter day in 1888 two cowboys, the Wetherill brothers, were riding along the edge of a canyon in southwestern Colorado looking for cattle. Suddenly, across the steep, narrow canyon they saw a city of stone tucked in an enormous overhang. Hundreds of ancient, vacant windows and doors stared back at the cowboys. Towers, both square and round and up to four stories high, loomed above over two hundred rooms and twenty-three kivas. The brothers named their discovery Cliff Palace. In the ensuing years they removed and sold artifacts from Cliff Palace and other cliff dwellings. In 1891, they assisted an archaeologist from Sweden, Gustaf Nordenskiold, in the excavation of several mesatop ruins and cliff dwellings flanking the fingers of Mesa Verde (Spanish for Green Mesa). Most of the artifacts unearthed from these early digs are now in private collections and foreign museums.

In 1906, Mesa Verde became a national park (it is now also designated as a world heritage site). The passing of the Federal Antiquities Act made it illegal to disturb ruins on public property. Although the ruins may represent the dwellings of only one-tenth of the Anasazi population of the Four Corners region (it is estimated that over thirty thousand people lived in villages to the northwest, in Montezuma Valley), they are the best known of the Anasazi sites. Nearly four thousand sites, among them roughly six hundred cliff dwellings, have been located in the park. Several of these sites, including mesatop ruins and cliff dwellings, are open to the public.

Figure 17:
Anasazi architecture is so similar to that of historic Pueblo Indians that it is assumed that
Pueblos are direct descendants of the Anasazi. Dances at Hopi circa 1895 similar
to this may have occurred in Anasazi plazas in southwestern
Colorado over seven hundred years ago.
Photo courtesy of the Museum of New Mexico.

A tour of Mesa Verde National Park should begin at the Far View Visitor Center, after a long and winding drive up to Chapin Mesa. Nearby, several mesatop ruins, including Far View House and Far View Tower, a possible ceremonial structure, can be seen. What appears to be a rain-filled reservoir called Mummy Lake, with visible steps leading down into it, could have stored up to half a million gallons of water for the occupants of the adjacent villages. It is presumed the storage facility was used primarily for drinking water, although the structure's use as a reservoir is debated among several archaeologists.

Continuing south down Chapin Mesa one arrives at the Site Headquarters and Museum, where informative dioramas and hundreds of artifacts can be viewed. A short but somewhat steep walk down into the adjacent canyon leads to Spruce Tree House, one of the best-preserved cliff dwellings. Some of the 114 rooms still have red and white painted plaster wall decorations. Two of the eight kivas have been restored, the ground-level roofs of which form the main courtyard where most of the chores were done. The natural ceiling of the over-hang is black from the soot of thousands of Anasazi fires. A short walk to the south leads to a petroglyph panel, where the Anasazi carved images of mountain sheep, turkeys, humans, hand prints, and various spirals and lines into the rock face.

The west loop of Ruins Road leads to a series of Anasazi sites that show the evolution of the culture from about A.D. 600 to 1200. Here Basketmaker pithouses represent the earliest habitations while the more recent cliff dwellings, including Square Tower House, Little Long House, Fire Temple, New Fire House, and Oak Tree House, can be viewed across the canyons.

The east loop of Ruins Road winds around to the largest cliff dwelling, Cliff Palace, described above. Visitors can walk down a stair-way to the ruin and exit up ladders, routes that follow the original

Figure 18:
By around A.D. 1200, numerous Anasazi were leaving many of their mesatop pueblos and building apartments in protected overhangs. Were nomadic enemies invading, or did dwindling resources cause serious competition among the Anasazi? Diorama photo courtesy of Mesa Verde National Park.

Anasazi paths, which were small incised indentations in the cliff face just large enough to grip with fingers and toes.

At Balcony House it is possible to appreciate the defensive nature of the cliff dwellings since one exits through the same narrow tunnel through which one must crawl to enter the dwelling; an ancient intruder would have been totally vulnerable to armed guards posted at the tunnel. Between the first and second stories of one of the buildings is an original balcony used as an entrance to the upper rooms. Another unique feature of Balcony House is a protective wall at the cliff edge, suggesting concern for small children who played in the courtyard.

West of the Far View Visitor Center lies Wetherill Mesa, where two impressive cliff dwellings can be visited (summer only). Long House, the second largest of the cliff dwellings, has more than 150 rooms and 21 kivas. A large outdoor "great kiva" may have served as the ceremonial center for other villages throughout the area.

In Step House Cave, named for the Anasazi stone steps leading into the overhang (still visible from the modern stairway), four Basketmaker pithouses have been excavated. One was partially restored to illustrate wall and roof construction. On the ceiling above the more recent cliff dwelling are paintings, perhaps representing stars. The images may be of Navajo or Ute origin, perhaps painted several hundred years after the cliff dwelling was abandoned.

Mesa Verde National Park is one of the most popular tourist attractions in Colorado so consider visiting off-season to avoid the crowds. Although not as many ruins are open during off-season months, the park is still beautiful, particularly when the mesa is blanketed with snow. Campgrounds, showers, picnic areas, restaurants, and motels are available in nearby communities. For more information, contact Mesa Verde National Park, Box 8, Mesa Verde, CO 81330; (303)529-4465.

Other Anasazi Sites

Ute Mountain Tribal Park, located just south of Cortez, is an extension of the Anasazi villages of Mesa Verde National Park. The Utes offer interesting tours of cliff dwellings, rock art, and historic Ute sites. The cliff dwellings, which are similar to those of Mesa Verde National Park, are mainly located in Lion Canyon and include Fortified House, Tree House, Lion House, Morris No. 5, and Eagle Nest House. These sites are not far from Cliff Palace and Balcony House (as the crow flies) and may have been an associated community.

Figure 19:
Named after the Spanish explorers who documented them in 1776, the Dominguez and
Escalante ruins at the Anasazi Heritage Center exhibit features and masonry similar to
structures at Chaco Canyon, over a hundred miles to the south-southeast.
This suggests the complex may have been a northern trade center for the Chaco Anasazi.
Photo courtesy of Curtis Martin.

Tours are led by Ute guides, with visitors traveling through the park in their own cars. Tours last most of the day, and special arrangements can be made for overnight tours. Camping is available. Reservations can be made by contacting the Ute Mountain Tribal Park, Ute Mountain Indian Reservation, Towaoc, CO 81344; (303)565-3751.

Another Anasazi ruin open to visitors in Colorado is Lowry Pueblo, located ten miles west of Pleasant View on a county road off U.S. 666. This is a series of mesatop ruins, occupied from roughly A.D. 1100 to 1300. The interconnectedness of the villages is exemplified by a great kiva and several "streets" leading from the main part of town to smaller communities.

The Dominguez and Escalante ruins at the Anasazi Heritage Center, on Colorado 184 south of Dolores, are managed by the Bureau of Land Management. The two sites are mesatop ruins (first documented

by the Dominguez and Escalante Expedition of 1776) that have archi-
tectural similarities to Chaco Canyon sites in New Mexico. Consequently, the sites have been termed "Chaco outliers" and may have
served as the northernmost trading center for the Chaco Canyon culture. The short trails to the sites are wheelchair accessible. The adjacent
Anasazi Heritage Center consists of an informative museum with hundreds of artifacts and fascinating interpretive displays, including a
replica of a pithouse. Other mesatop ruins near the center will be open
soon for visitation. For more information, contact the Anasazi Heritage
Center, 27501 Highway 184, Dolores, CO 81323; (303) 882-4811.

Some of the most intriguing of the Anasazi sites are in Hovenweep
National Monument located west of Mesa Verde National Park on the
Colorado-Utah border. Defying the effects of time, over half a dozen
tall stone towers still stand, some clinging to huge boulder outcrops in
canyon bottoms, others rising like sentinels on ridgetops. It is not
known exactly what these towers were used for—defense, storage, ceremonies, or some other purpose. To get to Hovenweep National Monument, take the gravel road out of Pleasant View or U.S. 163 and
SR262 out of Blanding, Utah. Be prepared for hot weather in the summer and muddy roads after a rainstorm. A visitor center and camp-
ground are provided, and the drive itself is worthwhile. Write or call
Mesa Verde National Park for more information.

Finally, the U.S. Forest Service manages some ruins in one of the
most spectacular topographical locations in the Southwest. The Chim-
ney Rock Pueblo perches on a small triangular mesa one thousand feet
above the Piedra River Valley, east of Pagosa Springs just off Colorado
151. The architecture of the rooms and kivas indicates they were constructed by skilled masons from Chaco Canyon, New Mexico, the hub
of Anasazi culture to the south. Two rock spires tower above the ruins
to the east. The dramatic setting of the site and the fact that the ridge
was an unlikely spot for a farm village (water had to be carried up from
the valley floor) suggest that the builders chose the location for ceremonial rather than practical purposes. For a tour of the site, contact
the U.S. Forest Service Ranger Station in Pagosa Springs.

Children and adults can sign up for numerous classes, including
artifact identification, rock art recordation, and excavation of Anasazi ruins located near Crow Canyon Archaeological Area northwest
of Cortez, Colorado. For a course catalog, call 1(800)422-8975 or
(303)565-8975.

Suggestions for Further Reading

Dozier, Edward P. *The Pueblo Indians of North America*. New York: Holt, Rinehart and Winston, 1970.

Ferguson, William M., and Arthur H. Rohn. *Anasazi Ruins of the Southwest in Color*. Albuquerque: University of New Mexico Press, 1990.

Houk, Rose. *Anasazi*. Tucson, Ariz.: Southwest Parks and Monuments Association, 1992.

Matlock, Gary. *Enemy Ancestors*. Flagstaff, Ariz.: Northland Publishing Co., 1988.

Matson, R. G. *The Origins of Southwestern Agriculture*. Tucson and London: University of Arizona Press, 1991.

Nabhan, Gary Paul. *Enduring Seeds: Native American Agriculture and Wild Plant Conservation*. San Francisco: North Point Press, 1989.

Noble, David Grant. *Ancient Ruins of the Southwest*. Flagstaff, Ariz.: Northland Publishing Co., 1991.

————, ed. *Understanding the Anasazi of Mesa Verde and Hovenweep*. Santa Fe, N.M.: Ancient City Press, 1991.

————, ed. *Houses Beneath the Rock: The Anasazi of Canyon de Chelly and Navajo National Monument*. Santa Fe, N.M.: Ancient City Press, 1991.

Titiev, Mischa. *Old Oraibi: A Study of the Hopi Indians of Third Mesa*. Albuquerque: University of New Mexico Press, 1992.

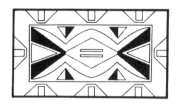

4

The Fremont Culture
in Western Colorado

▲ ▲

MOST PEOPLE WHO LIVED NORTH OF THE ANASAZI and west of the
Rocky Mountains of Colorado remained hunters and gatherers,
never adapting to the farming life. In the plateau country south of
Grand Junction, this Archaic lifestyle is often called the Uncompahgre
Complex after the plateau of that name (see "The Archaic Hunters and
Gatherers"). However, for over a thousand years, the area of southern
and eastern Utah and northwestern Colorado was also home to a culture that combined hunting and gathering with limited farming. This
culture is generally called the Fremont, named after the Fremont River
in southeastern Utah where sites of this type were found. Colorado
archaeologist Alan Reed calls this culture "Formative" and believes
that, with the exception of areas in Dinosaur National Monument,

Douglas Creek, and Glade Park, the Fremont tradition did not spread
into west-central Colorado (Reed 1984).

Five geographic variants have been identified in Utah. In Colorado,
Fremont sites in Dinosaur National Monument and Glade Park, south
of Grand Junction, appear to be influenced by the Uintah variant of the
Uintah Basin in northeastern Utah. The Douglas Creek sites south of
Rangely exhibit traits of the San Rafael variant of southeastern Utah.

ORIGIN OF THE FREMONT PEOPLE

The origin of the Fremont people is unclear. Perhaps early Anasazi
traders, their packs full of seeds and their heads full of stories, told the
northern Archaic hunters and gatherers of a better life that was possible. These northerners may have been originally Great Basin dwellers
of the Numic language stock, to which the later Ute, Paiute, and
Shoshone tribes belong.

James Truesdale, archaeologist at Dinosaur National Monument,
proposes that the canyons of the Green and Yampa rivers were good
sources of tool stone and animal and plant foods for the Archaic peoples. In time the area was lived in year-round and became so popular
and overcrowded that limited agriculture was the only way to provide
for the permanent Archaic occupants of the canyons. Increased farming, pithouse dwelling, and a unique style of rock art are the traits that
distinguish the Archaic and Fremont cultures.

Excavations at Dinosaur National Monument revealed that Fremont farmers were growing corn there as early as A.D. 408 and possibly
much earlier. Corn, bean, and pumpkin patches probably dotted the
side canyons of the Green and Yampa rivers. Small gardens may have
flourished in south-facing alcoves, watered by natural seeps.

However, the fact that northwestern Colorado and much of Utah
have less rainfall kept the Fremont from farming to the extent the
Anasazi did. The presence of houses and pottery, though, suggests the
Fremont remained in one place for at least part of the year.

Fremont pithouses have been excavated at Dinosaur National Monument, and a pithouse probably constructed during the Fremont period
was found at Battlement Mesa south of the Colorado River near Parachute. Fremont pithouses were not as elaborate as those of the Anasazi.
Four posts supported each roof, and they usually had no ventilator

Figure 20:
With a sharp stone chisel, a Fremont man pecks a figure
that possibly represents a god or well-adorned member of the group.
The figure appears to hold a mask or human head.

shafts or entrance ramps. Although the Fremont people sometimes built single houses with stone foundations, they never constructed connecting rooms, and their villages remained small.

FREMONT ARTIFACTS

Fremont pottery consisted of round-bottomed, wide-mouthed jars, often with handles attached for easy carrying. Plain gray or black was the most common color found in Dinosaur National Monument. Elsewhere, they made black-on-white designs. Some excavated sites contained Anasazi pottery, probably obtained through trade.

Small, corner-notched arrow points are so numerous in Fremont sites it is obvious that hunting still occurred, along with limited farming. With the increase in population, however, mountain sheep and deer may have moved elsewhere, making agriculture all the more important. Wild plants, small game, and insects, including calorie-rich grasshoppers, were eaten along with the farm crops.

Analysis of pollen found in a recently excavated Archaic/Fremont/Ute site in the Jones Hole/Ely Creek area suggests the following wild plants were the most popular, eaten raw, cooked, or brewed for tea: prickly pear cactus (probably both pads and fruit), Mormon tea, wild rose and pea, saltbush, ragweed, tansy, mustard, Jerusalem artichoke, juniper berries, pinyon nuts, Indian rice grass seeds, sunflower seeds, and amaranth. The Fremont people parched the seeds, ground them into flour, and formed the flour into cakes as their Archaic ancestors had done.

Tube-shaped pipes carved from stone were found in the overhangs of Dinosaur National Monument, indicating that the Fremont people smoked some sort of tobacco consisting of herbs, bark, or a mixture of plants. As was the case with most historic tribes, the Fremont people may have smoked as an offering to the spirits or whenever people gathered together for business reasons.

Moccasins made of the leg hides of mountain sheep were worn instead of sandals. The hair and the dewclaws were left on the hide (dewclaws are the small appendages growing above the hoofs of deer or sheep), perhaps serving as hobnails to protect the soles of the moccasins.

In several Fremont sites in Dinosaur National Monument, corn cobs were impaled with sticks, which perhaps were corn skewers to hold hot corn on the cob while eating or to carry it during a ceremony.

Bone artifacts yielded through excavation include awls with sharpened points and the hollow leg bones of birds, ground on the ends and used as decorations, perhaps as beads. Bone fishhooks, pendants, and gaming pieces were also made by the Fremont people. Similar bone gaming pieces were used in gambling games by the later Plains Indians, and the Fremont people may have been in contact with ancient Plains hunters from the Wyoming area.

Smooth stone balls about the size of baseballs are often found at Fremont sites in Dinosaur National Monument and other parts of western Colorado; and carved depressions the exact size of the balls have been observed on boulders in some Fremont sites. Perhaps the balls were used in a game in which they were rolled, thrown, or kicked into the depressions similar to the way the Tarahumara Indians of Copper Canyon in northern Mexico kick hard balls as they run in bare feet or toeless sandals.

Unfired clay doll-like figurines decorated with bits of clay representing noses, eyes, and ears have been excavated from sheltered overhangs in Dinosaur National Monument. In other areas Fremont figurines were decorated with skirts, earrings, necklaces, and shoulder ornaments, and may have represented the lavishly attired men and women of the culture.

Baskets and juniper bark bags full of corn kernels are some of the perishables that survived the centuries because they were in the dry, protected overhangs. In some Fremont sites northwest of Grand Junction, baskets were found that had been lined with gilsonite, a sticky black substance that made them waterproof and today is used for asphalt.

One of the most beautiful artifacts from the Fremont culture was discovered in an overhang in Dinosaur National Monument. Inside a pouch fashioned from the hide of a deer's face and scalp was a headdress made of the bright red and yellow feathers of two species of the flicker, the front of which was decorated with ermine fur.

Fremont artifacts and the lifestyle of limited farming spread into Utah and south into the Colorado canyons of the Roan and Book cliffs north of Grand Valley (near present-day Grand Junction). The Fremont may have also farmed the broad canyon bottoms and uplands of Glade Park (south of Grand Junction, Colorado National Monument, and the red rock canyons west of the monument) ranging as far east as Meeker, Colorado; evidence of this is a carved stone figurine probably of Fremont origin found at a site in the Piceance (PEE-ahnts) Basin between Rifle and Meeker.

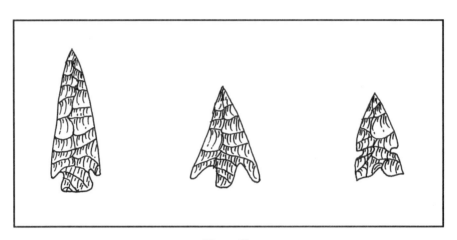

Figure 21:
By approximately A.D. 500 the Anasazi and Fremont peoples had replaced their spears and atlatls with bows and arrows. Projectile points hafted to arrows were smaller than spear points. Arrowheads from left: Rosegate corner-notched (Fremont), Rosegate corner-notched (Anasazi), desert tri-notched (Ute/Shoshone).

On the sandstone cliffs flanking Douglas Creek along Colorado 139 are several rock art paintings possibly of Fremont origin. The canyon is called Canyon Pintado, or Painted Canyon, named by the Spanish explorers Dominguez and Escalante as they passed through the area in 1776 while looking for a route from Santa Fe to the California missions. Fremont rock art, which is among the most impressive of all the prehistoric styles, is described in detail in Chapter 11.

Also in Canyon Pintado are several small stone structures locally referred to as "towers." No pottery or tools or other domestic evidence lies near the structures, suggesting they were not houses. Archaeologist Richard Hauck has noted certain lunar and solar alignments related to the structures and suggests the Fremont people were using them to determine or celebrate solstices and possibly other astronomical events (Hauck 1992, personal communication). Since the soil in the canyon of Douglas Creek is very salty, crops were probably grown in more fertile, alluvial fans where smaller canyons entered Canyon Pintado. Fremont houses probably were built in these side canyons.

It is not known what happened to the Fremont people. Artifacts typical of their culture began to disappear by about A.D. 1150, although some groups probably remained longer. A radiocarbon date from a Douglas Creek masonry site indicated use up to A.D. 1500, suggesting the Fremont were in the area when the Numic-speaking Ute and Shoshone groups entered Colorado. The drought that was one of the major causes of the Anasazi evacuation of the Four Corners area may have also affected northwestern Colorado and northeastern Utah. A Fremont site in Dinosaur National Monument yielded more farm crops than wild plant foods in the lower levels while the upper levels (the time of the long drought) contained no corn, beans, or squash but many wild plant seeds and pollen as well as deer bones. The Fremont people appeared to be hunting and gathering more than farming during the time they last used the sheltered site. In this regard, it is interesting that some Utes, who were traditionally hunters and gatherers rather than farmers, believe they are descendants of Fremont people. Shield-figure rock art motifs of the Eastern Shoshoni could indicate a link, but as yet there is no archaeological evidence supporting Fremont ancestry for either historic tribe. It is also possible that some Fremont people migrated to Hopi villages, perhaps accompanying their Anasazi neighbors. Some evidence points to this. During the late 1200s some Hopi farmers of northern Arizona began to grow corn with pronounced dents in the kernels, very much like Fremont corn. Also, the Hopi made spoon handles similar to Fremont figurines.

PLACES TO VISIT

At the sites listed below, precautions must be taken not to touch or harm the rock art in any way.

Colorado

MUSEUM OF WESTERN COLORADO
4th and Ute
Grand Junction, CO 81501
(303)242-0971

The museum offers an informative display of Fremont and Ute artifacts.

RANGELY MUSEUM
434 W. Main Street
Rangely, CO 81648
(303)675-2612

The museum houses exhibits of the Fremont and Ute cultures.

Utah

BUREAU OF LAND MANAGEMENT
2370 South 2300 West
Salt Lake City, UT 84119
(801)977-4300

Contact the BLM for directions to Fremont rock art sites in several locations.

CAPITOL REEF NATIONAL PARK
Torrey, UT 84775
(801)425-3791

Among other sites of interest visitors can see Fremont rock art on several canyon walls. Ask at the Visitor Center for locations.

DINOSAUR NATIONAL MONUMENT
Jenson, UT 84035
(801)789-2115

Visitors can see Swelter Shelter, named by the archaeologists who excavated it, and a panel of Fremont petroglyphs several miles northeast of the Dinosaur Quarry. Ask for directions at the Visitor Center or Dinosaur Quarry.

FREMONT INDIAN STATE PARK
11000 Clear Creek Canyon Road
Sevier, UT 84766
(801)527-4631

This state park is the largest Fremont site ever excavated; there are magnificent rock art panels, interpreted at a fine new museum.

Suggestions for Further Reading

Aikens, C. Melvin. "Fremont Culture: Restatement of Some Problems." *American Antiquity* 37, no. 1 (1972): 61–66.
——— . "Plains Relationships of the Fremont Culture: A Hypothesis." *American Antiquity* 32, no. 2 (1967): 198–209.
Parker, Kathleen. *The Only True People: A History of the Native Americans of the Colorado Plateau*. Moab, Utah: Thunder Mesa Publishing, 1991.
Reed, Alan. *West Central Colorado Prehistoric Context*. Denver, Colo.: State Historical Society of Colorado, 1984.
Truesdale, James A. *Archaeological Investigations at Two Sites in Dinosaur National Monument: 42UN1724 and 5MF2645*. Division of Cultural Resources Selection Series No. 4. Denver, Colo.: National Park Service, 1993.
Wormington, H. M. *A Reappraisal of the Fremont Culture*. Denver, Colo.: Denver Museum of Natural History, 1955.

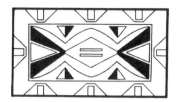

5

Prehistoric Cultures
of the Plains

▲ ▲

WHILE THE ANASAZI AND FREMONT CULTURES thrived in much of western Colorado, the Archaic hunters and gatherers of the Plains evolved as well, although they were not influenced by the advanced culture of the Anasazi (the Rocky Mountains may have been too great a barrier) but by people from the Midwest. Several hundred years before the Four Corners area became agricultural land, complex farm cultures were already developing in Ohio and Illinois. These people, called the Adena and Hopewell, cleared the thick woods for fields and built large ceremonial burial mounds and earthworks in the shape of animals, especially serpents. Beautiful jewelry, made of stones and shells obtained through trade from faraway places, was placed in their tombs. These farmers constructed villages that lined the rivers with houses built of logs. And they made pottery in which to cook—long before the Anasazi did.

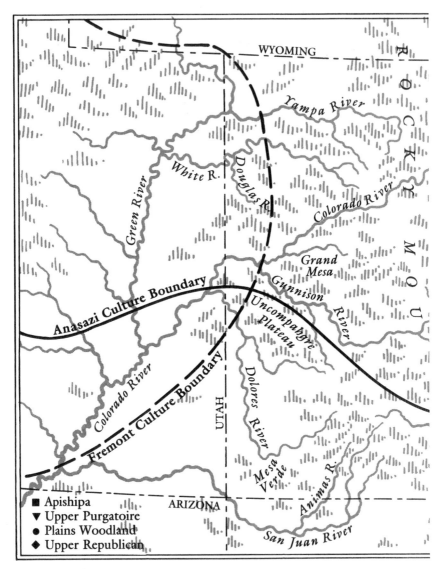

Figure 22:
(This page and page 63)
The Rocky Mountains served as a cultural barrier
between the Formative peoples of
western and eastern Colorado. Cultures of the
Oklahoma and Texas
panhandles and some as far away as the
Missouri and Mississippi rivers influenced
pottery types, housing styles, and farming practices
of Formative peoples on the
east side of the mountains.

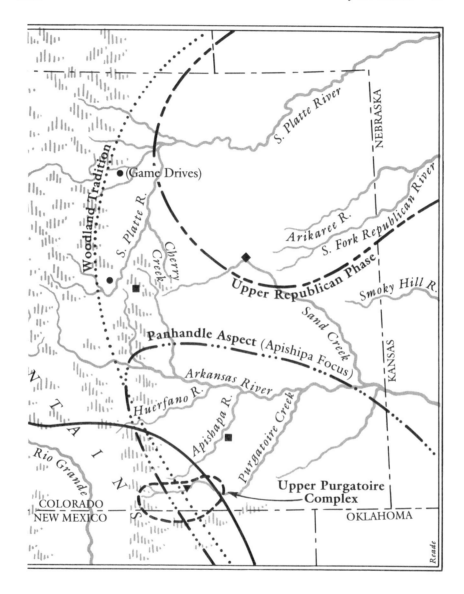

THE PLAINS WOODLAND CULTURE

Gradually, the ideas of these midwestern farmers, also known as the Mound Builders, began to influence people to the west. People living along the Missouri River passed the ideas on to those who lived along the major rivers of Colorado's vast Plains—the South Platte, Arikaree, Republican, Smoky Hill, and Arkansas. The ideas of the Mound Builders which reached people in Colorado, about A.D. 100, mainly concerned pottery, house building, and corn growing, but even these did not have a major influence. The culture of Colorado's first pottery makers is called the Woodland, or Prairie, culture.

A few houses of the Woodland people have been discovered in southeastern Colorado near Golden. Excavation of these features showed that the Woodland people often lived in shallow pithouses. But they may have also built the first aboveground dwellings in Colorado. One such house in southeastern Colorado was circular, the same as pithouses built during that same period. The occupants had built a low stone wall surrounding the ground-level floor. Like pithouses, large holes lined the interior of the wall, indicating the roof was supported by eight large posts. Roofs of both kinds of houses were made of sticks and mud.

Where rock shelters were present, they were probably preferred over houses. In the rock outcrops in the foothills near the town of Morrison, west of Denver, rock shelters protected Woodland families from winter snows and kept them cool in the heat of summer. In one excavated rock shelter, older and more recent artifacts suggested centuries of occupation; but distinctive cord-marked pottery and corner-notched arrowheads indicated that Woodland people, now armed with arrows instead of spears, had also lived in the shelter.

The pottery of the Woodland people differed from that of the Anasazi. While the Anasazi coiled long ropes of clay around and around to form a pot, the Woodland peoples made a pot by pressing thin slabs of clay together. A hand or a flat stone was then placed inside the pot while the outside was paddled with a piece of wood (this is called the paddle and anvil method of making pottery, as opposed to the coiling method). The outside was decorated with a thin piece of braided cord made of plant fiber, which was pressed against the soft clay before firing. The cord marking was decorative but also helped bind the pieces of clay together. This type of pottery is called cord-marked pottery. Pots were shaped like long cones with pointed bottoms so they could not sit flat, perhaps designed to fit in holes in the ground so they would not easily tip over.

It was during this period of the Woodland culture that bows and arrows largely replaced atlatls for hunting throughout the Colorado Plains (though not known, the source of this invention may have been the last migrants from Siberia). We know that bows and arrows were used at this time (about A.D. 500) because in Woodland sites in Colorado archaeologists found projectile points that are smaller than spear points in soil levels dating from this period. These smaller points are called arrowheads. The earliest arrowheads had notches in the corners, which were used to attach the points to the arrow shafts. Later arrowheads were side-notched. Bows and arrows had great advantages in hunting since game could be shot more accurately and at greater distances. Also, up to a hundred arrows could fit in an arrow quiver while only a few spears could be carried at a time.

Although pottery, houses, and limited farming were introduced to the Colorado Plains through the influence of the people of the Midwest, hunting and gathering still provided most of the food. Deer, buffalo, elk, and rabbit were favored meat sources.

It is thought that group hunting that employed game drives became very popular at this time. A typical game driveline consisted of rock walls and logs piled over ten feet high fanning out from a ridge crest in a V shape. The sheep were chased upslope into the wide part of the V and funneled towards the point, where hunters hid in shallow pits. The walls sloped inward at the top so the sheep, which were excellent jumpers, could not escape. The mountain sheep reeled about when funneled into the corral area at the end of the trap. When they circled back, hunters stood up in their pits and shot arrows into the confused herd.

The above information is based on the discovery of a game drive near Sawtooth Mountain, west of Denver. Artifacts found on the ground surface by archaeologist Steve Cassells and crew near the V-shaped rock walls suggest the drive was used for many generations (Cassells n.d.).

On the Carrizo ranches in Baca and Las Animas counties in southeastern Colorado rock walls have also been found leading out from cliff edges, probably used as corridors through which bison were chased over cliffs. Along the Continental Divide west of Denver, thirty-five game driveline sites have been documented within a stretch of fifteen miles. Artifacts found at some of the drives suggest use by Woodland peoples, although they were probably also used by later hunters.

Archaeologist James Benedict suggests an interesting seasonal migration route probably taken by Archaic peoples who lived in winter base camps in the foothills of the Front Range from roughly A.D. 570 to 1235. This area was chosen because the sandstone "hogback" region receives less snowfall than the Plains and is kept warmer by chinook winds, providing relative shelter from the elements.

Careful study of source material for tools led Benedict to conclude that when spring arrived, small groups of people headed north from their

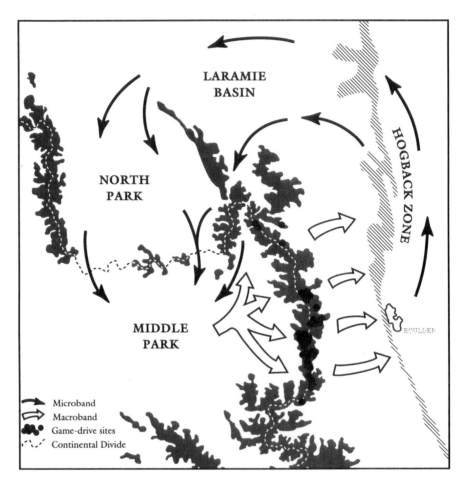

Figure 23:
Archaeological evidence suggests that
Archaic peoples who wintered near
present-day Boulder followed a seasonal migration
route beginning in the spring.
They headed north then west over a snow-free
pass to hunt in North Park,
then south to Middle Park in midsummer,
where they quarried stone
to make new tools. Come fall, they traveled east
to the Continental Divide
to hunt mountain sheep in communal game drives;
then, well stocked with meat, they headed back
to the sheltered hogback for the winter.
Reproduced by permission of the Regents of the University of Colorado
from Alpine and Arctic Research, *27 no.1 (1992).*

Figure 24:
At the crest of the Continental Divide, hunters funnel mountain sheep into a game driveline
consisting of natural and fabricated rock walls. Such game drives probably occurred in the
fall when the sheep were fat, having eaten the high mountain grasses all summer long.

winter camps. The bands of fifteen to fifty individuals took with them
cord-marked pottery, stone knives, corner-notched arrowheads, and
grinding slabs made of sandstone found only in the hogback region.

Near the present-day Colorado-Wyoming border, they found a pass
snow-free as early as mid-May and followed it west to North Park.
(Two passes further south were snow-free a month later, and all three
were probably used to make the most of the resources.) In North Park
wild plant foods such as cattail and bitterroot, as well as game, including
deer, antelope, buffalo, and elk, were abundant. As the snow melted
further south, they headed to Middle Park, where they continued to
hunt. They also replaced their worn tools with new ones chipped from
quality jaspers and cherts found in quarries near Table Mountain and
the Kremmling area. Middle Park was probably a festive region in midsummer, where small bands joined together for ceremonies, games,
courtships, and marriages.

By late August, the large bands climbed eastward to the Continental Divide, where elk and mountain sheep were plump and the snow

had finally melted off the game drive structures. Here, archaeologists have found tools made of Kremmling chert and Table Mountain jasper. Also, worn pieces of grinding slabs made of sandstone from the hogback region have been found, suggesting the people had to haul these tools with them all the way from their winter homes since no replacement material was available.

After a month of hunting, gathering berries, and enjoying the fall weather, snowfall forced the people to pack their loads of dried hides and meat and trudge east to their foothill winter camps. Knowing there was a supply of sandstone down below, the now completely worn grinding slabs were all left at timberline (Benedict 1992).

THE UPPER REPUBLICAN CULTURE

By the time a few diluted ideas had trickled into Colorado from peoples in the Midwest, the southern Hopewell culture in Mississippi and Louisiana had advanced to become the impressive Mississippian culture. This culture is known for the construction of gigantic platform mounds and huge cities surrounded by protective wooden and earthen walls. The cities were built in river valleys where vast cornfields grew. Ideas and trade goods from Mexico influenced the Mississippians in the form of doll-like effigies, parrot and macaw feathers, and human sacrifices.

The Woodland villagers along the Missouri River through Kansas, Nebraska, and South Dakota were the first to be influenced by the Mississippian culture. They built circular houses of earth, some of them large enough to house several families. The probable descendants of these people are the Mandans, Pawnees, and Arikara, who lived in similar houses when first observed by non-Indians.

From the villages along the Missouri River, some ideas of the Mississippian culture spread via people living along the Republican River (which flows into the Missouri) northwest into Nebraska. Here, around A.D. 1000, square and rectangular houses were built with posts holding up the roofs. Also, cord-marked pottery similar to Woodland pottery was made, but the pots were rounded instead of cone shaped. Along the Republican River, corn was grown and was more important in the diet than it had been during the Woodland period.

In Colorado, sites of this period, known as the Upper Republican, are not as impressive as those in Nebraska. The only solid evidence of the influence of the great Mississippian culture is the round pots found at Colorado sites dating from A.D. 1100 to 1300 (the same period of time that the Anasazi cliff dwellings were built and the whole area soon abandoned). Several Upper Republican sites have been excavated in eastern Colorado, two near Limon. In addition, north of the South Platte River side-notched arrowheads and sherds from rounded pots were found in rock shelters.

THE APISHAPA CULTURE

Corn cultivation and village life never quite took hold in the Plains of central and northeastern Colorado. But while the Anasazi in south-western Colorado were farming on the mesatops, the Indians in the southeastern part of the state learned how to store large amounts of wild food, a practice which enabled them to live in permanent houses for at least part of the year.

Projectile points and pots were similar to those farther north (arrowheads were side-notched, and pots were round). Clustered on canyon rims, the circular houses were built of huge rock slabs, and often tall rock pillars supported the wooden roofs.

At a site located near the Apishapa (a-PISH-a-pa) River, a southern tributary of the Arkansas River southeast of Pueblo, at least six houses made of stone slabs are perched near the edge of a cliff. Some slabs are standing upright while others lie on top of each other on the ground, forming walls. This type of upright slab architecture as well as wild seed storage and buffalo hunting are typical of the Apishapa culture, which flourished from roughly A.D. 1100 to 1400.

Apishapa-like houses also have been recently excavated at the Fort Carson Military Reservation near Colorado Springs. One of these, called the Avery Ranch site, revealed a huge C-shaped structure, the walls of which were made of massive sandstone blocks and slabs. Wooden juniper posts were placed between the rocks to support a roof of posts and brush. Two smaller slab-walled structures were excavated nearby. The small structures may have been the foundations of houses where two families lived. The large structure may have been a communal work area where buffalo meat and bones were cut up, hides were scraped and tanned, and goosefoot seeds and other wild plants were cooked.

Many bison bones were found in what could have been the large communal work area and throughout the site, suggesting that a bison kill had occurred nearby. Some bones had been broken to extract the edible marrow while others had been further broken to get out the bone grease.

Scraping tools were also excavated at the site, indicating that buffalo hides had been scraped there. Charred goosefoot seeds were found
throughout the site, and although some corn cobs were noted, it
appears the Apishapa people at the Avery Ranch site preferred gathering and cooking tiny goosefoot seeds to growing corn. Pottery jars
were used to cook the wild food.

The facts that mass killings of bison often occurred in the fall due
to their herding habits and that goosefoot seeds become edible in the
fall suggest that the Avery Ranch site may have been occupied from the
fall through the winter. The people lived mostly on dried buffalo meat,
bone marrow, stored goosefoot seeds, and other wild foods. These
foods could be sealed and protected in storage cists—holes dug into
the ground, lined with rocks, and sealed with large rock slabs.

The Fort Carson Apishapa sites and others found further south in
Pinyon Canyon (as well as those throughout most of southeastern Colorado) are all located in sandstone canyon environments. The Apishapa
people seem to have centered their culture on bison hunting and wild
food gathering. Perhaps with improved methods of storing foods they
could afford to stay in one place for a limited time and build houses to
live in during the winter. Here, they waited until spring when they left
their homes of stone and brush to follow bison and elk herds and
gather ripening plants. Before leaving, they may have planted a few
gardens with corn, hoping they would grow while they were gone.

Known Apishapa sites are on private or government-restricted property. Permission from the owners is needed to visit them.

THE UPPER PURGATOIRE CULTURE

West of the historic town of Trinidad, in southeastern Colorado, the
Purgatoire (PURG-a-tore-ee) River flows down from the Sangre de
Cristo Mountains. Some local people call it the Picket Wire River
because the original French name, which is still spoken incorrectly, was
difficult for early settlers to pronounce. Several years ago, the Purgatoire River was dammed west of Trinidad. Before the dam was built,
however, archaeologists recorded over three hundred sites and excavated some of them. These excavations revealed a previously unknown
culture that may have thrived in this one area and nowhere else.
Because it was identified on the Upper Purgatoire River, the culture, or
complex, was named after it.

The Upper Purgatoire Complex consisted of a combination of traits from several cultures in other areas. Pithouses, built from A.D. 1000 to 1100, are similar to some found on the eastern Plains. More recent houses built of adobe bricks made of mud and grass look like Pueblo houses of that time along the Rio Grande in New Mexico or adobe-brick houses from the Oklahoma Panhandle. Pottery was obviously influenced by the Rio Grande Pueblos. The corn grown by the people of the Upper Purgatoire could have come from either the Pueblos, the Oklahoma Panhandle, or both.

To summarize, in the centuries following A.D. 100 the Indians of the Colorado Plains basically followed their old lifestyle of gathering wild food and hunting game. Although slightly influenced by the grand civilizations of the Midwest and farmers from Oklahoma, life generally continued as it had for the last several thousand years. No evidence has been found to tell us what happened to the people who lived on the Colorado Plains before the arrival of the historic Indians. It is probable that as new migrants drifted into the area from the north, the original occupants were overpowered and joined the newcomers.

PLACES TO VISIT

The Woodland and Upper Republican cultures of eastern Colorado were somewhat influenced by the Mound Builders (Adena and Hopewell cultures) and Mississippian people, who lived in large villages in the Midwest and had trade networks extending as far west as the Yellowstone National Park area. Although the cultural traits were considerably altered by the time they reached Colorado, it is interesting to visit the sites where they originated.

Illinois

CAHOKIA MOUND STATE HISTORIC SITE
P.O. Box 681
Collinsville, IL 62234
(618) 346-5160

Sixty-five of the original 120 mounds of the Mississippian culture (circa A.D. 900 to 1100) can be visited at the largest prehistoric site in America. The museum contains artifacts, dioramas, and a reconstructed Mississippian village.

Ohio

HOPEWELL CULTURE NATIONAL HISTORICAL PARK
16062 State Route 104
Chillicothe, OH 45601
(614) 774-1125

Twenty-three mounds built by the people of the Hopewell culture during the first two centuries A.D. can be visited. The site, administered by the National Park Service, has a museum containing many artifacts, including the famous Hopewell "effigy pipes."

SERPENTS MOUND STATE MEMORIAL
3850 State Route 73
Peebles, OH 45660
(513) 587-2796

Although often associated with the earlier Adena culture (800 B.C. to A.D. 1), the quarter-mile-long serpent effigy mound may have been built by later Indians around A.D. 1000. Exhibits in the museum illustrate the Adena culture and different interpretations of the mound's construction.

OHIO HISTORICAL SOCIETY
1982 Velma Avenue
Columbus, OH 43211
(614) 297-2332

Reconstructed houses, dioramas, and hundreds of artifacts interpret the Hopewell, Adena, and other prehistoric and historic cultures of the Ohio River Valley.

For additional sites to visit in Ohio, call 1-800-BUCKEYE.

Suggestions for Further Reading

Drass, Richard R., and Peggy Flynn. "Temporal and Geographic Variations in Subsistence Practices for Plains Villagers in the Southern Plains." *Plains Anthropology, Journal of the Plains Anthropologist* 35, no. 128 (1990): 175–90.
Zier, Christian J., Stephen M. Kalasz, Margaret A. Van Ness, Anne H. Peebles, and Elaine Anderson. "The Avery Ranch Site Revisited." *Plains Anthropology, Journal of the Plains Anthropologist* 35, no. 128 (1990): 147–73.

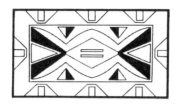

6

Historic Cultures
of the Plains

▲ ▲

E AST OF THE ROCKY MOUNTAINS the flat to gently rolling Great Plains stretch for hundreds of miles. Trees only grow along rivers and streams. Before settlers came to the Plains, the land was a sea of tall grass supporting over 30 million buffalo. Today, most of the natural grass is gone, and farms and ranches sprawl across the land. The Ogalalla aquifer, the vast underground store of water reaching from North Dakota to Texas and eastern Colorado to western Missouri, has been pumped for decades to water fields of corn and hay. The aquifer was named for a band of Lakota (Sioux) that lived in South Dakota and eastern Wyoming. The water table of the Ogalalla aquifer lowers each year, making the future of the Plains ecology unknown. Some think it might be wise to let the land grow native grasses and support protein-rich, low-fat buffalo again.

During the winter months the temperature plunges. The snow of howling blizzards forms massive drifts against the prairie hills. In the summer the sky is generally a searing blue, but it can suddenly turn black when huge, funnel-shaped tornadoes twist across the land. Fist-sized hailstones beat down, sending prairie dogs, coyotes, rabbits, and rattlesnakes rushing for shelter in their underground homes. Then, as quickly as it came, a summer storm disappears and steam rises from the ground.

THE ARRIVAL OF THE HORSE

One blazing summer day in the year 1541 some Indian buffalo hunters saw a sight in the distant haze that baffled them. Snaking down a hill were over two hundred men covered with hard, shiny skin that reflected the sun and seemingly attached to huge dogs. As they came nearer, the hunters were shocked to find the men were white-skinned and had hair on their faces. What the Indians saw were the armor-covered soldiers of the Coronado Expedition sent from New Spain (Mexico) to find cities of gold rumored to be located on the Plains. Although the Spaniards were disappointed in their search, Spanish horses eventually became as valuable as gold to the native hunters of the Plains.

The buffalo hunters learned that a horse could carry four times the load a dog could and travel twice as far each day, even though Indian dogs were strong, big, and long-bodied. Before horses, Indians hunted buffalo on foot when herds were in the area; but it took days, sometimes weeks, to catch up to them, and the buffalo might move on as soon as camp was set up. By contrast, horses could carry all the camp equipment, and riders on horseback could easily keep up with the herds.

With the arrival of horses scattered groups of hunters and gatherers banded together to hunt the far-roaming buffalo herds. As the Plains Indians became raiders, the warriors left the women and children in protected camps while they sought their enemies on horseback. Their loved ones no longer had to suffer the consequences of warfare along with them. The few Indians living on small farms along the rivers of southeastern Colorado also soon saw the advantages of horses. These useful animals, along with the buffalo, helped create a powerful, exciting culture that thrived in Colorado from the late 1700s until the mid-1860s, after the Civil War.

Figure 25:
Cattle, carts, and the pale-skinned, bearded Spanish equestrians of the
Coronado Expedition awed Apache hunters. Acquisition of the horse
dramatically changed the lifestyles of the Plains Indians.

In this culture horses became the focus of many activities. A man's wealth was measured by the number of horses he owned. As a child he cared for foals; when older, he watched over the camp's herd with other young men and was given a fast horse of his own. A boy was taught that stealing horses from rival tribes or ranches was a necessary skill. Much time was spent training a horse to ride close to stampeding buffalo—a dangerous feat since a hazard as insignificant as a rodent hole could trip the most intelligent horse, sending both horse and rider to the ground where they would be trampled to death. A good buffalo horse was worth several pack horses. The best buffalo horses were wild mustangs that had been captured after becoming accustomed to grazing alongside herds of buffalo.

Mexican and Indian strays probably formed the first wild horse herds in Texas around 1650. The herds grew and spread from there north into Colorado, especially along the Arkansas River Valley and east of Colorado Springs. Capturing wild horses was not too difficult if done in the spring when they were half-starved from winter. At that time of the year the horses were usually full of fresh grass and water and not in shape to run very far. To capture horses, one hunter would lie flat on his horse's back, ride close to a herd, and then charge into the herd, scattering the horses. Other men would ride from behind low hills, where they had been hidden from view, and capture the horses. George Bent, son of the Cheyenne Owl Woman and the famous trader William Bent, described capturing horses in the 1860s:

> Each hunter had a long slender pole with the noose of his lasso fastened to the end of the pole. As he overtook the mustang he was pursuing, he rode up alongside and slipped the noose over the wild horse's head. He then "choked down" the mustang until it was subdued, then threw it, put a rawhide halter on its head, and "tailed it up" to a tame horse. Gentle old mares were usually taken along to be employed in this work. The wild horse's head was tied close up to the mare's tail. This was called "tailing" the mustang. Old mares were best because the wild horses soon became very friendly with them and followed along after the mares without giving much trouble (Hyde 1987, 35–37).

The horses remained tied to the mares' tails all the way back to camp. While still tied, a man would gently rub a horse's nose, ears, and back. After a while he would place a buffalo robe on its back and lead the mare and wild horse around the camp. Hobbling the wild horse, the man would untie it from the mare and pile more robes on. When the horse became used to the weight, the man would mount it while it was still hobbled. The next day the man would untie and unhobble the horse and ride around with the mare next to it. In this gentle manner, the wild mustangs were broken.

The majority of wild horses lived south of the Arkansas River, in Comanche, Kiowa, and Apache country. These tribes naturally owned the largest herds. A group of Kiowas, Comanches, and Apaches camped on the Arkansas River near Bent's Fort in southern Colorado reportedly had their horses grazing for fifty miles along the river.

These tribes supplemented the wild mustangs they captured with horses stolen from ranches in Texas, Mexico, and New Mexico. Only a few men would go on a horse raid. They traveled on foot, a very dangerous undertaking since they could rarely escape mounted enemies if caught in the open; consequently, they walked in ravines whenever possible. Most horses grazed within a few miles of the villages, but the most desirable ones were herded into the camps every evening and staked near their owners' houses. The raiders would wait until dark, then slip into camp and attempt to steal the best horses.

THE BUFFALO, GIVER OF LIFE

Almost all necessities of the Plains Indians of Colorado came from the buffalo. Babies, wrapped in the soft hides of buffalo calves, sucked on buffalo meat and lived on a diet centered around buffalo the rest of their lives. Their mothers ground buffalo dung into a fine baby powder (moss was also used, with "diapers" of soft hides). Fresh buffalo meat, especially the tongue, was enjoyed the most; however since buffalo were difficult to hunt in the winter strips of meat from buffalo killed in the summer were sliced thin, dried in the sun, and stored—food known by non-Indians as jerky. Pemmican was also made from dried buffalo meat and berries.

Strict rules were followed during a buffalo hunt. No individual could start hunting without the others. If the herd was disturbed before the hunters assembled, those responsible for frightening them would have their tipis torn down, their weapons and horses destroyed, and their clothing torn. In some tribes the offenders were flogged by the soldier societies (see "The Cheyennes").

Hunting buffalo on horseback was thrilling and dangerous. The hunters wore only breechcloths and guided the horses with their legs or knees so their hands would be free to throw spears or shoot bows and arrows, or later, repeating rifles. The dust from the panic-stricken, charging buffalo made it hard to see, and hunters had to ride close enough to get a good shot. Before firearms, each hunter's spear or arrow was marked so he could tell which buffalo (or enemy) he had killed. Many Indians preferred using arrows to guns for just this reason. Right-handed marksmen guided their horses to the right side of the buffalo, and the spear or arrow was thrust or shot into the kidneys. Some bows were so strong that an arrow shot from them would go in one side of a buffalo and out the other. The hunt usually lasted about

Figure 26:
A good buffalo horse was trained to run among a stampeding herd
to allow its rider a close shot.

ten minutes. Although the horses could run as fast as the buffalo, they could not keep up the rapid pace for long. There was only enough time to shoot a few lances, arrows, or bullets.

Hunters also stalked buffalo on foot (as their Archaic ancestors had) when there were no buffalo horses, when the snow was deep, or when there were few buffalo in the herd. This activity was a challenge that showed the skill and cunning of the hunters. Covered with wolf skins, they would mingle with the herd and silently shoot many buffalo cows with arrows, without the herd noticing. Guns, of course, could not be used since the noise would create a stampede.

A carcass was butchered by at least two people. Some sources say that a buffalo was butchered while lying on its back. Others claim that because of the hump, a dead buffalo was butchered lying on its stomach. When butchered in this position, sharp stone knives were used to cut the skin along the back, and the hide was pulled down on each side of the animal. The skin served as a mat on which the best meat, sliced from the hump, was placed. The front legs were then stripped of meat, then the back legs, pelvis, vertebrae, and head. The soft parts of the animal, such as the liver, kidneys, brains, part of the nose, the marrow of the leg bones, blood, and fat, were eaten raw at the butchering site.

When the meat was dragged back to camp, everyone feasted. After pulling meat-ladened travois (TRAV-wah) to the village, the dogs scampered back to the kill site and devoured the scraps. Mother dogs ate their fill and returned to camp to regurgitate the chewed meat for their puppies.

The sheer number of necessary items made from buffalo parts testifies to the ingenuity of the Indians and to the importance of the buffalo to Plains culture. The hides were used for numerous purposes. Hides taken in summer were staked out on the ground and scraped by women with scrapers made of buffalo bone then made into tipi covers. In the winter sometimes they left the hair on the hides to make warm sleeping robes or mittens, caps, and moccasins. Hairless hides were also made into stiff boxes called parfleches (PAR-flesh-es) in which clothing, food, tools, cooking utensils, and other items could be carried. Rawhide (untanned skin) was also made into cooking kettles and round, tublike boats, which were not used for river travel but for carrying things across water. Arrow quivers—cases to carry arrows—and moccasin soles, drums, and saddles were also made from rawhide. Both broken tools and broken bones were splinted with rawhide. From rawhide of a bull, good rope was made which was tied when wet so it would shrink when dry; thus it could tightly bind a travois or a stone axe to a wooden axe handle. The thick neck skin from a bull was used to make battle shields for warriors. Although buffalo hide was too thick for most clothing (whenever available, deer, elk, or antelope hide was made into shirts, dresses, and breechcloths), the thin, soft hide of buffalo calves was made into underclothes.

Drinking cups and spoons were made from buffalo horns. The hooves provided glue. The sinew, or tendons, from along the animal's back were made into bowstrings and sewing thread. Needles were made from sharp pieces of bone. In the winter children scooted down hills on sleds made of buffalo ribs.

Since people on the move had little use for breakable baskets or pots, buffalo stomachs were cleaned thoroughly and served as waterbags, food carriers, and cooking pots. Hot stones were added to liquid rather than placing the pots directly over the fire. A real treat was hot buffalo blood boiled in a buffalo stomach. (Plains Indians supplemented buffalo meat with deer, antelope, rabbit, and wild turkey as well as plant foods such as wild potatoes and onions, spinach, and prairie turnips.) Because there was little firewood available on the Colorado Plains, except for trees growing along the rivers, dried dung, commonly called "buffalo chips," was used as fuel for cooking fires.

THE VILLAGES OF THE PLAINS

Before the arrival of horses among Plains tribes, small hide tents that could be carried by dog travois sheltered the Colorado Plains hunters and gatherers. A travois consisted of two poles and a crossbar tied in the shape of an A. The top of the A lay across a dog's back, and the spread-out poles forming the base dragged along the ground. The tents and other goods were lashed onto a net or poles forming the crossbar of the A. After the arrival of horses larger travois carrying heavier items could be pulled by them, allowing the construction of huge tipis made of buffalo hide.

Twelve to twenty buffalo hides were sewn together to make a tipi cover, depending on the wealth of the family. Generally, hides of cows taken in the summer were used for lodge skins while hides taken in the winter were used for warm robes. First, the hides were stretched and pegged to the ground, where women scraped off the flesh with bone scrapers, turning the hides to scrape off the hair. Then the tanning mixture of soapweed, grease, liver, and brains was rubbed in and left to dry overnight. The next day, the skins were worked over a string of tight sinew or through the hole of a buffalo shoulder blade until they were fairly soft. Then three straight poles (the Utes used four) were tied towards their tops and set up like a tripod. More poles were laid against the tripod, and the lower ends were spread out to form a large circle. The top of the tipi cover was tied to the top of a separate pole, and both were heaved up on the framework. The cover was spread around the poles and pinned together with long, wooden pegs. New tipis were made waterproof by allowing a fire to smolder inside. Two smoke flaps were moved by poles as the wind changed to let out smoke from the center fire; these were closed when there was heavy rain or snow.

Various adjustments were made to the tipi interior to control the temperature. When the weather was hot, the edges of the tipi were raised to let air through; when the temperature dropped, a skin liner on the inside or bunches of grass on the outside kept out drafts. An animal skin covered the oval-shaped doorway. Beds were made of grass, soft deerskin, or, in the winter, thick buffalo robes. The family usually slept on the left side of the door while the right side was saved for guests. Babies slept in cradleboards hung from the poles. Backrests made of willow branches made sitting more comfortable.

In most Colorado tribes, women owned the family tipis and everything in them. It took only a few minutes for several women to erect a tipi. Women often painted designs on hides and hung them on the insides of the tipis while men decorated the outsides with images representing their war adventures or visions they had experienced. When enough hides were available, the tipis were usually replaced every spring.

The circular shape of the tipi had special meaning. For some tribes, the circle was an unbroken line symbolizing the unity of the people and the equality of all things of the earth. The sun and earth, from which life came, were circular. Also, the Prayer Circle (Medicine Wheel) is a common motif represented in ancient rock art and other mediums including modern jewelry designs. The circle is often divided into four parts, representing not only the four directions and four races but the heart, soul, mind, and body as well as the four seasons of life. In the Medicine Lodge constructed for the Sun Dance (see "Beliefs"), the circular shape of the lodge represents the universe while each post surrounding the lodge represents some object of creation.

Traditionally, an entire camp might be set up in a circle. Each clan was assigned a place within the circle to pitch its tipis, and wide walkways divided the clan groupings. Guards were usually camped on the outside to protect the people. Tipis were erected with the doors facing east, so the lodges would be sheltered from the blasting winter winds that usually blew from the west. When people opened their tipi door in the morning, they would greet the rising sun. At night, the fires lit up the tipis, and they looked like hundreds of giant lanterns.

Tribes had favorite campsites where they stayed seasonally. Generally, in the summer camps were located on the Plains by rivers where cottonwood trees provided firewood and shade and where grass for horses was plentiful. The lush grasses of North Park and South Park located on the east side of the Rocky Mountains attracted animals, and consequently hunters, during the summer. There were often battles in these areas because enemies of the Plains tribes, particularly the Utes, were frequently encountered at these sites. In the fall before the winter winds blasted, the camps were moved west, closer to the protection of the Rockies.

Several guards known for their bravery usually slept outdoors near the camps, in the rain, hail, or snow, to watch for horse raiders. Some had an equally important job—to watch buffalo. If a nearby herd started moving during the night, hunters were warned so they could follow the herd.

When an entire camp moved due to a change of seasons or to be closer to a large buffalo herd, there would be a flurry of activity as dawn began to break. Young men and boys would round up the horses while women would take down the tipis and load them, along with the family belongings, onto the horse and dog travois. Young children and older people unable to ride horses would ride on the travois, and women would ride horses with small children on their laps and babies in their cradleboards hung on the saddle pommels.

A moving camp of Plains Indians could be several miles long. Scouts rode in front to look for buffalo, enemies, and good campsites. The chiefs and hunters followed, and armed warriors rode on each side of the women and children. According to George Bent, the Indians spread out as they traveled and ". . . there were no well-marked trails in the plains. The Indians knew the whole country like a book and took any route they pleased. They traveled by landmarks from one stream to the next. As the Indians did not travel in 'Indian-file,' as the whites seem to suppose, they did not leave a deep-marked trail, and after the village had gone on, the trail would soon disappear and leave no mark in the grass" (Hyde 1987, 182). By contrast, trails were more clearly defined in the plateau and mountain regions, where rugged topography limited the available travel routes, usually to animal trails. Some of these ancient trails are still in use today. When the new camp was reached, tipis were set up along a stream, near trees which provided firewood and poles to make meat-drying scaffolds. Level ground was needed not only for lodges but for stretching and drying buffalo hides.

CLOTHING AND HAIR

Babies were wrapped in soft animal skins and secured in cradleboards the first year or two of their lives. Infants were tied snugly to the boards, according to the Cheyennes, to simulate the comfort of the

Figure 27:
Plains women's and girls' deer hide dresses were typically T-shaped,
fringed, and richly beaded with geometric designs.
Photo courtesy of the Colorado Historical Society.

Figure 28:
Fortunately for small children, heavily beaded
buckskin clothing and ornate jewelry were worn
only on special occasions.
Photo courtesy of the Colorado Historical Society.

mother's womb. Little boys usually wore nothing until they were almost eight years old, at which time they donned breechcloths. These were long strips of soft leather and later, cloth passed between the legs and tied to the waist with a cord. The excess leather flaps hung down in front and back. Young girls wore dresses made of deerskin that was tanned by their mothers to make it soft.

Older boys and men also wore only breechcloths and moccasins in the warmer months. During ceremonies they often painted their faces and bodies with designs. In cold weather or at ceremonies, men also wore leather leggings, often with flaps of fringe. Leggings protected the legs while riding and were later adopted by cowboys, who called them chaps. Shirts made of two deerskins sewn together were worn over the leggings. Fringed sleeves, sometimes decorated with horse hair or weasel skins, were often attached to the shirts, and the scalps of enemies were sometimes sewn on for decoration. In addition, some clothing was decorated with paint made from plants and minerals.

Women wore T-style dresses of deer hide, the yoke made of one hide, the rest of the dress made from another. There were often fringes on the sides and borders of dresses that swayed gracefully when the women walked or danced. Beads of stones, juniper berries, animal horns, and elk teeth were sewn onto dresses for decoration. Leggings were worn under the dresses.

Both men's and women's clothing was often decorated with flattened porcupine quills (where available), dyed different colors and sewn into the leather to make designs. Later, beads obtained from white traders almost entirely replaced this quill work. Then men's shirts had solid bands of beads over the shoulders and along the sleeves; the sides of their leggings were also beaded. The yokes of women's dresses were beaded in square, triangular, or rectangular designs, or combinations of all these shapes.

Figure 29:
During warm months, or sometimes when hunting buffalo on horseback, men wore only a breechcloth of deer hide or fabric, drawn between the legs and tucked under a belt in front and back. (Goes Uphill, Arapahoe). Photo courtesy of the Denver Public Library.

Hair was worn loose or parted in the middle and braided. Some tribes painted the part line red. The fat from bear or buffalo was rubbed into the hair to keep it in place. When a loved one died, women often cut their hair short and did not wash or brush it until the mourning period was over—sometimes a year or longer. People of the Kiowa tribe cut their hair only on the right side. As a result, in sign language, the sign for Kiowa was a cupped hand passed around the right side of the face in a circular motion.

GAMES, PLAY, AND MUSIC

Since prehistoric times all American Indians have played games. The Plains Indians had games that taught young boys skills in hunting and fighting such as throwing spears through rolling hoops to improve aim. Boys played in mock battles and had to recite what kind of "coup" points each "warrior" earned (see "Raiding and Warfare"). They also had contests to see who could shoot arrows the straightest and fastest or, in winter, who could slide a stick across the ice closest to a certain spot. A person was considered a fast shot if he could shoot three arrows in the air before the first one touched the ground. Swimming contests were held on summer days when boys swam on their backs as fast as they could with a foot stuck out of the water and a blob of mud on the big toe.

Girls played with toys made to teach them tasks they would pursue as women. They placed buckskin dolls lovingly on squirrel skin beds inside miniature tipis and used tiny spoons of buffalo horn to feed the dolls from small bowls made from tree knots.

Footraces, including relay races, were popular and improved running skills. Sometimes the women of different tribes would play tug-of-war or shinny, a ball game similar to modern hockey. Naturally, horse racing was enjoyed by all.

Tops carved of wood and spun with a whip of cordage were favorite toys among children of all ages. Bull roarers, flat pieces of wood tied to strings which made a roaring sound when whirled overhead, were also popular. Guessing games were played by everyone, especially on winter nights inside the warm tipis. A favorite one was moccasin. To play this game, three moccasins were placed on the ground with a small rock in one, and people tried to guess which moccasin held the rock. Many varieties of this game were played, including one version where the rock was held in one hand or the other. Such games are still played by Indians today.

Gambling was very popular. Plains Indians bet on all games and often anything else which had an unknown outcome. Shirts, tools, tipis, entire horse herds, and even wives were bet, which made winning exciting and losing devastating. (Modern bingo casinos on reservations, built to provide tribal income, reflect the traditional love of gambling, although non-Indians patronize the casinos more than Indians.)

Figure 30:
A game enjoyed by women of many tribes was shinny, which was played with sticks and a
ball—somewhat similar to hockey. Behind these Ute women are the Book Cliffs of
western Colorado or eastern Utah.
Photo courtesy of the Colorado Historical Society, 1908.

Music was very important to Plains Indians. At night, the rapid beat of drums could be heard miles from a camp. Drumming was (and is) an important form of expression of individual feelings and enabled spiritual contact. Drum making was an exacting skill learned only by a few people. Special ceremonies required dancing, and the drums kept the rhythm going (rhythms generally consisted of four beats). Victory dances were held when men returned from successful horse raids or battles of revenge. People also danced to celebrate such events as a boy's first animal kill and a girl's coming of age.

All songs sung among the tribes had symbolic meaning. Songs were "copyrighted" by individual families by an unwritten law. These songs, along with other musical skills, were passed down in families through generations (Jennie Parker 1994, personal communication). Songs were accompanied by drums, shakers made of small bones and dewclaws, and rattles fashioned of dried gourds filled with pebbles or other small objects. Sometimes wooden flutes were played, producing a beautiful melody drifting through a tipi camp. Often a young man courted a girl near her tipi by playing special tunes he had composed.

RAIDING AND WARFARE

From the time a boy could get his legs over the back of a horse, he dreamed of battle. During winter evenings inside his family's tipi his grandfather showed numerous scars and proudly explained how he had gotten each one. There was no better honor than dying in battle.

Most battles resulted from raiding—to steal horses or get back ones that had been previously stolen. Horse stealing was not considered a crime but an honorable act requiring skill and courage. Although it was not the intention of a horse raid to kill, sometimes people died while defending or stealing horses. If, during a horse raid, many men were killed by the enemy, the wives or relatives of those men might gather together a group of warriors to avenge the deaths of their loved ones. Such war parties often attacked at dawn when the enemy camp was unprepared.

Even during battles of revenge, killing an enemy was not considered as brave as simply touching him. This act is called counting coup (pronounced "coo," meaning "hit" in French). With his hand, spear, or special coup stick, a warrior rode up to an enemy and touched him. Although the enemy might be shot by another warrior, the one who touched him received the most honor. It was also more honorable to kill with a spear or war club than with a bow and arrow or a gun because it was more dangerous than shooting arrows or guns from a distance. Nearly every act of war was valued according to how much courage it required, although the value placed on various acts differed from tribe to tribe. Some thought taking an enemy's horse ranked almost as high as counting coup. Others thought taking an enemy's gun was more worthy. Getting wounded deserved recognition, but rescuing a wounded tribesman ranked higher in most tribes. Back at camp, warriors proudly told of their deeds and rarely lied about coup. Coup was so important that everyone was watched carefully by others, and one risked being exposed and humiliated by lying.

The wearing of feathers in the hair was not due to whim but had special significance. Among the Cheyennes, for example, the particular manner in which feathers were worn indicated the society to which a man belonged. In some tribes a feather worn straight up meant the warrior had killed someone with his fists. A feather placed in the hair horizontal with the ground often meant the warrior had counted coup on a live or dead enemy. Among the Sioux, a tribe that often visited

Colorado, a V-shaped slash in one side of a feather signified that the warrior had cut the enemy's throat and scalped him. A similar slash on the other side of the feather meant he had been third to count coup on an enemy. Headdresses made of eagle feathers were worn only by men who had counted coup many times in battle, each feather representing a specific coup count.

Plains tribes also honored skills in battle through military societies. The Cheyennes, for example, had five societies, the Fox, Elk, Shield, Bowstring, and Dog (or Crazy Dog), each performing its own dances and songs and wearing distinctive clothing styles. The Dog Soldiers became the most feared warriors on the Colorado Plains (and beyond) and eventually evolved into a distinct band of their own.

Figure 31:
Most Indians were pampered as children because parents knew their adult lives would be difficult. A boy such as this Shoshone might die as a young warrior (Washakie's grandson). Photo courtesy of the Denver Public Library.

Weapons of war consisted of bows and arrows, war shields, and, later, repeating rifles. Bows were only three or four feet long, so they could easily be carried while riding a horse. Arrows were about two feet long. Almost one hundred arrows could be carried in a quiver, a long leather bag that hung over the shoulder. Even after the repeating rifle was available through trade with non-Indians, the bow and arrow were often used, particularly when game might be easily frightened by gunshots. Also, enemies had a harder time figuring out from which direction arrows were coming than gunshots.

When a young man was ready to go to war, he made a shield from the tough hide of a buffalo neck. A personal design was painted on the shield, giving the shield protective powers. Arrows could not go through a well-made shield but bullets could. The war shield was sacred and was kept in a cover until battle.

Special designs were painted on men's faces and horses before battle, often with red pigments, representing strength. Early explorers called Indians redskins because of this practice. On returning from a successful battle, black paint, representing victory, darkened the faces of the proud warriors of some tribes.

Before a battle, a warrior said a prayer and sang a war song to make him brave. If he was a seasoned and respected chief, he might don a specially made war bonnet representing certain personal traits and exploits, then charge into battle. His determination to fight with honor, to count coup, often led to his death.

A dead Plains Indian was wrapped in buffalo robes and placed on a platform to keep animals from the body. A warrior's shield was wrapped with him, and his favorite horse and sometimes even his wife and slave were killed so they could accompany him to the Spirit World. Red pigment, representing Mother Earth, was frequently painted on deceased members of the tribe so the spirits of their relatives would recognize them. Loved ones often gashed their own arms and legs, cut off a finger, or cut their hair as part of the mourning ritual. A woman might cut her hair and sometimes not comb it for a year after the death of her husband.

The most honored people in the Plains tribes were the chiefs. (While the Utes resent the term "chief" since it is a word non-Indians have applied to their leaders, most other tribes accept the term.) In many tribes, there were two kinds of chiefs, war chiefs and peace chiefs. These positions were not inherited but had to be earned.

A war chief might be a leader for just one raid or battle, or he might be so successful and respected that he would retain this position for many years. By contrast, because the war chief set the rules of battles and led the attacks, he might lose his position if a battle was unsuccessful. The characteristics of a peace chief had to include compassion, generosity to those less fortunate, bravery, and intelligence. It was believed that even the most fearless warrior would not make a good peace chief if he lacked any of these traits. A peace chief rarely led a battle charge, leaving the honor to more skillful fighters. In constant communication with the camp police (such as the Dog Soldiers of the Cheyenne), he was a peace keeper, often settling disputes without taking sides. He was also responsible for deciding when and where to move the camp and for selecting a soldier society to police the village. When representatives from enemy tribes came to talk of peace, it was the peace chief's duty to host them while they visited the camp. Nobody could harm an enemy while he was under the protection of the peace chief.

BELIEFS

The Colorado Plains Indians believed that there was a power beyond that of humans. The beliefs and ceremonies that centered around this power are called supernaturalism, and supernatural beings, or gods, were honored. Appeal to the gods, or religion as non-Indians call it, was part of the Plains Indians' daily life and could not be separated from it. All things in nature were there for a reason, and humans were connected to them all. Ceremonies and magic were used to "call" animals being hunted and to honor buffalo and bring them back after their winter migration. When an animal was killed, the hunter thanked the spirit of the animal for giving itself so the hunter and his family could eat. Although each tribe had its own way of practicing religion, there were four important elements of religious practice common to many Colorado tribes: the vision quest, the Sun Dance, the sweat lodge, and the medicine man.

THE VISION QUEST

Visions were the most important part of religious life. They were sought to bring success in hunts, warfare, and raiding, as well as to bring good health. Visions were real to the person who sought them, and nobody lied about seeing a vision. Often a person would seek a vision on a high hill or mountaintop. For a period of four days the person on a vision quest would not eat and would be exposed to the elements and suffer lack of sleep. Then, following this time of deprivation, if the seeker had a true heart and a belief in the spirits, he might experience a vision.

During the vision, a person or animal would teach the vision quester, often an adolescent boy, certain songs he must sing for luck in hunting or in battle and describe specific totems to put in his medicine bundle. If the spirit was an animal, then that animal could never be killed by the one experiencing the vision. If a person was unfortunate enough not to experience a vision, that person might "buy" a copy of someone else's medicine bundle and receive its power—although this option was inferior to having a medicine bundle resulting from a personal vision. Dreams were often as important as visions since they could predict the future or guide somebody when a decision had to be made. Certain members of the tribe were often sought to explain the meanings of particularly noteworthy dreams.

THE SUN DANCE

Roughly twenty Plains tribes performed the Sun Dance. The Cheyennes, Arapahoes, and Sioux practiced it the most elaborately (the Cheyennes and Arapahoes lived in Colorado, and the Sioux often raided there). The following summarizes the basic rites of the Sun Dance as followed by most of the Colorado Plains tribes, although each had its own variations based on individual belief systems.

The Sun Dance was performed at the request of a person who vowed to sponsor it if some of his or her loved ones' problems would be solved. This request also might involve a more universal problem that affected the whole tribe. Sun Dances are still performed today for the same reasons. The ceremony was usually held in the late spring or early summer, when the buffalo grass was a certain height, although it was sometimes held in the fall. In prereservation days a Sun Dance in the spring served to gather all the bands together after the long winter.

The first four days of the ceremony were spent asking the Great Spirit for the renewal of all life: to bring new babies, buffalo calves, grasses, and other plants to the world. On the fourth day the Sun Dance Lodge was built. A man was chosen to find the perfect tall cottonwood tree for the center pole of the Sun Dance Lodge. After the

Figure 32:
This nineteenth-century sketch of a Sioux Sun Dance portrays the tearing of the flesh by hanging from the Sun Dance pole or by dragging buffalo skulls. Feather headdresses may not have been worn during the ceremony. Courtesy of the Denver Public Library.

tree was located, there was great excitement as other men galloped off on their horses to cut it down. After the tree was cut, the men treated it as they would an enemy, rushing up to it and counting coup on it. When it was dragged back to camp, offerings were placed in the fork of the pole, and it was set up in the center of the dance area. A wall of posts and branches was built around the pole, and a roof of poles and branches completed the circular Sun Dance Lodge, called various names, including Offerings Lodge, by the Arapahoes.

On the fifth day warriors gathered around the center pole and danced as they stared at the top of the pole. They blew whistles made of eagle bone and prayed for power. Some dancers did not drink water or eat for four days.

On the eighth day, those who had vowed to make a sacrifice had their flesh pierced with skewers, often made of sticks or eagle claws. The skewers were placed under the chest or back muscles, and ropes were tied from the skewers to the top of the center pole. The dancers then strained until they tore out the skewers from their muscles and flesh. Often the piercing was done through the back muscles, and buf-falo skulls were attached to ropes hooked through the skewers. The men danced and dragged the skulls until the skulls pulled loose, usually in a few hours. Sometimes dancers were pierced through the chest and hoisted up into the air so only their weight would rip out the skewers.

The Sun Dancers sacrificed themselves for the good of others. Women could offer sacrifices by cutting small pieces of skin from their arms or by offering their children's outgrown clothes, which were left to the elements. Although this may not seem like much of a sacrifice, it is necessary to keep in mind how time consuming it was to make clothes out of animal hides.

The Sun Dance was made illegal by the United States government from 1904 to 1935. It is currently practiced by some tribes, particularly the Sioux in South Dakota, the Northern Cheyennes in Lame Deer, Montana, and the Northern Arapahoes on the Wind River Reservation in Wyoming (the Utes perform a version of the Sun Dance that does not involve self-torture). It is reported that Sun Dances were held more often than usual during the Vietnam War to bring peace to the world.

THE SWEAT LODGE

Sweat lodges (also called sweat houses) were common not only in Colorado but among American Indians everywhere. Sweating purified, or cleansed, the body and soul. Sweats were taken before and after performing ceremonies, before hunting, to cure illness, or whenever a sense of well-being was desired.

The sweat lodge was a dome-shaped structure of branches, often willow, covered with skins. Although it was small it represented the entire universe. Rocks were heated on a fire outside and brought into the center of the small lodge, where seven or sometimes more people could sit cross-legged. Water was then poured over the rocks, and people inhaled the hissing steam that filled the small enclosure, which was the sacred breath of the earth. Even though the heat and steam were often unbearable, they might cure disease or a wound of the body or mind. People left the sweat house refreshed, feeling closer to each other and the Great Spirit. Sand was often rubbed on the skin to dry it off.

Sweat lodges still are used by many American Indians of all tribes whenever a person has a problem and needs the prayers of friends and

help from the Great Spirit. They are also used prior to certain ceremonies, particularly among the Navajos, who used to live in southwestern Colorado. Sweats are held on the Ute reservations in Colorado and
Utah; in communities in Oklahoma, Montana, and Wyoming (where
other Colorado Indian tribes were relocated); and in Colorado cities,
particularly in Denver, where there is a large American Indian population. In prisons Indians often hold sweats to exercise their religious
freedom—a practice that helps the prisoners maintain a connection to
their traditional life in an alien environment. Sweats are also becoming
popular among non-Indians, something which is offensive to many traditional people, who think non-Indians are not using sweats for the
correct purposes.

MEDICINE MEN AND PRIESTS

Medicine men, often called shamans by non-Indians, played important
roles in the religion of the Colorado Plains Indians. They had special
powers given to them by the spirits, frequently through visions. A person was obligated to obey the spirits, even if he did not want to
become a medicine man. With their power and knowledge of medicinal herbs and plants, medicine men could cure the sick, call animals to
be hunted, locate enemy tribes, and help find lost or stolen property.
To prove their power, they sometimes performed feats of magic. For
example, Cheyenne and Arapahoe medicine men often walked barefoot
on fire. Kiowa medicine men were forbidden to exhibit their power,
however; if they did so, it was believed they would suffer penalties of
misfortune, a belief that still exists today.

Doctoring was one of the most important jobs of a medicine man,
who often cured patients with knowledge of medicinal plants. If medicinal plants did not work, a medicine man often "sucked out" a foreign
object, such as a piece of bone or an insect, that had made the person
sick. The patient's health often improved when he or she saw the
object that had caused the illness. Medicine men are still sought by traditional American Indians for curing certain physical and psychological
problems. Occasionally, a medical doctor will suggest the patient seek
the help of a medicine man to augment a modern cure (the practice of
seeing a physician as well as a medicine man is not considered a con-
flict—many American Indians often consult both).

With the exception of the Kiowas, most tribes had priests. These respected people differed from medicine men in that they presided over ceremonies instead of healing the sick. Ceremonies were supervised so that all stages of the rituals, such as songs, dances, and offerings, were performed correctly. Priests spent years learning hundreds of rituals and songs. They also were in charge of sacred objects such as the Cheyenne Sacred Arrows and the Arapahoe Flat Pipe. Today, priests still supervise important ceremonies, although they also might hold jobs as teachers, bankers, or carpenters.

PLACES TO VISIT

Colorado

COLORADO HISTORY MUSEUM
1300 Broadway
Denver, CO 80203
(303)866-4686

The museum has displays and dioramas of Colorado Plains Indian cultures.

Suggestions for Further Reading

Bains, Rae. *Indians of the Plains.* Nahwah, N.J.: Troll Associates, 1985.
Baldwin, Gordon C. *Games of the American Indian.* New York: W. W. Norton and Company, 1969.
Bancroft-Hunt, Norman. *The Indians of the Great Plains.* Norman: University of Oklahoma Press, 1992.
Koch, Ronald P. *Dress Clothing of the Plains Indians.* Norman: University of Oklahoma Press, 1977.
Mails, Thomas. *Mystic Warriors of the Plains.* New York: Marlowe and Company, 1995.

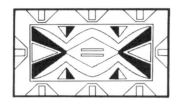

7

General History of the Plains Tribes

▲ ▲

*F*OR CENTURIES THE WINDY COLORADO PLAINS have been the home of many Indian tribes. Around 1700 the Jicarilla Apaches of southeastern Colorado were pushed into New Mexico by the Comanches, northerners armed with French guns. For seventy years eastern Colorado served as the home base from which the Comanches plundered neighboring tribes and Spanish settlements.

The Kiowas, formerly mountain people like the Comanches, entered Colorado around 1775. They and their allies, the Prairie or Kiowa-Apaches, were better armed than the Comanches and displaced the famous horse raiders south of the Arkansas River. Soon, however, all three tribes were allies and became the masters of the southern Plains.

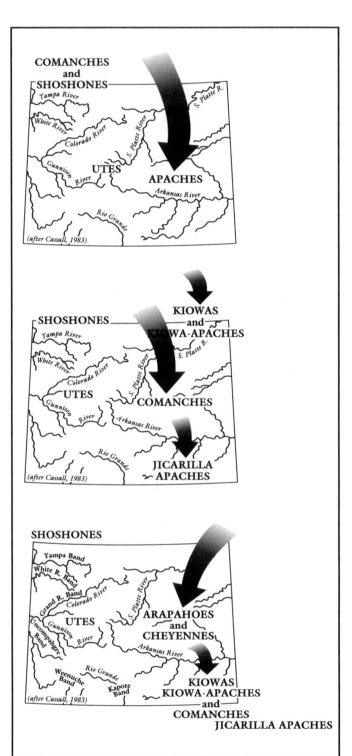

*Figure 33:
Although the
Utes occupied
western Colorado
for over five
hundred years, a
succession of
different tribes
occupied the
eastern part of
the state, all
living off the
buffalo and
acquiring horses
from their
southern
neighbors.*

Fur trappers encountered Arapahoes in Colorado as early as 1806. These Indians had been displaced from their Great Lakes homeland by other Indians armed with French guns but soon found that buffalo hunting on horseback was more to their liking than farming. The Arapahoes moved into the territory that had been abandoned by the Kiowas and Comanches. Soon the Arapahoes were joined by their Great Lakes neighbors, the Cheyennes. These tribes became strong allies and with their friends the Sioux raided the Crows, Shoshones, Utes, Pawnees, and their southern neighbors, the Kiowas and Comanches.

EARLY COMMERCE WITH TRAPPERS AND TRADERS

Although each tribe had different origins and somewhat varied belief systems, their history after the arrival of non-Indians was basically the same. The Plains Indians of Colorado were tolerant of mountain men, the trappers and traders who brought blankets, kettles, knives, fire-starters, beads, cloth, and other items for which the Indians traded beaver pelts and finely tanned buffalo robes. Felt made from the beaver pelts was used to make the fashionable tall hats sported by east-erners and Englishmen. Warm furry buffalo robes were used as blankets to tuck around chilly feet and legs during sleigh and wagon travel or were made into coats, saddles, and belts. Indian women occasionally married trappers, considered by some to be good husbands because of their wealth of beads, ribbons, and other trinkets with which women loved to decorate their clothing. These women prepared their husbands' beaver pelts, cooked their food, taught them the language and customs of the tribe, and kept them company during the long days and nights in the wilderness, even though such isolation was difficult for the women, who were accustomed to having their families around all the time.

A trapper-trader named William Bent, who would later marry into the Cheyenne tribe, established a thriving trading post about 1833 with his brother Charles and partner Ceran St. Vrain. The adobe-walled building, which came to be known as Bent's Fort, was located on a bluff above the Arkansas River, near present-day La Junta in southeastern Colorado. This site was chosen because it was close enough to the mountains to attract the mountain men but east enough

Figure 34:
Established along the Santa Fe Trail around 1833, Bent's Fort
provided a lively setting for mountain men and Colorado Plains Indians
to trade hides for basic commodities such as flour, coffee, pots,
and cloth. It was the news center of the Southwest Plains.
Drawing by Lachlan Allan MacLean, 1846, courtesy of the Museum of New Mexico.

to be within the hunting range of the southern Plains tribes. The post became the center of commerce and social life for trappers, traders, and travelers on the Santa Fe Trail as well as for all the local Indian tribes. Here the Cheyennes and Arapahoes would bring in buffalo robes the women had patiently tanned. While engrossed in barter, their enemies the Kiowas and Comanches might be riding towards the fort with stolen Cheyenne horses to trade—situations such as this kept things lively at Bent's Fort. Of further historical interest is the fact that Bent's half-Cheyenne son George, who had been educated in St. Louis, lived with his mother's people during the Indian wars of the 1860s after fighting with the Confederates during the Civil War and being threatened by Union veterans when he returned to Bent's Fort. George remained with the Southern Cheyennes for the rest of his life; his letters describing this period, published in the book *The Life of George Bent*, provide a wealth of historical information from the perspective of the Southern Cheyennes.

Soon other trading posts were built along the east side of the Rockies, connecting Bent's Fort with Fort Laramie on the North Platte in today's Wyoming (Fort Laramie was named after the French trapper La Ramie, who was killed in the Colorado Rockies). A steady stream of commerce was established between Bent's Fort, Fort Lupton, Fort St. Vrain, near Platteville, and other smaller trading posts near the base of the Rocky Mountains. Today, the trading route roughly follows U.S. 50 from La Junta to Pueblo, Interstate 25 to Denver, U.S. 85 to Greeley and Cheyenne, and Interstate 80 west to Laramie. This busy commercial route followed the northern border of Comanche and Kiowa country along the Arkansas River and sliced directly through the heart of Arapahoe and Cheyenne country as it headed north (see Figure 35, pages 102–103).

Although the Cheyennes traded with the newcomers, the Arapahoes, better known for their trading prowess with other tribes, took full advantage of their position by utilizing their natural commercial skills. One of Bent's traders, John Poisal, married MaHom, a young Arapahoe, and taught English to her brother, Niwot, or Left Hand. This bright young man, through his trading experiences, became fluent not only in English but in several Indian languages as well. This ability, along with his belief that peace was the only way the tribes could survive, later made Left Hand a valued and respected Arapahoe leader. (A mountain and the town of Niwot, northeast of Boulder, the site of the Southern Arapahoes' favorite winter camp, are named after Left Hand.)

The 1830s were prosperous years for Indians and non-Indians alike, both reaping the benefits of trade. In 1840, the Southern Arapahoes and Cheyennes made peace with their old enemies the Kiowas and Comanches. The peace was requested by all tribes after each one had suffered devastating losses at the Battle of Wolf Creek in northwestern Oklahoma. In 1837, a group of forty-two Cheyenne Bowstring warriors were discovered by Kiowas while the Cheyennes scouted the Kiowa camp to steal horses. All forty-two men were killed by the Kiowas. As a result, a great force of revengeful Cheyennes and Arapahoes attacked a Kiowa camp. Comanches and Jicarilla Apaches camping nearby helped fight the Cheyennes and Arapahoes. The bloody battle took the lives of so many people that everyone was alarmed. The tribes made peace, hoping the bond would present a unified force against their common enemies—the Utes as well as encroaching Texans and Mexicans.

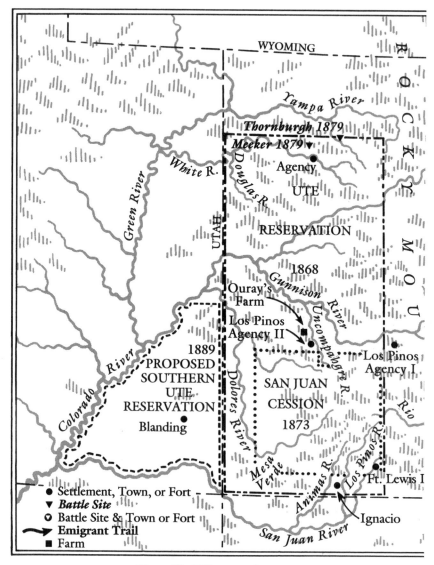

Figure 35: (This page and page 103)
Emigration trails, settlements, forts, trading posts, reservations, and
battle sites in Colorado, 1832 to 1889.

The all-Indian peace meeting of 1840 was a dramatic occasion.
Organized by the Cheyenne Dog Soldiers, thousands of Cheyennes,
Arapahoes, Comanches, Kiowas, and Jicarilla Apaches pitched their
tipis along the Arkansas River near Bent's Fort. For days gifts were
exchanged between the former enemies; the Kiowas and Comanches

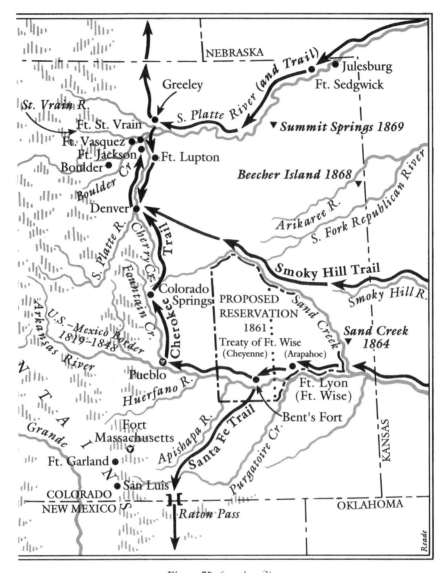

Figure 35: (continued)

gave away thousands of horses, so many that almost every person of every tribe received a horse, some receiving several. A great feast was held after the gift giving. The peace that was established above the Arkansas River that summer was never broken. Together the former foes often rode into Kansas and Nebraska to raid the Pawnees and

Delawares or west into the Rocky Mountains to attack the Utes. In general, the unified tribes remained friendly with the traders since their business was too valuable to lose.

CONFLICTS WITH SETTLERS

Despite peace between the tribes, the year 1840 marked the beginning of the end of the free life of the Plains Indians as well as the fur trade era (the last rendezvous was held on the Sisk-ke-dee (Green) River in Wyoming that year). This was due to traffic along the Santa Fe and Oregon trails as wagon trains of gold seekers and homesteaders traveled west in search of new lives. As they rolled along the arteries of Colorado's Indian country, the Arkansas and South Platte rivers, they burned the timber, shot the buffalo and other game, and allowed their thousands of oxen and horses to deplete the grasses of the Indians' traditional campsites.

Emigrant trains traveling just north of Colorado along the North Platte River en route to Oregon, Salt Lake, and the gold fields of California began to feel the sting of Indian raids as the Indians saw their game and land being destroyed. Although the Colorado tribes as a whole refrained from such attacks, the chiefs had difficulty restraining individual angry warriors from joining in the raids.

As a result of these circumstances, the United States government appointed the first Indian agent, famous mountain man and guide Thomas Fitzpatrick, to work out a treaty with the Plains tribes. Fitzpatrick wanted to hold the treaty meeting at Bent's Fort. However, due to loss of business because of increased tensions along the Santa Fe Trail and silk hats replacing those made from beaver pelts, Bent blew up his adobe buildings with dynamite after he was discouraged at the low price the government had offered him to purchase his post for a military fort. He built another home thirty-five miles downstream and moved his Cheyenne wife and five children to the place known as Big Timbers, which later became known as Fort Wise.

In 1851, Fitzpatrick then chose Fort Laramie, just north of the Colorado border on the North Platte, as the place to hold his treaty negotiations. After months of traveling among the tribes throughout the Plains, he finally assembled over ten thousand Indians around the post. But even before the council began, the thousands of horses had eaten up all the grass, and the treaty site had to be moved to Horse Creek, thirty-seven miles away. When the council was finally held, the Cheyennes and Arapahoes were the Colorado Indians represented. Also present were the Sioux, Arikara, Assiniboines, Gros Ventres (northern relatives of the Arapahoes), Shoshones, and Crows. The other Colorado tribes, the Comanches, Kiowas, Apaches, and Utes, did not attend the meeting, perhaps because they considered their territory to be outside the range of the depredations along the northern emigrant route.

The remarks of Chief Cut Nose expressed the feelings of his fellow Arapahoes as well as the other Plains tribes when he addressed the United States government's representative during the council:

> Grand Father, I thank the Great Spirit, the Sun and the Moon, for putting me on this earth. It is a good earth, and I hope there will be no more fighting on it—that the grass will grow and the water fall, and plenty of buffalo. You, Grand Father, are doing well for your children, in coming so far and taking so much trouble about them.
>
> I think you will do us much good; I will go home satisfied. I will sleep sound, and not have to watch my horses in the night, nor be afraid for my [family]. We have to live on these streams and in the hills, and I would be glad if the whites would pick out a place for themselves and not come into our grounds; but if they must pass through our country, they should give us game for what they drive off (Trenholm 1986, 136).

Fitzpatrick spoke of the destruction of the grazing lands and buffalo by the emigrants and pledged the tribes protection from further depredations. In addition, $50,000 worth of annuities (flour, sugar, rice, beef, coffee, cloth, and other basic commodities) would be distributed every year for the next fifty years. The agent also promised that the land traditionally used by the Indians would be theirs forever. The Southern Arapahoes and Cheyennes were guaranteed the country between the Arkansas and Platte rivers and from the Continental Divide east to central Kansas, an area that included most of eastern Colorado (Figure 35, pages 102–103). The Indians were pleased with the government's intentions

and promised they would not further harass emigrants traveling
through their land. In addition, they gave the government permission
to establish military posts and roads. The tribes and Fitzpatrick left
Fort Laramie with hopes for a peaceful future due to agreements that
became known as the Fort Laramie Treaty.

During the next two years, however, thousands more emigrants,
soldiers, and surveyors passed through Indian land, breaking up and
killing buffalo herds and destroying the grass and timber. Fitzpatrick
reported that the Sioux, Arapahoe, and Cheyenne people were starving
half the year. Not only people were suffering; the Indians lamented the
poor condition of their horses, which were ridden long distances by
hunters trying to find food.

Along with the devastating destruction of natural resources, the
emigrants brought measles, smallpox, whooping cough, and cholera.
Within a twenty-year period the population of Northern and Southern
Arapahoes was reduced from ten thousand to three thousand people.
Entire Comanche bands were wiped out by cholera and smallpox
brought by gold seekers headed for California from Texas. George
Bent wrote that at least half of the Cheyennes died from cholera:

> Then, in '49, the emigrants brought the cholera up the
> Platte Valley, and from the emigrant trains it spread to
> the Indian camps. "Cramps" the Indians called it, and
> they died of it by hundreds. On the Platte whole camps
> could be seen deserted with the tepees full of dead bod-
> ies, men, women and children. The Sioux and
> Cheyennes, who were nearest to the road, were the
> hardest hit, and from the Sioux the epidemic spread
> northward clear to the Blackfeet, while from the Chey-
> ennes and Arapahos it struck down into the Kiowa and
> Comanche country and created havoc among their
> camps (Hyde 1987, 96).

In addition, alcohol began having a destructive impact. Although its
sale to Indians was illegal, traders reaped enormous profits trading
watered-down whiskey for tanned buffalo robes and other furs. One of
the most notorious trading posts involved in the illegal whiskey traffic was
the ramshackle adobe community of Pueblo. The results were that within
ten years, many Cheyenne men had become alcoholics. The women of

Figure 36:
Declining food resources left children such as these Arapahoe boys
vulnerable to malnutrition and disease.
Photo courtesy of the Denver Public Library.

the tribe who had spent weeks tanning beautiful buffalo hides agonized as their husbands traded them for whiskey. Many warriors found alcohol an escape from their frustrations at watching their families starving, not being able to live their lives in the traditional way, and having no way to thwart the emigrants who were responsible for their state of affairs.

For frontiersmen like Jim Beckwourth, a renowned mountain man who was usually critical of the whiskey traders, the economic opportunity of selling whiskey was too tempting to pass up. Whiskey traders, for a nominal sum, could purchase a forty-gallon cask of alcohol and add four gallons of water to each gallon of whiskey. This resulted in two hundred gallons, or sixteen hundred pints, and for each one of these the trader could get a buffalo robe. The robes were worth five dollars each, which meant a profit of a total of eight thousand dollars for the initial purchase of a barrel of whiskey.

Despite the fact that the Indians were upholding their part of the treaty, even under miserable, starvation conditions, the government reduced the time of annuity distribution from fifty years to fifteen. More soldiers entered Indian land, establishing posts throughout the area, a military presence that angered the Indians. The Smoky Hill Trail, which cut through the heart of the last good buffalo ranges in east-central Colorado, was established, and thousands more wagons rumbled across the Plains, some families settling along the streams.

In 1853, agent Fitzpatrick made a treaty with the Kiowas and Comanches (similar to the Fort Laramie Treaty), whereby the tribes were guaranteed their land south of the Arkansas River. With the sad knowledge that the treaty probably would not be upheld, the mountain man and friend of the Indians died of a sudden illness in February of 1854.

Although the chiefs of the Colorado tribes urged peaceful relations with the emigrants, a few frustrated warriors, mostly Cheyennes, attacked travelers on the Oregon Trail. Others stole stock from settlers to feed their starving families. In 1857, a military command intent on punishing the Cheyennes ordered one of their villages burned. With it was destroyed up to twenty thousand pounds of buffalo meat which was to feed the entire band that winter.

In the spring of 1858, gold seekers invaded the foothills of the Rockies. A town of cabins and tents sprang up at the confluence of the South Platte River and Cherry Creek (later to become the town of Denver), a favorite Arapahoe campsite. The Indians watched in amazement as the founders of the adjacent towns of Auraria and Denver fought over the incoming merchants with their wagons full of goods, each trying to convince the newcomers of the advantages their town had over the other. George Bent wrote: "When Auraria secured a new merchant there was gloom in Denver, and when Denver succeeded in capturing another grocer there was gnashing of teeth in Auraria." Denver won the battle in 1859 when two large wagon trains were "both secured by Denver," and "Auraria then turned up its toes and died" (Hyde 1987, 106).

Other settlements were going up on land that belonged to the Platte River Indians, according to the 1851 Fort Laramie Treaty. Arapahoe leaders, including Left Hand, were deeply concerned about the fate of their people. They were constantly restraining warriors from fighting the intruders while trying to feed their people through trade with miners. Some disgusted warriors disregarded the leaders' plea for peace and raided several ranches along the Platte River. Left Hand and Little Raven, another prominent Southern Arapahoe chief, were concerned for the safety of the women and children of the tribe and moved their villages along the Arkansas River near Bent's Fort.

Increasing raids on the settlers, compounded by rumors of a general Indian uprising, encouraged Colorado's Governor Evans to propose another treaty. From what he considered to be reliable sources, Evans learned that the Sioux, located in the Dakota Territory northeast of Colorado, had finally rebelled after their starving families received rotten rations, or none at all. They had been on a killing spree and were planning an all-out attack along the Platte rivers. The attack would occur in the spring of 1864, when they hoped to receive more ammunition.

It was originally rumored that only some of the Cheyenne bands had pledged to join the Sioux in the war. Robert North, a non-Indian who had been, according to George Bent, "loafing around the Arapaho camp, living on the Indians and keeping an Arapaho wife," informed Evans that he had heard that in addition to the Cheyenne bands, the Comanches, Kiowa-Apaches, Kiowas, and Northern Arapahoes had smoked with the Sioux and were plotting a war in the spring. According to North, only the Southern Arapahoes and a few Cheyenne bands had refused to smoke. George Bent and other sources claim the majority of Indians were too busy trying to provide for their families to plot a war (Hyde 1987, 119–21).

Governor Evans was now convinced of the Indian rebellion. The army purchased Bent's new fort and named it Fort Wise after the governor of

Virginia (the name was later changed to Fort Lyon in honor of a Union commander). Here a treaty was signed by the peaceful Cheyenne chiefs Black Kettle and White Antelope, as well as with the Southern Arapahoe chiefs Little Raven and Left Hand. The Fort Wise Treaty would give the Cheyennes and Southern Arapahoes a six-hundred-square-mile reservation in eastern Colorado, roughly between the Arkansas River and Sand Creek, as well as enough money to purchase farm tools, although most of the area included sandy wasteland and was unfit for agriculture. In exchange, they would give up the rest of their territory. The Cheyennes and Southern Arapahoes did not want to move to the reservation. The Cheyennes wanted to stay near the Smoky Hill and Republican rivers (eastern Colorado), the only remaining region where there were still enough buffalo—there were no buffalo in the area proposed for the reservation. Although one Southern Arapahoe family moved to the Sand Creek Reservation, the rest kept moving along the Arkansas River in search of game.

The isolated raids and rumors of an Indian uprising continued to terrify Colorado settlers. Governor Evans, frustrated that he could not enforce the Fort Wise Treaty and persuade the Indians to move to the reservation, was intent on proving that peace was not possible. Consequently, he sent messengers to the tribes to either report to military posts or be considered hostile.

Chiefs Black Kettle and Left Hand traveled to Denver to tell Governor Evans they wanted peace, but because Evans wanted an excuse to eradicate all the Indians, he did not want to meet with the friendly chiefs. Instead, the governor sent the chiefs away with the impression they would be safe at Fort Lyon. He then conferred with Colonel John M. Chivington, an ex-minister and Civil War hero (leader of the victorious Battle of Glorieta Pass in New Mexico) who was intent on winning an Indian battle for political reasons. Evans told Chivington where he thought Black Kettle's band might be camping and implied an opportunity for glory.

When the peaceful chiefs brought their starving, bedraggled bands to Fort Lyon, they were told they could not stay there because no rations were available. Instead, they were ordered to go to a place along Sand Creek, about seventy-five miles to the northeast. Promises were made that they would be safe from American troops intent on killing all Indians who had not surrendered.

Chivington then led a group of volunteers who had been waiting to fight Indians for months from Denver toward Black Kettle's peaceful camp. George Bent, who was living with his wife, a Cheyenne named Magpie, among Black Kettle's band on Sand Creek, wrote: "This regiment had been hastily recruited from among the worst class of frontier whites—toughs, gamblers, and 'bad-men' from Denver and the mining camps, rough miners, bull-whackers, and so on" (Hyde 1987, 148). When Chivington arrived at Fort Lyon with his rag-tag troops, he had the place surrounded so nobody could leave to warn the Indians. He threatened George's brother Robert and the old mountain man Jim Beckwourth with death if they didn't lead the troops, now reinforced with six hundred more soldiers, to Black Kettle's camp (Beckwourth had to return because of the intense cold). At Black Kettle's camp there were mostly women, children, and old men since many of the warriors had gone hunting. The peaceful Chief Left Hand and his extended family, possibly up to fifty Arapahoes, were also camped with Black Kettle's Cheyennes.

Chivington's men attacked at dawn on November 29, 1864. As the soldiers charged the sleepy villagers, Black Kettle reportedly stumbled out of his tipi, hastily tied an American flag to a pole, and stood in front of his lodge, thinking the soldiers were confused. He yelled at the frightened Indians that the soldiers were mistaken and would cease shooting as soon as they knew they were attacking Indians who were at peace with the United States government. According to one report, as Black Kettle stood by the flag he was shot nine times but miraculously did not die.

According to another soldier's report, Chief Left Hand was shot as he ran towards the troops with his hands outstretched—the Plains Indian sign for peace. Since his body was not found, he probably escaped and died that night. The Cheyenne leader White Antelope, feeling guilty that he had induced his people to camp at Sand Creek by telling them they would be safe and that the non-Indians were good, did not wish to live. While others fled, he sang his death song as he stood before his tipi with arms folded and was shot to death.

As women and children ran up the creekbed, they were slaughtered by the soldiers' bullets. Some frantically dug pits in the sand of the riverbed and hid behind the low dirt walls. Little Bear, a Cheyenne friend of George Bent's, ran with the women and managed to escape with some. Bent wrote that Little Bear told him, "After the fight I came back down the creek and saw these dead bodies all cut up, and even the wounded scalped and slashed. I saw one old woman wandering about;

her whole scalp had been taken off, and the blood was running down into her eyes so that she could not see where to go" (Hyde 1987, 154).

George Bent, who had been shot in the hip, was with the survivors as they struggled up the creek and camped in the open that night. He reported:

> That was the worst night I ever went through. There we were on that bleak, frozen plain, without any shelter whatever and not a stick of wood to build a fire with. Most of us were wounded and half naked; even those who had time to dress when the attack came, had lost their buffalo robes and blankets during the fight. The men and women who were not wounded worked all through the night, trying to keep the children and the wounded from freezing to death. They gathered grass by the handful, feeding little fires around which the wounded and the children lay; they stripped off their own blankets and clothes to keep us warm, and some of the wounded who could not be provided with other covering were buried under piles of grass which their friends gathered, a handful at a time, and heaped up over them. That night will never be forgotten as long as any of us who went through it are alive. It was bitter cold, the wind had a full sweep over the ground on which we lay, and in spite of everything that was done, no one could keep warm. All night the Indians kept hallooing to attract the attention of those who had escaped from the village to the open plain and were wandering about in the dark, lost and freezing. Many who had lost wives, husbands, children or friends, went back down the creek and crept over the battleground among the naked and mutilated bodies of the dead. Few were found alive, for the soldiers had done their work thoroughly; but now and then during that endless night some man or woman would stagger in among us, carrying some wounded person on their back (Hyde 1987, 157–58).

One Arapahoe woman named Kohiss escaped while holding a baby in front of her, a child on her back, and another by the hand. As she

Figure 37:
One of the few child survivors of the Sand Creek Massacre of 1864, this Arapahoe
girl was raised by a woman in Central City, Colorado.
Photo by Albert McKinney, courtesy of the Denver Public Library.

ran from the soldiers, bullets ripped through all of them. Although two of her children were killed, incredibly she and the baby survived, and Kohiss lived out her life in Oklahoma to the age of 104. Her many scars reminded all who saw her of the brutal massacre.

Bent reported that a total of 137 Indians were slaughtered, 109 of whom were women and children. Chivington falsely claimed he and his men had killed 400 to 500 Indians in a bloody battle.

At first most Denverites rejoiced as the soldiers bragged of their exploits, but soon the gruesome details of the massacre became known. During the ensuing investigation, soldiers such as Silas Soule, an officer who refused to send his troops into the camp and watched the massacre from the bluffs, testified against Chivington and described the atrocities of that day. Soule was later killed by one of Chivington's men; and Chivington resigned as commander of Colorado's military district so he would not be court-martialed.

Following these events, some Southern Arapahoes left Colorado and with Little Raven's band roved the Oklahoma Panhandle and southern Kansas. But there was now no hope for peace between non-Indians and other Colorado Indian tribes. The rumored consolidation of tribes that Governor Evans had been warned about for so long finally occurred, prompted by the Sand Creek Massacre.

On January 7, 1865, over one thousand Cheyennes, Northern Arapahoes, and Sioux warriors attacked the stage station and store at Julesburg, in northeastern Colorado. George Bent reported that the Indians seized so many goods it took three days to haul all the supplies back to their camp. He also claimed they found the army payroll; while the Indians cut up the bills and tossed them to the wind, Bent stuffed them in his pockets.

These Indians, at least, finally had enough food to eat. Bent wrote:

> The camp was well supplied with fresh beef and had a big herd of cattle besides; then there were whole wagon loads of bacon, hams, big bags of flour, sugar, rice, cornmeal, shelled corn, tins and hogsheads of molasses, groceries of all sorts, canned meats and fruit, clothing, dress goods, silks and hardware. . . . Most of these things the Indians had never seen before, and they were all the time bringing things to me and asking me what they were and what they were used for. I remember an

old Indian who brought me a big box and wanted to
know what was in it. It was full of candied citron and I
told him what it was for. Another thing that puzzled
the Indians was the canned oysters (Hyde 1987, 179).

When bolts of cloth were found, warriors liked to gallop at full speed over
the prairie while the cloth unwound and streamed dramatically behind.

There was so much feasting and celebration that there were fires all
through the nights in the villages, the drumming often lasting until
dawn. According to George Bent, "On a still night you could hear
them [the drums] for miles and miles along the valley" (Hyde 1987,
199). The drumming was so loud and incessant that the few remaining
buffalo were driven away, and the soldier societies had to prohibit the
celebrants from drumming. Singing continued, however, as it did not
appear to disturb the buffalo.

For the next two years the Cheyennes, Northern Arapahoes, and
other Plains tribes continued their rampage, stealing horses, raiding
wagon trains, and cutting telegraph lines. Colorado was virtually cut off
from the other states, and martial law prevailed. Many residents and government officials called for total extermination of the Indians, but others
apologized for the Sand Creek Massacre and tried to make treaties.

In October of 1867, roughly five thousand Comanches, Kiowas,
Kiowa-Apaches, Cheyennes, and Arapahoes gathered along Medicine
Lodge Creek, approximately seventy miles southwest of Fort Larned,
Kansas. The wooded hollow was a favorite winter camp of the Indians.
In a grove surrounded by tall elm trees, the tribes signed the Medicine
Lodge Treaty by which they agreed to allow safe passage of emigrants
and ensured the safety of the railroads. The treaty forced them onto
reservations in Kansas and Oklahoma—the mountains and plains of
Colorado were now officially "off limits." George Bent described what
the treaty meant to his tribe: "This was, in a way, the most important
treaty ever signed by the Cheyennes, and it marked the beginning of
the end of the Cheyenne as a free and independent warrior and hunter,
and eventually changed his old range, from Saskatchewan to Mexico,
to the narrow confines in Oklahoma" (Hyde 1987, 285).

Not only did the Medicine Lodge Treaty signify the end of true
independence for eastern Colorado tribes, it also marked the beginning
of a forced, humiliating dependence on the United States government
for food, protection, and education.

Many Indians did not hear of the treaty, others did not understand it, and some chose not to. Consequently, attacks by frustrated warriors occasionally still occurred.

In 1868, Northern Cheyenne and Sioux warriors attacked over fifty men who were under Major George Forsyth and Lieutenant Beecher at what is now known as Beecher Island in northeastern Colorado—a stretch of land which was surrounded mostly by a dry streambed but offered trees for shelter. The Indians had the men trapped on the island for nine days. It was during this Battle of Beecher Island that the greatly respected Cheyenne warrior Roman Nose was killed. Although Roman Nose had been through many battles, he was considered invincible because of a war bonnet he possessed. This war bonnet had been connected with a vision Roman Nose had as a boy while fasting for four days, in which he had seen a snake with a single horn on its head. One of the most famous Cheyenne medicine men, White Bull, later made a war bonnet for Roman Nose, which had a headband with only one buffalo horn rather than two, rising over the center of the forehead. No materials made by non-Indians, such as thread, cloth, or metal, were used to fashion the war bonnet, and White Bull told Roman Nose that he must never eat anything that metal had touched; if he followed these instructions, the war bonnet would make him invincible. As a result, whenever Roman Nose was a guest in another person's lodge, before he ate any food the warrior always asked if it had been prepared with metal utensils. However, a few days prior to the Battle of Beecher Island he had neglected to ask this important question and later learned that a Sioux woman had lifted his bread from a pan with an iron fork.

Knowing the protective power of his war bonnet had been broken, Roman Nose was hesitant to lead a charge against army troops without going through the proper purification ceremony. However, he was asked to do so, and not wanting to disappoint his fellow warriors, Roman Nose consented. As he led the charge towards the island, he was shot in the small of the back. At first, nobody knew he had been shot since he stayed on his horse, rode back to the Indian line, and only then lay down on the ground. He died the next morning.

That same year Black Kettle, the Southern Cheyenne who had pleaded for peace only to be attacked at Sand Creek, asked for protection from the soldiers at Fort Cobb, Oklahoma. Again he was refused and led his band to the Washita River, where they were attacked by Colonel George Armstrong Custer. Many Cheyennes were killed, and all their tipis, clothing, and food were burned. The attack occurred on November 29, 1868, exactly four years to the day after Black Kettle had survived the Sand Creek Massacre. This time the man who only wanted his people to live in peace was not so fortunate. He and his wife were shot as they tried to escape on the same horse, their bodies falling in the creek and being trampled by cavalry horses.

In the early summer of 1869, the Cheyenne Dog Soldiers, under the leadership of White Horse and Tall Bull, were still hunting along the Republican River while most of the Cheyennes, along with the other tribes, were struggling to survive on the reservation land in Oklahoma. In midsummer they were pursued north by Major Eugene A. Carr, who had been hunting them all winter (one of Carr's scouts was William F. "Buffalo Bill" Cody). A flooded South Platte River halted the advance of the Dog Soldiers and their families so camp was made at Summit Springs, about ten miles south of present-day Sterling, in northeastern Colorado. While the Cheyennes were eating their midday meal, Carr's troops, led by Pawnee scouts, attacked the village. Sentries had seen the enemy approach, but their signals went unheeded—fires the Cheyennes had set to destroy their trail had made the air too hazy to see the lookouts. Consequently, the attack was a total surprise. Almost the entire village of Dog Soldiers under Tall Bull was wiped out by United States troops. The Northern Cheyennes were escorted to a reservation in Wyoming, and later moved to another one at Lame Deer, Montana. The few Southern Cheyennes who had yet to surrender did so at Camp Supply, Oklahoma, where they shared the reservation with the Southern Arapahoes.

The Kiowas, Kiowa-Apaches, and Comanches of southeastern Colorado suffered a fate similar to that of the Arapahoes and Cheyennes. Diseases, reduction of the buffalo herds, and devastation of the grazing land enraged the tribes; but unlike their northern neighbors, the Kiowas and Comanches in general had less desire to cultivate peaceful relations with the intruders. Their territory ranged far south into Texas and New Mexico, and they had been at war with the Mexicans, and later, Texans for decades. Now they raided non-Indian settlers along the Santa Fe Trail as well.

Increased Indian attacks during the 1850s alarmed settlers to such a degree that the Texas Rangers pursued a policy of extermination. One band of Comanches was mistakenly attacked while returning from a peace meeting with United States officers.

During the Civil War, most soldiers were called east to serve, and Comanche and Kiowa raids continued unimpeded along the Santa Fe Trail. As previously mentioned, at the Medicine Lodge Creek council in Kansas, the tribes were assigned reservations in Indian Territory.

The Comanches, Kiowas, and Kiowa-Apaches were sent to the southwestern Oklahoma area near Fort Sill but continued raiding in Texas. The Comanches, Kiowas, and Kiowa-Apaches faced the same dilemma as did the Cheyennes and Arapahoes. To settle on the reservations in Indian Territory meant starvation; if they left to hunt, they would be attacked by the army. In violation of the Medicine Lodge Treaty, non-Indian buffalo hunters slaughtered thousands more buffalo. A futile Indian attack on the hunters only brought an onslaught of United States troops.

Prominent Kiowa leaders who resisted confinement to the reservation included Kicking Bird, Big Tree, Satanta, and Satank. Noted Comanche leaders who resisted were Ten Bears, considered one of the finest orators of the time, Iron Mountain, Horseback, Toshaway, and Mowway.

In 1875, military authorities rounded up suspected leaders of the depredations and sent them to Florida prisons. The rest of the roving bands were confined to the Oklahoma reservation. The Kiowas, Kiowa-Apaches, and Comanches had finally been defeated.

COLORADO TRIBES IN INDIAN TERRITORY

Life in Indian Territory, later called Oklahoma, was not pleasant for the tribes that had formerly ranged along the mountains and rivers of eastern Colorado. Confinement brought more diseases, including measles, tuberculosis, and whooping cough. Commercial hide hunters had exterminated the buffalo by 1879 (the last wild buffalo in Colorado were observed in Lost Park in 1897). The starving people in Indian Territory were often forced to kill their horses to survive. All tribal populations declined drastically.

In 1890, new hope was kindled among many displaced tribes by the introduction of the Ghost Dance. It was believed that if the dance were performed faithfully, soon the world would be rid of all non-Indians, all dead relatives would come back to life, the buffalo would return, and the world would be as it used to be before the arrival of non-Indians. Government officials benefited from this belief because if many Indians thought all settlers would soon be gone, it was easier to get them to accept a document called the Dawes Act.

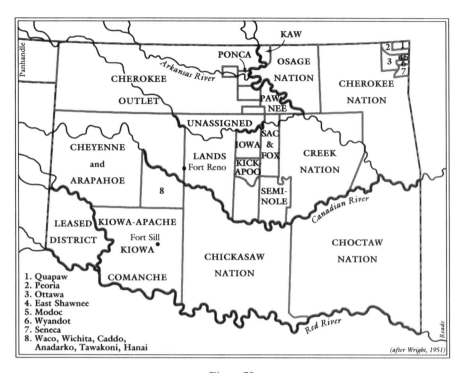

Figure 38:
Original Indian reservations in Indian Territory (Oklahoma)
prior to the Allotment Act (Dawes Act) of 1887.

Better known as the Allotment Act, the Dawes Act was passed in 1887, supported by land-hungry settlers as well as people sincerely concerned about the future of the people in Indian Territory. Even a few Indian leaders, such as the famous Comanche Quanah Parker, believed the law would bring equality and prosperity to the Indian people. In the end, however, the Dawes Act did more to deprive Indian people of their land and culture than any other action of the federal government, including open warfare. Under its terms, each Indian received 160 acres to which clear title was given after twenty-five years. The remaining reservation land was opened for home-steading. All mineral rights were lost along with this "excess" land. When the Indians acquired title to their allotments, many sold their land to pay off debts. Soon, those who had sold out were not only poverty-stricken but landless as well.

The federal government was intent on "Americanizing" Indians. Prior to the turn of the century a policy of assimilation was carried out: Indians were not allowed to perform traditional dances and ceremonies, to sing and gather together, or to visit other families of the same tribe. The policy was not as successful as the officials had hoped. Many tribes such as the Cheyennes, Kiowas, and Comanches continued their religious practices in defiance of the government. The Arapahoes used a strategy of placation, performing their sacred ceremonies but calling them Christmas or Thanksgiving celebrations, or dances to benefit the Red Cross.

In the late 1800s, another religion called Peyotism was introduced on the reservations. Peyote cactus buttons, which grow only along the Rio Grande in Texas and in Mexico, were eaten as an offering to God. Visions, so important to traditional tribal spiritualism, were experienced while the participants sang songs and said prayers for loved ones. The religion stressed goodness and high morals, and many alcoholics gave up drinking after joining the Peyote cult. Although Peyotism declined during World War II, it was soon revitalized by a younger group. Today, it is known as the Native American Church, and many Christian elements are incorporated into the ceremony. The Native American Church is pan-tribal and has served to unite Indians from all over the United States.

During the early 1900s several events undercut the economy of the remaining Indian farms in Oklahoma Territory. First, dishonest merchants inflated farm equipment prices and repossessed plows and tractors when a single payment was missed. The small parcels of land owned by families continued to be sold to pay the bills. The Depression hit hard, and many Indians moved to towns and cities to find jobs. Although the Oklahoma Indians were scattered and retained few allotments, the Oklahoma Indian Welfare Act of 1936 helped bring structure to the fragmented tribes. The bill allowed tribes to adopt constitutions, secure federal charters, and establish business committees to foster economic development. Additional relief came with New Deal programs such as the Works Progress Administration, Emergency Relief Administration, Civilian Conservation Corps, and the National Youth Administration.

The 1930s also saw a reversal in federal policy. John Collier was appointed commissioner of the Bureau of Indian Affairs and immediately stressed the importance of preserving Indian arts, crafts, dancing, and language. Although many Indian men earned great distinctions during World War II, their families at home suffered when the 1930 relief programs were terminated. Soldiers returning home, however, brought new ideas and leadership abilities, and many became businessmen and successful farmers and ranchers.

Indian communities benefited from several social programs initiated in the 1960s and 1970s. These programs provided educational opportunities, housing development with increased sanitation and facilities, job training, and general economic development. Unfortunately, during the 1980s there was a drastic reduction in these programs.

Although discrimination and unemployment remain constant battles for the Oklahoma Indians who used to live in Colorado, a fierce pride in their heritage is obvious. Ceremonies and close family ties keep their traditions alive. Beautiful arts and crafts are exhibited throughout the state. Benefit dances are held almost weekly by families who want to raise money for certain causes or for people in need. National powwows (competitive and noncompetitive intertribal dances) are held throughout the summer in various Oklahoma communities.

PLACES TO VISIT

Colorado

BENT'S OLD FORT
35120 Highway 194
La Junta, CO 35120
(719)384-2596

Located east of La Junta along the Arkansas River and the old Santa Fe Trail, the fort, reconstructed by the National Park Service, is a fascinating place to experience the history of mountain men and American Indians. Interpreters and books provide a wealth of information about the Cheyennes, Arapahoes, Kiowas, Kiowa-Apaches, and Comanches, who traded at the fort.

COLORADO HISTORY MUSEUM
1300 Broadway
Denver, CO 80203
(303)866-3682

The museum displays crafts, clothing, and artifacts from many tribes that inhabited Colorado. Dioramas depict the day-to-day lifestyles of the Plains Indians.

DENVER ART MUSEUM
100 W. 14th Avenue Parkway
Denver, CO 80203
(303)575-2793

The museum includes excellent displays of Colorado Indian materials; special programs are also presented.

DENVER INDIAN CENTER
4407 Morrison Road
Denver, CO 80219
(303)936-2688

The center for American Indians of all nations to obtain information about educational and vocational programs, health care, and so forth.

DENVER MUSEUM OF NATURAL HISTORY
2001 Colorado Boulevard in City Park
Denver, CO 80203
(303)370-6363

The museum houses fine collections of Colorado Indian clothing, tools, and crafts; often special programs and exhibits are hosted.

FORT GARLAND MUSEUM
Fort Garland, CO 81133
(719)379-3512

The renovated and reconstructed adobe fort houses historic exhibits pertaining to its function to protect the settlements of the San Luis Valley from the Utes. Several rooms are furnished as they were in the nineteenth century during the military occupation. Excavation of the fort grounds is on-going.

FORT VASQUEZ STATE MUSEUM
13412 Highway 85
Platteville, CO 80651
(303)785-2832

The museum offers interpretation of the history of the fur trade and how it affected the local Cheyenne and Arapahoe tribes.

KOSHARE INDIAN MUSEUM
115 W. 18th
La Junta, CO 35120
(719)384-4411

MARCH POWWOW
For information contact:
Denver Chamber of Commerce
1445 Market Street
Denver, CO 80202
(303)534-8500 (or contact the Denver Indian Center)

The Powwow is held every March for four days in the Denver Coliseum. After the grand march with hundreds of people from all Indian nations participating, competitions are held for various dance categories that include stylized dances which stem from traditional hunting practices, war activities, and rituals. Drummers and singers from individual tribes provide music. Authentic Indian crafts are sold in booths surrounding the interior of the coliseum. A real sense of American Indian community is obvious at this exhilarating powwow.

MASSACRE/BATTLE SITES
Most of the sites of Indian/United States Army confrontations are located on the Colorado State highway map but are on private land. They include: the Sand Creek Massacre site, the Beecher Island Battlefield site, and the Summit Springs Battlefield site. The landowners should be contacted before visiting the sites. *Please respect their privacy.*

Montana

NORTHERN CHEYENNE TRIBE
P.O. Box 128
Lame Deer, MT 59043
(406)477-6284

Offices of the Northern Cheyenne tribe include offices of the Tribal Council chairman, Business Council, and Education, Health, and Housing.

Oklahoma

AMERICAN INDIAN EXPOSITION
Box 705
Anadarko, OK 73005
(405)247-6651

This is one of the finest American Indian fairs in the country. It includes a parade; a pageant with traditional songs and dances presented by many tribes, including Comanches, Kiowas, Kiowa-Apaches, Apaches, Cheyennes, and Arapahoes; competitive powwow dancing all five nights; crafts demonstrations and sales; traditional food booths; horse racing; and an archery competition.

BATTLE OF THE WASHITA HISTORIC SITE
Highway 47A
Two miles west of Cheyenne, OK
(405)497-3929

This is the location of the slaughter of Black Kettle's Cheyenne band in 1868.

BLACK KETTLE MUSEUM
Highway 47 and U.S. Highway 283
Near Cheyenne, OK
(405)497-3929

The museum contains exhibits describing the Battle of the Washita along with artifacts from the site.

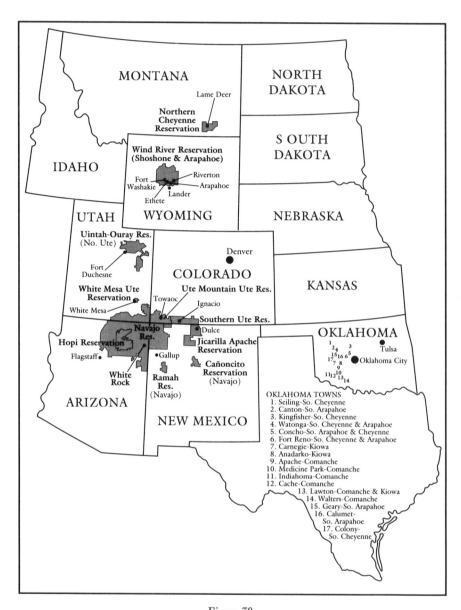

Figure 39:

Reservations and communities of today's Colorado Indian descendants.
Now only the Ute Mountain Utes and Southern Utes retain reservation land
within the state. Eastern Shoshones share the Wind River Reservation
with the Northern Arapahoes in Wyoming. Northern Cheyennes
live on a reservation headquartered in Lame Deer, Montana.
Kiowas, Kiowa-Apaches, Comanches, Southern Arapahoes,
and Southern Cheyennes live in various communities
throughout western Oklahoma.

INDIAN CITY USA
Highway 8
Three miles east of Anadarko, OK
(405)247-5661

The site features eight reconstructed Indian villages, including Kiowa tipis and Apache wickiups. Arts and crafts are displayed at the museum and gift shop. Special Indian programs occur throughout the year.

KIOWA TRIBAL MUSEUM
Tribal Office Complex
Carnegie, OK 73015
(405)654-2300

The museum exhibits traditional clothing and tools of the Kiowas. In the fall the museum hosts a powwow at which there is traditional Kiowa dancing as well as food. There is a Kiowa Gourd Dance and an arts and crafts show during the Fourth of July weekend.

SOUTHERN PLAINS INDIAN MUSEUM AND CRAFTS CENTER
Highway 62
East side of Anadarko, OK
(405)247-6221

This is a sales outlet for the Oklahoma Indian Arts and Crafts Cooperative; all arts and crafts are authentic and of excellent quality.

Wyoming

ST. STEPHENS INDIAN MISSION
P.O. Box 250
St. Stephens, WY 82524
(307)856-7806

The purpose of this Catholic mission and foundation is to provide religious and educational programs and other services to the Arapahoe and Shoshone tribes on the Wind River Reservation. The mission publishes *Wind River Rendezvous*, a magazine which includes articles about the history of the Shoshone and Arapahoe tribes as well as articles about current mission activities.

SHOSHONE/ARAPAHOE TRIBES
Business Council
533 Ethete Road
Ethete, WY 82520
(307) 332-6120

This and other tribal business councils are elected to advise tribal members of projects to pursue that would provide employment and economic benefits to the tribes.

Suggestions for Further Reading

Hubbard, Shirley. *Indians of Colorado. The Colorado Chronicles, Volume 3.* Frederick, Colo.: Platte 'N Press, 1981.

Hughes, J. Donald. *American Indians in Colorado.* Boulder, Colo.: Pruett Publishing Company, 1987.

Lavender, David. *Bent's Fort.* Lincoln and London: University of Nebraska Press, 1954.

Lowie, Robert H. *Indians of the Plains.* Lincoln and London: University of Nebraska Press, 1982.

Wright, Muriel H. *A Guide to the Indian Tribes of Oklahoma.* Norman: University of Oklahoma Press, 1951.

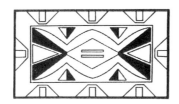

8

The Mountain Tribes

▲ ▲

VARIOUS INDIAN TRIBES MADE FREQUENT VISITS to Colorado to trade, raid horses, or hunt buffalo. The Pawnees farmed the river bottoms in Kansas and Nebraska but left their huge earth lodges in the spring to hunt up the Platte, Republican, and Smokey Hill rivers into Colorado (Pawnee Buttes, called Rattlesnake Buttes in James Michener's novel *Centennial*, rise above the flat plains north of Raymer, Colorado). The Brule and Oglala bands of the Lakotas (Sioux) frequently left their Black Hills homeland in South Dakota and joined the Northern Cheyenne and Arapahoe tribes to raid their mutual enemies. Likewise, raiders from the Crow tribe of eastern Montana came south to steal horses. The Wyandottes, Potawatomis, Kickapoos, Delawares, and Shawnees were eastern tribes forced to relocate in eastern Kansas and

Nebraska; buffalo and horses tempted all these tribes to travel to the Rockies. And the Delawares and Shawnees later became valued scouts, fighters, and hunters for the United States military in Colorado.

THE UTES

The first historic American Indians to live in Colorado were the Utes, distant relatives of the Shoshones. The Utes may have arrived in Colorado from five hundred to eight hundred years ago after several centuries of migrating east from the desert regions of California and Utah, or, as some Utes believe, possibly northern Mexico. Uto-Aztecan is the broad language group to which the Ute language is assigned, the same group to which the languages of the Aztecs, Hopis, Paiutes, Shoshones, and Comanches belong. The Anasazi's move to defensible locations in cliffs around A.D. 1200 may have been prompted by Ute (or Navajo) raids, although it is most accepted that the latter tribes probably did not enter the area until the 1500s.

Beliefs

Utes believe their people have always lived in Colorado, and some claim the Fremont people are their ancestors. Although Ute pottery and rock art are not like that of the Fremont people, it is possible that the drought beginning around A.D. 1275 that lasted almost a quarter of a century discouraged the pursuit of farming by the Fremont and caused some to revert back to a hunting and gathering lifestyle. This was the same drought that probably contributed to the abandonment of the Four Corners region by the Anasazi, and some Fremont may have joined them.

The Utes' origin story relates that the Creator, Sinawaf, cut up sticks and put them in a bag. Coyote, the trickster, watched him and became very curious. While Sinawaf was away, Coyote opened the bag and out came many people, all speaking different languages. The people spread far and wide and soon began to fight each other over land. Sinawaf was angry with Coyote because he wanted to distribute the people evenly so they would not fight. Some people remained in the bag—the Ute people. Sinawaf said they were very brave and could defeat the others.

Figure 40:
Although the Lakotas (Sioux) considered the Black Hills of South Dakota home, they often
joined their Cheyenne and Arapahoe neighbors to raid mutual enemies in Colorado.
Photo by J. R. Anderson, courtesy of the Colorado Historical Society.

Utes valued the healing properties of hot springs and considered them sacred places; the Northern Ute leader Ouray frequently bathed in the hot springs near present-day Ouray to ease the severe pain of his arthritis. Although bitter enemies, the Utes and Arapahoes considered Manitou Springs to be neutral territory, and reportedly would not fight when encountering each other in the sacred area. However, early descriptions of the springs by settlers refer to stone walls erected around the springs, indicating the need for protection, or at least privacy. An 1847 account by Frederick J. Ruxton describes the offerings left by Ute, and perhaps Arapahoe, worshippers at Manitou Springs: "The basin of the spring was filled with beads and wampum, and pieces of red cloth and knives, whilst the surrounding trees were hung with strips of deer-skin, cloth, and moccasins. The Indians regard with awe the 'medicine' waters of these fountains as being the abode of a spirit who breathes through the transparent water, and thus, by his exhalations, causes the perturbation (rippling) of its surface" (Pettit 1990, 23).

Ute religion, as in the case of most American Indian groups, was a part of everyday life. Each morning the Utes raised their hands to the

Figure 41:
Occupying their huge earth lodges in Kansas and Nebraska only long enough to plant
and harvest their cornfields, the Pawnees spent most of their time hunting buffalo,
often following rivers west into Colorado.
Photo courtesy of the Denver Public Library.

sun and ritually enveloped their bodies in its warmth. Evil did not exist in their world, only discordance which could be overcome by giving bad thoughts and things to the ancestors, the only ones who knew how to turn them around. Power was often brought by "the little people," dwarfs who hid behind rocks or trees and shot tiny arrows into a person (the Shoshones have a similar belief and call these little people *NunumBi*).

Dances were not only social events and times of feasting and games but were often of a religious nature. After the first thunder of spring, the Bear Dance, or *mama-kwa-nhhap*, drew friends and relatives from miles around. In a three- to four-day ceremony they thanked the Great Spirit for their survival of the harsh winter and celebrated the renewal of life, symbolized by the "Bear" coming out of hibernation. The "Bear," their brother and protector, was represented by the rubbing of a notched stick (a rasp), producing the sound of growling and claw sharpening. The rasp also represented thunder, another spring event.

Inside a dance arena of brush, the men walked to the center of the enclosure forming a line to face the women, who selected partners by walking over to the men and waving their shawls at their choices. Singers, accompanied by rasps and drums, began the song, and the dancers moved two steps forward and three steps backward in time. On the last day of the dance, the "Cat Man," who supervised the dance, broke the lines into couples. The women tried to outlast the men, and the dance did not end until someone had fallen with exhaustion, or was tripped by a fellow dancer.

Figure 42:
Every spring the Bear Dance brought Utes together to celebrate the renewal of life.
This also was a time of socializing, feasting, and courting.
Photo courtesy of the Colorado Historical Society.

Clothing and Personal Adornment

While many people in the barren basin country of Utah had to wear clothing fashioned from tules and sagebrush, the Colorado Utes perfected the art of hide tanning and made attractive shirts, leggings, and dresses from the deer, elk, antelope, and mountain sheep that were plentiful in the Colorado mountains. The Ute women of Colorado were known by other tribes, and, later, Spanish and American traders, for making the softest and whitest buckskin in the region. These women preferred doe skins for dresses, using one for the back and one for the front. The neck end of the skin would be the top of the dress, the upper legs forming the dress sleeves. The tails usually were cut off from the dress bottom but occasionally were left hanging down in the center. Three skins were required for a yoked dress, one entire skin forming the yoke and sleeves, the other two comprising the front and back. Early dresses were plain, but later ones were decorated with trade beads, fringe, deer dewclaws, or elk teeth. A woman usually owned two dresses and washed them in soap made from yucca roots.

Hard-soled moccasins were worn with knee-high leggings tied with buckskin thongs. When trade beads became available, moccasins saved for special occasions were elaborately beaded. Several buckskin bags hung from a woman's belt in which she usually kept two awls (one small, one large, used to punch holes in hides to sew them together), crushed minerals to use as face paint, and a knife hafted to a handle wrapped in buckskin.

The Ute men in Colorado wore a buckskin breechcloth, leggings tied to the belt, and a buckskin shirt. The shirt was smoked brown or yellow and was made with two skins forming the front and back with an additional skin used for sewn-on sleeves. A distinctive V-shaped flap was sewn in the shirt front, outlined with a band of beadwork. There were wider beaded bands over the shoulders that extended almost to the waist and also bands that followed the shoulders down the sleeves to the wrist. Enemy scalps often decorated the shirts.

Men's moccasins were similar to women's. During the winter both might wear sagebrush stockings or moccasins with buffalo hide soles and uppers of deer or elk hide with the hair worn inside. Rawhide overshoes were sometimes worn while hunting, made warmer by stuffing bark or buckskin rags between the moccasins and overshoes.

During the day a baby was usually wrapped in buckskin and laced onto a cradleboard that was decorated with fringe and, later, trade

Figure 43:
Beautifully beaded leather-covered Ute cradleboards
were often constructed of rods of rabbitbrush.
Photo by Kolberg Hopkins,
courtesy of the Denver Public Library.

beads. According to Northern Ute Betsy Chapoose, rods of rabbit-brush often were woven to make the frame (Betsy Chapoose 1994, personal communication). A boy's cradle was painted white, a girl's, yellow. Mattresses and pillows filled with eagle down or deer hair padded the baby. The cradleboard could be quickly attached to the mother's tumpline worn over the shoulders in case of attack by an enemy tribe. At night, the baby was placed in a small bag of buckskin or on a pile of soft animal hides. A small child wore little clothing but often wore a belt with a long loop attached. During a sudden attack the mother could pick the child up, sling the child over her back, and run. Older children wore clothing of animal skins, similar to adults.

Ute women were fond of dark red rouge made from the crushed mineral pigment they carried. Deer fat mixed with the rouge protected skin from wind and sunburn. Wreathlike willow hats also protected women's faces from summer sun, while men often wore painted rawhide visors. Dried leaves of certain fragrant plants, which were carried in small rags, served as perfume from both women and men.

Women's hair hung loose or was braided. Men often wore beads near their hair parts and otter skins on their braids. During battle, eagle feathers might be stuck in the braids. Both sexes painted their hair parts red and often painted their bodies with colored earth. Men sometimes applied white paint to their entire bodies then scratched designs through the paint.

Most Utes owned rabbit skin blankets for wearing and sleeping. Jackrabbit skin was cut in a continuous spiral and twisted around buckskin strings. The furry ropes then were twined together. If the blanket was large enough, it could be laid on and wrapped around a person, like a sleeping bag. Sleeping mats were also made of willow twined together with bark cordage.

Besides personal clothing, blankets, and jewelry, a typical Ute family living in Colorado owned the following possessions: a buckskin bag and rawhide parfleche (bag or box) for clothing, a buffalo hide parfleche for meat, a berry basket, parching tray, cups and ladles of wood and horn, and several baskets or pots for boiling.

History and Culture

Small family units of Utes followed traditional hunting and gathering practices to procure food. Various methods were used to lure and trap game animals. Pits were dug along game trails where hunters waited patiently for deer to walk by, and the shrill cry of a fawn made with an aspen leaf in the mouth lured does within killing distance. Buffalo and antelope were stalked, and elk were hunted in the winter when they easily floundered in deep snow. One historic account describes a swift hunter running after an antelope and catching it by the hind leg. Sometimes antelope were also hunted on horseback in relays. A solitary hunter might reflect sunlight into the eyes of an antelope with a mirror, causing the curious animal to come close to investigate.

The meat of the antelope, buffalo, elk, and deer was eaten fresh or dried for future use. To dry the meat, drying racks of small three-poled frames were built over smoldering fires, and the meat was hung on willow braces and left for two to three days. Then a long mano was used to pound the dried meat into a powder that was mixed with boiled bone grease and rolled into balls. Rawhide bags or boxes (parfleches) were used to store the balls of meat.

Deer meat, freshly cooked or dried, was the favorite meat of the Utes. Ribs from deer and other animals were hung on sticks next to cooking fires or roasted in coals. Rabbits and beavers were gutted and boiled—the cooking water of beaver meat being changed frequently to remove the strong taste of this meat. Beaver tails were a delicacy usually roasted in ashes. Sage hens and their eggs were eaten, as well as rattlesnakes, the latter skinned and roasted on coals.

Mountain lions were never eaten by the Utes because they were considered very dangerous and were much feared. Although terrifying tales of bears were told, if one were encountered, it might be killed. The only time bears were deliberately hunted, however, was when they were groggy from hibernation. Then a waving blanket in front of its den would cause strange shadows that the sleepy bear would investigate. When it stumbled out of the cave, the hunters shot it with arrows, spears, or, later, guns. Bear meat was cooked, the boiled bones making useful fat for future use. Coyotes and wolves were not hunted but were killed if found feeding on dead animals. Their fur was used to make saddle blankets or to sit on.

Eagles, prized for their feathers, were captured by hunters crouched in pits covered with willow branches. An eagle, baited by deer meat placed atop a pit roof, was grabbed by the legs and pulled into the pit. After needed feathers were pulled out, it was turned loose because the feathers of these birds were highly prized but the birds

were not eaten. Baby eagles were sometimes captured by a man lowered by rope to the nest. They were kept in brush cages and fed rabbits
until they were large enough that their feathers could be plucked.
Eagle feathers were worn in the hair and were attached to arrows while
the bones were made into whistles. Sometimes hunters made a living
out of capturing eagles and trading the feathers for horses.

The Utes in Colorado had advantages over their neighbors living in
the barren basin country of Utah, which was named after the tribe.
Because the Utes lived in a mountainous rather than in the drier region
of central Utah, they could afford the luxury of being discriminating
about their food sources. Unlike tribes that lived in central Utah, the
Utes did not eat porcupine, locusts, grasshoppers, horses, or dogs.
Since the dry habitat of central Utah would not sustain many horses,
the Colorado Utes also had more horses than the Utah tribes and considered themselves somewhat superior as a result.

The Utes used other food sources of their mountainous terrain to
good advantage. They tapped pine and aspen trees with hollow deer
bones to obtain the sap, which ran into bark buckets. The sap was a
sweet treat, eaten right away. Archaeologists occasionally find ponderosa pine trees with slashes of bark removed. Northern Ute Clifford
Duncan claims this was another way to obtain sweet sap and recalls as a
child watching older women happily preparing for trips of several days
in the mountains to obtain inner pine bark (Duncan 1994, personal
communication). Another source states that strips of inner bark were
tied in bundles and eaten later with salt (Martorano 1981). The Utes
requested permission of the tree before removing its bark, a ritual that
was followed with all living things they used; thus animals killed for
food were also asked permission and given thanks and offerings.
Juniper needles were brewed to make a medicinal tea. The liquid was
also put on the faces of unfortunate dogs who had been too friendly
with porcupines, since the tea dislodged the quills somewhat.

A cooking fire was made by rapidly rotating a stick of greasewood
between the hands into a small depression made on the side of a piece
of sagebrush wood. When the wood began to spark, shredded sagebrush or juniper bark placed next to the hearth would smolder and be
blown until it flamed. When available through trade, flint sparked with
a metal fire starter was used. Occasionally bullets were removed from
cartridges, and guns were shot at piles of dry bark, the gunpowder
causing sparks that set the bark on fire.

Vessels and utensils were made from a variety of materials. Some Utes made pottery but never to the extent the Anasazi did nor was it painted as the Pueblo pottery was. Because the Utes moved so often, their pottery was easily broken, and fine craftsmanship would have been wasted. To boil meat, a pot, which usually had a rounded bottom, was put near the fire, and ashes were placed around it. Most cooking, however, was done in pitch-lined, waterproof baskets with hot rocks heating the water to cook the meat.

Large "burden" baskets were used to gather berries. A basket full of berries was covered with leaves held down by a drawstring laced through loops on the rim of the basket. Another loop held a thong by which the basket would hang from a woman's neck while she picked the berries. Thin, straight sumac or willow branches were gathered to make the baskets. Bark was scraped off, and sewing splints were soaked in water. Then the splints were split in three pieces and sewn around the sumac or willow branches as the basket progressed upward. Some White River Utes dried buffalo heads to use for gathering seeds and berries. The slits left from the eyes and horns were sewn shut, then the heads were moistened and stuffed with bark as they dried.

Trays for parching seeds and seed beaters used to remove seeds from plants were also woven of sumac or willow. Hot ashes or charcoal were placed over the seeds in a tray, and the tray was shaken so the charred chaff would blow away. Seeds were then parched with hot coals as they were moved back and forth on a tray for about fifteen minutes. After the shells popped open, the grains were then boiled to make a nutritious cereal.

Woven bottles were made waterproof by boiling pinyon sap until soft and pouring it into them. Thongs were attached for carrying, and plugs of sagebrush bark hung from the necks of bottles by strings. Mountain sheep horns were heated and shaped into ladles and cups. Similar vessels were also made by charring the interiors of knots of wood from juniper, cottonwood, and pine trees.

In the spring a few families planted small plots of corn, beans, and squash then left them untended with the hope of a small harvest after returning from their seasonal circuits. In the river valleys, roots such as the yampa, camas, and wild onion were dug by women with sharp-tipped digging sticks. To cook them, pits about three feet deep were lined with hot rocks then a layer of damp grass. The roots were placed on the grass, covered with more grass, and topped with another layer of hot rocks. The pit oven was then covered with a mound of dirt, which steamed the roots overnight.

In mid to late summer camps were moved to the high mountain meadows, where women and children gathered a multitude of wild berries—raspberries, elderberries, serviceberries, and plump wild rose berries. According to historical accounts, the fruits growing at the top of berry bushes were often left for the birds to devour, while those at the very bottom were not picked so the smaller animals could eat them. Once the berries were collected they were dried in the sun and then stored.

In autumn when frost covered the mountain meadows, the Utes moved back down to lower regions such as the San Luis Valley or the Garden of the Gods near Colorado Springs. Along the western slope of the Rockies the valleys of the Colorado, Uncompahgre, and Gunnison rivers provided game, water, and firewood.

At this time of year pinyon nuts and seeds from juniper trees and those from delicate Indian rice grass were gathered in the nearby foothills. Meat was dried and stored along with nuts and berries for the long winter to come. The Utes, as did the Archaic people before them, stored dried food in sheltered overhangs for use during winter. The food was placed in grass-lined rawhide or sagebrush sacks and buried in holes covered with rocks, bark, grass, and dirt. Fires were burned on top of the storage pits to keep animals from smelling the food, but some Utes were probably nevertheless disappointed to find their cache ravaged by hungry wolves or bears at times.

Wickiups, the tipilike shelters made of juniper or pinyon poles covered with animal hides, provided the early Utes with shelter, along with natural overhangs. Hides, clothing, utensils, and other necessities were tied to travois, to be transported by dogs when the seasonal camps were moved.

At one time there were twelve or more bands of Utes scattered throughout Colorado, Utah, and northern New Mexico; historic accounts usually mention five or six major bands. The Mouache band ranged along the eastern slope of the Rockies, the San Luis Valley, and south almost to Santa Fe, New Mexico. They shared the San Luis Valley with the Kapote band, which hunted and foraged in the extreme northern and central part of New Mexico, down to the areas near the present-day towns of Chama and Tierra Amarilla. The Weenuche occupied southwestern Colorado, northwestern New Mexico, the canyon country of southeastern Utah, and the area surrounding present-day Mesa Verde National Park. The Mouaches and Kapotes are called the Southern Utes; the Weenuches are the Ute Mountain Utes.

The largest of the bands lived in west-central Colorado along the Gunnison and Uncompahgre river valleys. These were the Tabeguache (Taviwatch) or Uncompahgre Utes. North of them the Parianuc (Parusanuch), or Grand Valley Utes, lived along the Colorado River (once called the Grand River). The Yampa River Valley was home to the Yampa band, which also occupied North and Middle parks. When the White River Agency was established in Meeker, the Grand Valley and Yampa bands came to be known as the White River Utes. In the Uintah Basin near today's Dinosaur National Monument in northeastern Utah and northwestern Colorado, the Uintah Utes hunted and gathered. The Tabeguache, White River, and Uintah bands together are known as the Northern Utes.

The Utes were the first tribe to acquire horses, nearly thirty years prior to other tribes. Before that time they lived as their Archaic ancestors had; small groups of extended families moved often on foot to hunt migrating herds and gather wild foods as they ripened in well-known territories.

When Spaniards contacted the Utes in the mid-1600s, they traded knives, axes, kettles, wool blankets, and other goods for the soft, white buckskin hides the Ute women were famous for. However, they soon discovered Ute slaves were worth more than the hides. Hundreds of Ute children (and those from other tribes) were traded, or captured, to work in Spanish mines and on ranches.

Although the Ute slaves learned much about horses from watching Spanish horsemen in the adobe villages of New Mexico, they were not allowed to own the magnificent animals or they might escape. The Utes were quick to recognize the value of these "magic dogs"; perhaps as early as 1640 they began to raid Spanish ranches for horses and soon were galloping into camps of tribal enemies, swiftly stealing goods and capturing women and children. During the Pueblo Revolt of 1680, when all Spaniards fled the country for twelve years, many Ute slaves escaped with horses and made their way north. Large groups of Indians banded together to raid other tribes for more horses and to hunt buffalo.

The Utes became one of the most feared and powerful tribes in Colorado as they rode east onto the Plains to hunt buffalo and raid

Figure 44:
First to acquire horses from the Spanish, the Utes became the most powerful
tribe in Colorado. Although a mountain people, they often rode far out onto the Plains
to hunt buffalo and steal horses from their enemies.
Photo by H. S. Poley, courtesy of the Denver Public Library.

horses. They returned to their mountain homeland ladened with meat, hides, loot, and occasionally captive women who taught Plains crafts to the Utes. They learned to live in Plains-type tipis and to haul their camp supplies on horse travois. Although the Utes occasionally traded with the Navajos, Pueblos, Shoshones, and Comanches, they sometimes raided these tribes, along with their enemies, the Cheyennes, Kiowas, and Arapahoes. They pushed the Navajos out of the southwestern part of the state, where they had been living for generations.

To the Utes, war was only considered a necessary evil to acquire goods, horses, and captives. Unlike the Plains Indians, the Utes did not count coup or judge a man's bravery by his battle feats. Stealing a horse tethered next to a sleeping enemy was considered a deed of greater honor than killing anyone. Ute women, who did not weave or make fine pottery, appreciated the Spanish woolens, Navajo cottons, and Pueblo pottery their husbands brought back from distant raids.

Even though the Utes kept other tribes out of the Colorado mountains, they were friendly towards the first Spaniards who entered their country. In 1776, the priest-explorers Dominguez and Escalante traveled through western Colorado in search of a northern route from Santa Fe to California. They were led by Ute guides over Indian trails, passing through Dolores, over the Uncompahgre Plateau, and up onto the Grand Mesa. Although they had been told not to, Spanish packers accompanying the priests smuggled many trade items with them. The Utes did not want the Spaniards to leave with their goods and tried to frighten Dominguez and Escalante with tales of hostile Indians to the northwest. Undaunted, however, the explorers continued to the Uintah Basin (with a guide from there who happened to be visiting the Utes on Grand Mesa). Even though the expedition had to turn back towards Santa Fe because of the approaching winter, the reports of their travels through Colorado and Utah contained the first detailed written accounts of the Utes.

Figure 45:
Government-issued canvas tipis replaced those made of animal hides as game,
particularly buffalo, became scarce. Trees occasionally served as tipi poles.
Photo by Randall Wilcox, courtesy of the Denver Public Library.

Elsewhere, Spanish troops pursued Ute raiders who robbed miners and ranchers as well as Pueblos throughout northern New Mexico. Jan Pettit, in her book *Utes: The Mountain People*, quotes a Ute man as saying, "The Pueblo Indians planned for the Utes' raids. It was kind of like a game. They used to raise enough corn to eat, enough to plant new crops the next year, and enough for the Utes to steal" (Pettit 1990, 101).

Although such raids were swift and few people were killed—since the Utes did not want the source of their booty to move away—the raids became so distressing that in 1719 a force of Spanish soldiers, settlers, and Indians followed the Utes into the Colorado mountains to teach them a lesson. The retaliatory trip was unsuccessful, however, since members of the party rode through some poison ivy near present-day Dillon, and the miserable group of Spaniards returned to New Mexico.

In the later 1700s, the Utes engaged in lively trade with the Spanish who held annual trade fairs in Taos, New Mexico. Temporary truces allowed enemy tribes to barter with each other, as well as with the Spaniards. Navajo weavers made boldly striped "chief blankets" exclusively for the Utes, and Ute women wove baskets with Navajo designs to trade for the blankets.

In the 1830s and 1840s, caravans of Spanish traders started out from Santa Fe, New Mexico, with mules loaded with wool serapes, kettles, knives, and other goods to trade with the Utes of northwestern Colorado and northeastern Utah. The Spaniards traveled through the San Luis Valley, over Cochetopa Pass (in Ute, Buffalo Land), then north to the Gunnison River. Skirting the Black Canyon of the Gunnison, they followed old Indian trails to the site of Delta then on to the junction of the Gunnison and Colorado rivers (the present-day location of Grand Junction) and finally west along the Colorado River then north towards Rangely, probably by way of Douglas Creek. The route the Spanish traders followed is called the North Fork of the Old Spanish Trail. From Delta to west of Grand Junction the later Salt Lake Wagon Road followed a portion of the Old Spanish Trail. Ruts from this road, which was used to transport rations to the Utes at the agency at Colona, south of Montrose, are still visible in several places along Colorado 50.

When these Spanish traders arrived at the Uintah Basin west of Dinosaur National Monument, they traded their woolens for buckskin hides and slaves—the women and children the Utes had captured from

Figure 46:
A Ute woman inserts a pole in a smoke flap during a public demonstration
in the Garden of the Gods near Colorado Springs in 1913.
Photo by H. S. Poley, courtesy of the Denver Public Library.

tribes such as the Paiute (all tribes traded enemy captives as slaves, but the Spanish kidnapped thousands of Indians to sell as servants and ranch hands on Spanish *ranchos*). Slave trading was illegal among the Spaniards, but few cases were ever brought to trial; what little is known about the slave trade during this era comes from the few documented court cases.

Spaniards, and later fur trappers, could visit Ute country but were not allowed to stay. An exception was the trader Antoine Roubideau, who built trading posts on the Uinta River and close to the junction of the Gunnison and Uncompahgre rivers, near present-day Delta. However, the latter trading post was eventually burned by the Utes. Today, a replica can be visited in Delta (see "Places to Visit").

Figure 47: (This page and page 145)
Wearing traditional clothing, Chipeta and Ouray pose with other prominent Ute leaders
during a visit to Washington, D.C., in 1880. Top photo, this page, left to right, are: Galota,
Otto Mears, Savero (often spelled Severo), Shavanaux (also spelled Shavano), and Colonel
H. Page, Jocknick (?). Bottom photo, this page, left to right, are: Ignacio, Honorable C.
Schurz, Woretsiz (?), Ouray, General Charles Adams, and Chipeta.
Photo courtesy of the Denver Public Library.

Figure 47: (continued)
Top photo, this page, left to right, are: Ojo Blanco, William H. Berry,
Tapuch (?), Captain Jack, Tim Johnson, and Sour Wick.
Bottom photo, this page, left to right, are: Henry Jim, Buckskin Charley, Unknown,
William Burns, and Alhandra.
Photo courtesy of the Denver Public Library.

In the early to mid-1800s thousands of acres of Ute land were given to Spanish and Mexican citizens under Spanish land grants. Settlers increased in number in the San Luis and Arkansas valleys, building farms on the Utes' favorite camping grounds and plowing up valued root-digging areas. Game was shot by the intruders. Treaties were made and broken, each time the Utes' land shrinking in size. Although confrontations with the Utes occurred, astonishingly, the tribe as a whole did not fight. No amount of raiding by Utes seemed to discourage the flood of settlers. In 1852, however, Fort Massachusetts (Fort Garland) was established to discourage occasional Ute raids in southern Colorado, a military presence that angered the Utes.

Although there was some serious fighting between Indians and the United States military during this era, incidents involving killing were rare in Colorado. One such incident did occur in 1854. While some trappers, settlers, and friendly Utes were celebrating Christmas, a group of Mouaches under the leadership of Tierra Blanca, hurt because they had not been invited, attacked the party, killed fifteen of the celebrants, took the only woman and her two children captive, finished off the liquor, and raided a few nearby ranches. The Utes were pursued north by Fort Garland troops but disappeared into the mountains near Cochetopa Pass. In 1855, Kit Carson, Indian agent for the Utes, and Colonel Fauntleroy and his soldiers (along with four companies of volunteers) retaliated by attacking a group of raiding Utah Utes and Apaches near Salida, killing forty Indians.

There were many leaders responsible for the shaky peace that persisted through these devastating times. One of the leaders was Kaniache, a respected Mouache chief who signed the first treaty with the United States in Abiquiu, New Mexico, in 1849 (the first of many treaties that the United States would break). Another was Ouray (commonly pronounced "you-RAY," but Ute pronunciation is "OO-ray"), one of the most powerful of the Ute leaders, chief of the Uncompahgre Utes.

Ouray, whose mother was Apache, spent most of his childhood in Taos, New Mexico, where he lived with a Spanish family. There he learned to speak Spanish and English and also saw firsthand the power of the American military. In 1850, at the age of seventeen, Ouray gave up his "civilized" life and moved to western Colorado to be with his father, leader of the Uncompahgre band. His father died soon after Ouray arrived, but the young man stayed and learned how to be an effective warrior. He married a woman named Black Mare, who died shortly after their son, Paron, was born. Ouray then married Chipeta, a beautiful woman who had been caring for his son and continued to love him as her own after she married Ouray. When Paron was captured by the Sioux, Chipeta grieved as much as her husband. The two were rarely apart, and Ouray sought Chipeta's advice throughout his career as a leader of his people.

The Americans considered Ouray to be the spokesman for all the Utes, even though he represented only one band. In 1863, he signed the Tabeguache Treaty, which confined all Utes west of the Rockies and forced them to relinquish control of the mineral-rich San Juan Mountains. Ouray knew any resistance would lead to the killing of many Utes, but other bands were furious with his actions—many warriors thought it better to die fighting than to be wrenched from their land.

During this period rations were distributed to the Utes at various agencies. Often the rations were slow in coming and sometimes did not appear at all. Consequently, the hungry Utes had to hunt and gather in order to stay alive. One of the Ute agencies was in Denver at the junction of the South Platte River and Cherry Creek. Here, up to a thousand Utes would gather at ration time. The agent said they would "sometimes remain for several weeks, coming into town almost every day and walking around and gazing into the store windows for amusement" (Pettit 1990, 121). The site of the Ute camp can be seen today at Confluence Park, near 15th Street in lower downtown Denver.

The agency for the Uncompahgre and Grand River Utes was at Colona, south of the farm Ouray and Chipeta managed. The couple lived in an adobe house filled with American furniture and grew crops to set an example for their people. The site of their home is now the Ute Indian Museum just south of Montrose (see "Places to Visit").

Nathaniel Meeker ran the agency on the White River, just south of the present-day town of Meeker. In September 1879, he tried to convince the Utes to farm, an activity the Indians considered women's work. There was nothing in the treaties that stated that the Utes had to farm, and they were enraged when Meeker attempted to plow up one of their best horse pastures (some Utes claim it was a horse racetrack he wanted to plow). Meeker was shoved against a fence by a Ute named Johnson and immediately sent for military protection.

On September 22, 1879, Major T. Thornburgh and 178 men from Fort Steele, Wyoming, advanced towards the reservation. The Utes had heard of the merciless slaughter of innocent Indians at Sand Creek in southeastern Colorado sixteen years previously and feared a similar fate. Even Meeker sent a message to Thornburgh not to approach the reservation any closer and instead to come with only five soldiers to the agency to talk. Thornburgh, anxious to get his horses to feed and water, ignored the request and unlawfully entered the reservation at Milk Creek with his army. Almost immediately they were attacked by over 100 Utes under the leadership of Captain Jack, a White River Ute who had been raised by Mormons. The Utes cut the soldiers off from water and supplies. Thornburgh was killed, and the soldiers had only their dead horses for protection. For almost a week they suffered hunger, thirst, and the stench of rotting horses. Finally, the Utes left, having received word that Ouray and the Southern Utes would not assist them and that over 550 fresh soldiers had arrived from Wyoming.

Meanwhile, a few hours after Thornburgh and his men had illegally entered reservation lands, a man named Douglas and about twenty other Utes killed Meeker and the eleven other white men at the agency. They captured Meeker's wife, daughter Josephine (who was liked by her captors—she had been their teacher), and a young mother named Mrs. Price with her two children and held them captive for twenty-three days. Ouray convinced Douglas to release them near the present-day town of Mesa, close to Grand Junction. The captives, who later stayed with Ouray after they were released, were treated kindly at Ouray's home, and Chipeta even cried when the women left.

The Meeker incident reinforced the settlers' sentiments that the Utes should be forced from the area. Non-Indians were further enraged when the Utes burned thousands of acres of forests. Although this was an Indian tradition practiced to open the forests for easier horse travel, to make grasses more plentiful for game, to make future firewood gathering easier, and to concentrate game for easier hunting, settlers saw the fires as destructive and thought the Utes were setting them out of spite, which probably was the case under the circumstances.

Increased pressures to get rid of the Utes led to the establishment of even smaller reservations. The Uncompahgre (Tabeguache) Utes were given the Grand Valley area near present-day Grand Junction. However, after settlers realized it might have good farming potential, all the Northern Utes were gathered together in September of 1881 and forcibly removed to northeastern Utah, next to the reservation occupied by the Uintah Utes. The new reservation was named in honor of Ouray. (The two were later combined to create the Uintah-Ouray Reservation.)

The Northern Utes were not welcomed by their kinsmen because the Uintahs barely had enough resources to survive themselves. The land was described by Mormons as being so desolate that its only use was to hold the rest of the world together. Mormon leader Brigham Young highly recommended the area to Abraham Lincoln as a reservation for the Uintah Utes because his own followers would never consider settling there.

Ouray died before his people were torn from their homeland. Chipeta begged to stay on her farm, but the government refused her request; although non-Indian friends asked her to live with them, she bitterly abandoned her non-Indian ways and spent the rest of her life in a tipi with her people in Utah. Chipeta often visited the Glenwood Hot Springs to ease her arthritis and traveled to Grand Junction for several eye operations. Dying poor, blind, and lonely in 1929 at the age of eighty-one, she was finally returned to her farm. More than five thousand people attended her funeral. Her grave and that of her step-brother, John McCook, can be seen at the Chipeta Memorial Park on the grounds of the Ute Indian Museum south of Montrose. The graves lie near the spring where Chipeta and Ouray obtained their water when they lived on their farm.

On the Southern Ute Reservation Chief Ignacio did not want the land of his Weenuche band to be divided up into allotments. The Weenuches were moved to the corner of southwestern Colorado near Ute Mountain, west of Mesa Verde. They became known as the Ute Mountain Utes. For years the conservative band tried to keep their traditions alive by living in tipis—until the 1920s few lived in houses. Because they had no allotments to sell, they managed to keep their reservation land. A splinter group of Ignacio's band ranged off the Ute Mountain Ute Reservation, causing some trouble for local settlers. They were finally confined to an area south of Blanding, Utah, called the White Mesa Ute Reservation.

The Kapote and Mouache bands, led by Buckskin Charlie and Severo, accepted allotments. Many of these parcels were sold later to non-Indians. This land held by Utes is called the Southern Ute Reservation; its headquarters is in Ignacio, named after the Weenuche chief who struggled so hard to retain Ute land and culture.

The Utes, who had hunted throughout the entire state of Colorado, did not adapt well to life on the small reservations. Much of the land was unfit for farming, especially for a people who had no experience with

Figure 48:
Buckskin Charlie, shown with his wife, Towee, was a leader
of the Kapote band of the Utes. The Kapote band and
the Mouache band (under Severo's leadership), were allotted lands
that today are part of the Southern Ute Reservation,
headquartered in Ignacio.
Photo courtesy of the Denver Public Library.

Figure 49:
Although the Meeker incident of 1879 was the Utes' only major armed resistance against the
United States government, it resulted in the forced removal of all Northern Utes
to the Uintah-Ouray Reservation in northwestern Utah.
Photo courtesy of the Colorado Historical Society.

agriculture and considered it degrading and undignified. Attempts by the government to make farmers out of the Utes were unsuccessful at first, but gradually, encouraged by the success of other Indians, many began to cultivate hay, alfalfa, and wheat; some Ute produce even won prizes at county fairs. By 1925, most Utes lived in frame, log, or adobe houses. However, those who slept on the floor often caught colds from the drafts. Their tipis had been banked with straw, which blocked the winds.

Boarding schools of the era undermined traditional Ute culture, and parents did not want their children sent to these schools, where they were severely disciplined, forced to wear non-Indian clothing, and prohibited from speaking their own language. Several children died at the schools or while trying to find their way home after escaping from the institutions. The Teller Institute in Grand Junction attempted to teach Ute children, as well as those from other tribes, to farm, sew, read, and write. Some they taught to play musical instruments; the Teller Mandolin Band became so good that non-Indian bands in Grand Junction did not wish to compete with it. The school closed in 1911. Today, some of the brick buildings belong to the State Home on Indian School Road.

The Utes Today

The Ute Mountain Utes, because of their refusal to adopt non-Indian ways, remain the most traditional of the Utes. Their reservation surrounds the community of Towoac (TOY-yahk), located east of Sleeping Ute Mountain near Cortez, Colorado. Some cliff dwellings tucked into overhangs on their reservation just south of Mesa Verde have been stabilized, and the Ute Mountain Tribal Park is attracting tourists from all over the nation.

The tribe owns a pottery factory near Towoac, where pots and jars exhibiting modern designs are sold to tourists and to outlets all over the state. A large casino was recently built by the tribe along U.S. 666, south of Cortez. (In 1990, the Colorado legislature passed a bill allowing gambling in Colorado mountain towns; tribes, which are considered sovereign nations because they have their own governments, are allowed to offer the same games under the statutes of state and federal Indian gaming laws.) The casino provides jobs for over 375 people. The tribally owned Weenuche Construction Company, which employs from 170 to 300 people, built a pipeline in 1990 to provide the first treated domestic water to the reservation. It also constructed a canal from the McPhee Reservoir to the "toe" of Sleeping Ute Mountain on the southern portion of the reservation. The canal, part of the Dolores Project, will provide irrigation water for 7,600 acres that will be farmed by the Utes. Crops will be growing in the same fields where the Anasazi had their farms. The soil is rich there, evidenced by the numerous ruins of Anasazi farming villages that are currently being excavated in the project area as part of the mitigative effort to comply with historic preservation laws.

The Ute Mountain Ute tribal complex employs up to 275 people in various tribal administrative capacities. All of these organizations make the Ute Mountain Ute tribe the largest employer in Montezuma County (Lynn Hartmann 1994, personal communication).

Some Southern Utes who live in the "checkerboard" area near Ignacio (southeast of Durango) are farmers and ranchers. The term "checkerboard" refers to the ownership of the area's land; parcels of private land are intermingled with parcels of reservation land, a result of allotment sales and the original platting, which was designed to have non-Indians influence the Utes' farming activities.

Some local businesses owned by the Southern Utes bring in money for the tribe. Among these are the Sky Ute Motel in Ignacio as well as

Figure 50:
*Teller Institute's mandolin band played so well that other Grand Junction schools did not
want to compete with it. Photo courtesy of the Denver Public Library.*

Figure 51:
*In 1920s-style hairdos and clothing, Southern Ute girls study at an Ignacio boarding school.
Photo courtesy of the Denver Public Library.*

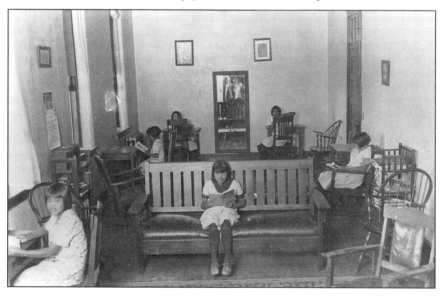

a modern racetrack and indoor rodeo arena. The tribe is also considering big-time gambling to attract tourists. Ute traditions and history are being researched and documented by the Ute Language and Culture Committee in Ignacio. The committee has compiled an excellent school curriculum for elementary and junior high school students.

Some Utes on the Uintah-Ouray Reservation, with headquarters in Fort Duchesne, Utah, benefit financially from oil and gas drilling on their allotted land. The area is a "checkerboard" area consisting of private land, reservation land, and a few remaining allotments. The primary employer on the reservation is the Ute tribal government in Fort Duchesne. Timber grows on the southern flanks of the Uintah Mountains, part of which is owned by the tribe, and logging is being considered to bring in money. The Utes also want to preserve a pristine portion of the forest for recreational use, including hunting. In general, however, the Northern Utes still suffer from unemployment and discrimination.

The Northern Utes are governed by a tribal Business Committee of six members, two from each of the three bands—the Uintah, White River, and Uncompahgre. Water rights is a major issue for the tribal government, as for many other tribes. The majority of water for the Central Utah Project (CUP), which is piped to the cities of Provo and Salt Lake, comes from the Uintah Mountains, much of it owned by the Ute tribe. In exchange for the Utes' contribution of their water to the CUP, a large irrigation project was proposed but never constructed. The Utes see this as one more promise broken by the government. The battle over the water rights issue has created bitter feelings between many non-Indians and the Utes.

Traditional ceremonies such as the Sun Dance and Bear Dance are still performed by all Utes. People from all three reservations travel to visit each other during these ceremonies. The first Bear Dances of the year are held in the spring on the Uintah-Ouray Reservation. Then, at the end of June the Ute Mountain Ute Reservation hosts the dance in Towaoc; the Southern Utes hold the Bear Dance in Ignacio the last weekend in May; and the last one of the year is held in August on the White Mesa Ute Reservation south of Blanding, Utah.

Although the Northern Utes are gone from Colorado, and the Southern Utes live on or near their reservation areas today, historical evidence of the Utes' past is continually being discovered in the valleys and on the ridges and mesas of their former homeland. A village of collapsing juniper-pole wickiups stands on a ridgetop in northwestern

Colorado, and an eagle
trap is perched on the
edge of a steep cliff.
Large ponderosa pines
on the Uncompahgre
Plateau bear the scars
of bark removal by
Utes who gathered the
inner bark for food.
Occasionally hunting
and storage platforms
are found high in the
tops of juniper and
pinyon trees. Small side-
notched arrowheads lie
in grassy forest mead-
ows. Fragments of pot-
tery provide evidence
of where Ute women
accidentally dropped
cooking pots while char-
coal shows where they
camped.

Figure 52:
Wickiups in North Park are reminders that Utes
once ranged a much greater territory that included
Colorado's mountains and plateaus,
as well as much of Utah.
Photo courtesy of the Denver Public Library.

A campsite called
the Harris site, dating
from the 1870s, the
years when the Utes last occupied the area, was recently excavated by the
Colorado Archaeological Society in a narrow red rock canyon snaking
down from the Uncompahgre Plateau northwest of Montrose. Artifacts
were found on a stream terrace, concentrated in two circles with center
firepits, indicating that the two areas where the artifacts were discovered
had been enclosed by tipis. Among the numerous artifacts found were
several bullets, a spoon, a silver hair ornament, tin can remains, bridle
fragments, and beads (Jonathan Horn 1992, personal communication).

Artifacts and features of the Utes whose ancestors lived in Colorado
for at least five hundred years tell us about the past. The people who
live on the Uintah-Ouray, Ute Mountain Ute, and Southern Ute reservations look to the future while preserving many of their important
values and traditions.

THE SHOSHONES

The tribe known as the Shoshones lived in the mountains and valleys of northern Utah, southern Idaho, and southwestern Wyoming. A few bands also ranged the Yampa and White River valleys in northwestern Colorado until about 1850 or 1860, when the Utes pushed them north into Wyoming. Game was plentiful for these people; there were even buffalo to hunt along the Snake River in southern Idaho.

The language of the Shoshones belongs to the Uto-Aztecan language group, the same as those of the Comanches, Utes, Paiutes, Hopis, and Aztecs. The Shoshones may have entered Colorado around the same time as the Utes, having migrated from the deserts of California and the Great Basin. The sign for Shoshones and their relatives the Comanches is a wavy hand at the waist, a motion that gave rise to the name Snake, by which the Shoshones were often known. In fact, the motion may represent the manner in which they constructed their houses long ago—by weaving grass between bent branches. The word *Shoshone* may mean "valley dwellers."

Beliefs

According to the Shoshones, the Creator, Appah (AP-ee), made the earth with the help of Wolf. Coyote, the trickster, created people and gave them fire but also brought pain, disease, and death to the world. The earth was a round disk, a central layer in a layered universe. The back-and-forth turning of the disk caused sunrises and sunsets. The lower disk, or underworld, was just like the earth, and the two were connected by a hole, the location of which was forgotten long ago. The Shoshones were often tormented by *NunumBi*, the Little People, who shot invisible arrows at unsuspecting humans, causing much discomfort.

Ancient myths and ceremonial dancing were (and still are) important to the Shoshones. In the spring the Circle Dance, or Grass Dance, is performed as well as a Bear Dance similar to that of the Utes. In the past Scalp Dances were performed in which women danced around scalp poles after successful battles against enemies such as the Blackfeet or Nez Perce.

Clothing and Personal Adornment

Adults wore blanket robes of antelope, deer, or bighorn sheep skin, with the hair left on in colder months. The warmest robes were of buffalo and beaver pelts. Summer robes were hairless and often made of elk hide.

Women's hide dresses were commonly decorated with porcupine quills rather than beads. When nursing, women wore dresses with open sides.

Men's shirts were long, reaching halfway down the thigh. The hides were of deer, antelope, bighorn sheep, and occasionally elk. Wide strips of quilled or beaded leather were sewn to the shoulders, and fringes decorated the sleeves. From the elbows down to the wrists, sleeves were fringeless and fitted the arm tightly. Men also wore leather vests and wide armbands.

Both women and men wore leggings. Women wore knee-high leggings of antelope skin; men's leggings were longer and fuller, each being made of almost a whole skin. The leggings were so long they served as a breechcloth, secured at the waist with a strip of leather. Fringe decorated the sides, often ornamented with hair from a slain enemy. Long beaded strips of leather were also added to the sides of the leggings.

Shoshone men and women wore moccasins made

Figure 53:
When game became scarce, Shoshone women replaced their hide dresses with ones made of trade cloth.
Photo courtesy of the Denver Public Library.

in one piece from the tanned hides of deer, elk, or buffalo. During the winter months, the buffalo hair was left on the hide and worn inside. Sometimes sagebrush was stuffed in the moccasins for added warmth. Men occasionally decorated the tops with skunk fur, leaving the tails trailing at the heel. Beads were used for decoration on men's and women's moccasins until about the turn of the century.

Explorers Meriwether Lewis and George Rogers Clark, who passed through Shoshone country in the early 1800s, were impressed with Shoshone "tippets," short cloaks made with collars of otter skin decorated with abalone shells. The otter's body trailed down the back, with the tail hanging down. Attached to the skin were from one hundred to two hundred and fifty small rolls of ermine fur, which were sewn in clusters to the otter skin. The ermine rolls covered the shoulders and body almost to the waist. Lewis claimed it was the most elegant piece of Indian clothing he had ever seen (Lowie 1909, 181).

Women and men generally wore their hair loose. Historic photographs often show men's "bangs" swept straight up in front. Necklaces of strung salmon vertebrae separated by small seashells worn by the Shoshones were later replaced by those made of long, cylindrical beads. "Collars" of embroidered leather or braided sweet grass were worn around the neck. Women wore necklaces of elk teeth while men preferred those made from the claws of grizzly bears they had killed. Both sexes wore earrings of beads and tiny shells, sometimes up to five in each pierced ear. Brass earrings became popular around the turn of the century; only one or two were worn in each ear.

History and Culture

For centuries the Shoshones hunted and gathered wild food and lived in brush and grass houses or tents of animal hides. They probably acquired horses from their southern relatives, the Utes, with whom they often fought. The Shoshones soon became buffalo hunters, adopting the clothes, tipis, and general lifestyle of Plains Indians. Like the Comanches, however, they did not adopt the Sun Dance (until recently, with many Christian overtones). Their most despised enemies were the Blackfeet in Montana and their eastern neighbors, the Crow, Sioux, Cheyenne, and Arapahoe tribes.

Figure 54:
Northwest Colorado was the southern extent of the Eastern Shoshones, who lived mainly
along the slopes of the Rocky Mountains from southwestern Wyoming to southwestern
Montana. Photo courtesy of the Denver Public Library.

When mountain men followed the beaver-filled streams into the
mountains of the Shoshones, they were generally well treated by the
Indians, who called the bearded strangers "dog-faced people." Many
trappers married Shoshone women and became closely tied to their
families.

In 1841, twenty-three trappers with a group of Shoshone allies met
a large party of Arapahoes, Cheyennes, and Sioux near Slater, Colorado
(northeast of Craig on the Little Snake River). The ensuing battle

Figure 55:
Codsiogo, an Eastern Shoshone, has braided hair
and wears armbands and a studded leather vest —
typical Shoshone attire of the late 1800s.
Photo courtesy of the Denver Public Library.

lasted twelve hours. When it was over, about one hundred Indians out of five hundred lay dead. Ten of the trappers were killed. Near Slater, Battle Creek and Squaw Mountain are reminders of the fight, the mountain named after the women who hid there during the battle (the term "squaw" is derogatory today).

In the early 1840s, the fur trade was coming to an end, but soon several thousand emigrants traveled the Oregon Trail through the heart of Shoshone country. They were headed for the Oregon coast, but on their way they hunted and scared the game and burned the trees along the streams for firewood. In addition, their thousands of horses and oxen ate all the grass along the Shoshones' ancient trail. Many Shoshones wanted to raid the settlers but were stopped by their respected chief, Washakie. This veteran warrior hated what the settlers were doing to his land and people, but, like Chief Ouray of the Utes, he realized the futility of fighting the whites and urged the Shoshones to remain at peace.

The Shoshones were forced to sign treaties which gave their land to non-Indian ranchers and farmers. The United States government wanted the Shoshones moved to Indian Territory (Oklahoma), but Washakie insisted his tribe be moved to their beloved Wind River Mountains of western Wyoming. The chief's wish was granted because

Figure 56:
*Shoshones and Comanches were late to adopt the Sun Dance. Although the dancers of these
tribes suffer from fatigue, thirst, and hunger, they do not pierce their skin.
Photo courtesy of the Denver Public Library.*

the government was grateful to him for keeping the peace. However,
the Shoshones had to share their reservation with the Northern Arapahoes, their longtime enemies.

The Shoshones Today

On the east side of the Rocky Mountains lies the Wind River Reservation. At the base of the majestic Wind River Mountains, the Eastern
Shoshones have shared the reservation with the Northern Arapahoes
since 1878, with each tribe retaining its own distinctive cultural traditions. Fort Washakie, named for their diplomatic and visionary leader, is
the center of tribal government as well as community life. Shoshones
also live near or within the towns of Burris and Crowheart, which lie
north and west of the mainly Arapahoe towns of Arapahoe and Ethete.

Most land parcels (allotments) given to individual Shoshone families in the 1890s were sold to non-Indian ranchers and farmers. The
Shoshone and Arapahoe tribes, however, maintained ownership of much
of the unallotted land on their jointly occupied reservation. Today,

Figure 57:
From 1840 until the turn of the century, Chief Washakie
encouraged peaceful relations with the Americans.
Refusing to have the Eastern Shoshones sent to Indian
Territory (Oklahoma), Washakie managed to have their
homeland surrounding the Wind River range in Wyoming
set aside as their reservation.
Photo courtesy of the Denver Public Library.

some of the few remaining allotments are farmed and ranched, while both tribes are promoting agriculture on the tribally owned lands as well.

Shoshone tribal government is separate from that of the Arapahoes, an arrangement dating back to a policy Washakie and the Arapahoe leader Sharp Nose established in 1892. A General Council, comprised of all adult tribal members, meets to discuss various tribal concerns such as programs, natural resource management, budgets, and personnel. The resolutions passed by the General Council are administered by the six elected members of the Shoshone Business Council. Cooperative programs and concerns shared with the Northern Arapahoes are managed by the Joint Business Council, comprised of six elected Shoshones and six elected Arapahoes.

In 1988, the Shoshone Tribal Cultural Center was established. Located in the historic Fort Washakie District, the center offers traditional craft classes to tribal members, sponsors the annual Treaty Day Commemoration in June (which is open to the public), and has a museum with historic exhibits as well as Shoshone arts and crafts. Shoshones from the center also visit schools and other organizations to inform the groups about Shoshone culture and history.

In addition to the Treaty Day Commemoration, other Shoshone events include the Crowheart Big Wind Powwow, Shoshone Indian Days, the Shoshone Stampede Rodeo, and the Shoshone Tribal Fair. For more information about these events, contact the Shoshone Tribal Cultural Center (see "Places to Visit").

PLACES TO VISIT

Colorado

BATTLE OF MILK CREEK MONUMENT

Located northeast of Meeker, off Colorado 13 on a dirt road (follow signs). At the site there is a stone monument built by Northern Utes at the request of the Rio Blanco Historical Society as a memorial to the Battle of Milk Creek, where in the fall of 1879 Utes kept General Thornburgh's troops from advancing to the Meeker Agency. It was dedicated in 1993 to all Indians and non-Indians who died in the battle.

FORT UNCOMPAHGRE LIVING HISTORY MUSEUM
205 W. Gunnison River Drive
Delta, CO 81416
(303)874-8349

A replica of Antoine Roubideau's trading post is the site of summer living history programs depicting life during the Indian trade and fur trapping era.

MUSEUM OF WESTERN COLORADO
4th and Ute
Grand Junction, CO 81501
(303)242-0971

The museum houses exhibits of Ute (and pre-Ute) artifacts and historic photos. The museum is also assisting the United States Forest Service in financing the Northern Ute History Project, involving Utes interviewing their elders about the lives of their ancestors in western Colorado.

UTE INDIAN MUSEUM
17253 Chipeta Road
Montrose, CO 81401
(303)249-3098

Here, Ute history is portrayed through historic photographs, dioramas, artifacts, tools, clothing, and an authentic tipi. The Chipeta Memorial Park, where Chipeta and her brother are buried, is adjacent to the museum.

UTE TRAILS

Hikers can follow the footsteps of the Utes on many old trails in Colorado. In the 1920s, the United States Forest Service marked a Ute trail over the Flattops north of Glenwood Springs in the White River and Routt national forests. An on-going project is to trace and map the trail and find those markers that still remain. Information about the project can be obtained at the United States Forest Service Headquarters in Glenwood Springs.

Another well-known Ute trail begins at the Garden of the Gods near Colorado Springs, one of the Utes' favorite wintering grounds. The trail winds north of Pike's Peak up to the Utes' sacred Manitou Springs, then on towards Ute Pass, roughly paralleling U.S. 24. In 1912, the trail was marked with marble markers by Chipeta and Buckskin Charlie, the Southern Ute Chief. Southern Utes, all proudly dressed in their traditional clothing, rode horseback or walked the trail they had not seen for over thirty years but remembered well. Information about the trail and Ute culture in general can be obtained at the Ute Pass Museum near Colorado Springs.

Wyoming

SHOSHONE TRIBAL CULTURAL CENTER
P.O. Box 1008
Fort Washakie, WY 82514
(307)332-9106

Located in the historic Fort Washakie District, the center offers traditional craft classes to tribal members and sponsors the annual Treaty Day Commemoration in June. The center also has a museum with historic exhibits and Shoshone arts and crafts.

Suggestions for Further Reading

Jefferson, James, Robert W. Delaney, and Gregory C. Thompson. *The Southern Utes: A Tribal History*. Ignacio, Colo.: Southern Ute Tribe, 1972.

Madsen, Brigham D. *The Northern Shoshoni*. Caldwell, Id.: Caxton Printers, 1980.

Marsh, Charles. *People of the Shining Mountains*. Boulder, Colo.: Pruett Publishing Co., 1982.

Pettit, Jan. *Utes: The Mountain People*. Boulder, Colo.: Johnson Books, 1990.

Smith, Anne M., collector. *Ute Tales*. Salt Lake City: University of Utah Press, 1992.

———. *Ethnography of the Northern Utes*. Santa Fe, N.M.: Museum of New Mexico Press, 1974.

Smith, David P. *Ouray: Chief of the Utes*. Ouray, Colo.: Wayfinder Press, 1987.

Southern Ute Tribe. *Exploration in Southern Ute History*. Ignacio, Colo.: Piñon Press, 1989.

Sprague, Marshall. *Massacre: The Tragedy at White River*. Lincoln and London: University of Nebraska Press, 1957.

Trenholm, Virginia Cole, and Maurine Carley. *The Shoshonis: Sentinels of the Rockies*. Norman: University of Oklahoma Press, 1964.

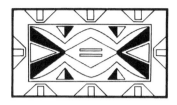

9

The Athabascans

▲ ▲

THE JICARILLA APACHES

Perhaps less than a century after the Anasazi abandoned the Four Corners area, people living in the Canadian region, known as Athabascans (a-tha-BAS-cans) moved south along the Rocky Mountains. These people were hunters and gatherers. As they moved into Colorado and further south, they broke up into several groups, acquiring slightly varied lifestyles in each area they occupied. In time, their languages also became somewhat different due to separation, the basic language being Apachean. One group that broke off from the rest is the Navajos, who lived primarily in southwestern Colorado and northwestern New Mexico, and later, in northeastern Arizona; another group is the Apaches.

Apaches may have moved onto the Colorado Plains after the long drought that ended around A.D. 1300, or perhaps even earlier. This makes the Apachean people (including the Navajos) the earliest Indian group in Colorado except for the Utes. The first Apaches to settle in Colorado are known as the Dismal River Apaches. To their diet of wild food they added corn that they grew along river valleys. These part-time farmers made a crude form of pottery that had a plain, unmarked surface. It is probable that the Dismal River Apaches occupied the same areas as the Apishapa and Purgatoire peoples, the prehistoric part-time gardeners and house builders of the Plains. The Purgatoire peoples may have been overwhelmed by, or married into, the Apache groups.

When Coronado and his armor-covered soldiers rode onto the Plains for the first time, they saw Indians hunting buffalo on foot and called them *Querechos* (ker-A-chos). These Indians, probably Apaches, eventually split into several groups. Most of them migrated south into New Mexico, Arizona, and Texas (the infamous Apaches Cochise and Geronimo were Chiricahua Apaches living in southeastern Arizona). But some remained in Colorado and were called *Apache de la Xicarilla* by the Spanish, "the people of the baskets," because the Jicarilla women were fine basketmakers. The Jicarillas call themselves the *Tinde*, "the People."

In most of Colorado the Apaches lived like other horse-mounted buffalo hunters—transporting their hide tipis on travois, packing their camp goods in parfleches, and raiding Spanish ranches for horses. However, they did not count coup or practice the Sun Dance.

Beliefs

Apache ancestors were thought to have come from the under-world. When the earth was new, great monsters roamed about threatening human beings. The monsters were slain by two culture heroes, who figure often in many Apache ceremonies. Coyote, the trickster, is another character who figures in many Jicarilla stories. Although Coyote usually gets into much mischief, he occasionally does something useful, such as obtaining fire for the Apache people. Many Jicarilla myths and legends are similar to those of other Apache groups, including the Navajos.

Clothing and Personal Adornment

While on the Plains, the clothing of the Jicarilla Apaches was similar to that of other Plains tribes—fringed dresses of deer hide for the
women and fringed shirts and breechcloths for the men. As they
migrated south, styles changed. When fabric became available, women
made dresses of cotton calico with a slit in the yoke for the head.
Sleeves were made in "squares," from sixteen to eighteen inches in
width. The long sleeves reportedly were used to wipe sweat from the
brows of busy women as they performed arduous tasks such as corn
grinding (Charlotte Vigil 1995, personal communication). One of the
most distinctive articles of clothing worn by Jicarilla Apache women
was a leather belt, which was sometimes up to seven inches in width
and often decorated with silver buttons.

Men's pants and breechcloths were gradually replaced with "government issue" pants. Photos from the 1930s show Jicarilla Apache
men clad in blue jeans with cuffs turned up to accommodate leg
length. Broad-brimmed felt cowboy hats were also popular.

In earlier times, men wore vests decorated with glass trade beads
called "seed beads." The beads were white, black, and navy blue in
color. Cloth belts and headbands were worn by the men, as well as
leather armbands and wristbands, often decorated with silver buttons.

History and Culture

The Jicarilla Apaches hunted or farmed throughout the Plains of
eastern Colorado and northern New Mexico during early historic
times. They also spent summers in the beautiful San Juan and Sangre
de Cristo mountains of Colorado and the Sandia and Jemez mountains
in northern New Mexico. Many of the Jicarilla Apaches settled in villages and farmed, much like the Pueblo Indians by whom they were
heavily influenced. A large Apache settlement along the Arkansas River
in Colorado (similar to any Pueblo village) was visited by Spanish soldiers in 1719, who called it El Cuartelejo, the faraway district.

The Apaches of El Cuartelejo and other eastern Colorado settlements obtained horses fairly early and lost no time in raiding Pawnee
villages in Kansas and Oklahoma for captives to be traded with the
Spanish as slaves. In the late 1600s, Comanches from the north

Figure 58:
*Although the Jicarilla Apache Reservation included some of their north-central
New Mexico homeland, the Apaches' timber was sold, and their best farmland
was leased to settlers by the federal government. Their means of subsistence gone,
most had to rely on ration day to get enough food to survive.
Photo courtesy of the Colorado Historical Society, circa 1929.*

obtained guns through trade with the French on the Missouri River. As the Comanches moved south to be closer to the source of Spanish horses, the Apaches could not hold their territory since they had not obtained guns from the Spanish. In 1709, Spanish soldiers met with the Apaches in southeastern Colorado and promised them protection against the Comanches, the Pawnees, and the Pawnee allies, the French. The Spaniards were eager to claim Colorado and hold it against the French intruders, who controlled the Missouri River trade. However, the Spanish soldiers were unable to keep the armed Comanches from uprooting the Apaches. Perhaps as early as the 1730s the Jicarillas were pushed out of Colorado into the mountains and foothills of northeastern New Mexico.

When New Mexico became part of the United States in 1848, Americans built forts to stop the Apaches from raiding—the only way this tribe knew how to survive since their hunting grounds had been taken over by non-Indian settlers. The Jicarilla Apaches were finally located on a reservation in 1887. The reservation, situated along the Continental Divide in north-central New Mexico, originally covered much of the Jicarilla homeland, but soon non-Indians claimed the best farmland and the United States government sold their timber and leased the southern reservation land to settlers. The growing season in the high country was too short to farm. The Jicarillas suffered from malnutrition and disease. Finally, in 1920, sheep were issued, and the Jicarillas became sheep ranchers.

The Jicarilla Apaches Today

In the 1930s, the Jicarilla Apaches established their own tribal government based in Dulce, New Mexico. Under the Indian Reorganization

Figure 59:
Cotton dresses and wide belts were typical fashions of Jicarilla Apache women
on the reservation headquartered in Dulce, New Mexico.
Photo courtesy of the Denver Museum of Natural History, 1940.

Act, which recognized American Indians as United States citizens, the non-Indian farmers were removed from reservation lands. The 1946 Indian Claims Act awarded the Jicarillas money for lands unjustly taken from them, from which some interest is generated. The tribe also developed its remaining natural resources—gas, oil, and timber.

Many Jicarilla Apaches practice their native religion. Traditional ceremonies such as the Puberty Fiesta, Bear Dance, and Relay Race are often held. The Puberty Fiesta occurs when girls come of age, and the purpose is to pray that the girls have a long and fruitful life. The Bear Dance is performed to cure people of certain illnesses. Both ceremonies are a time for socializing and feasting. The Relay Race is held each year in September near Dulce, New Mexico. Half the runners represent the sun and the animals, the other half the moon and the plants. If the sun runners, the *Olleros*, win, there will be many animals to hunt that year; if the moon runners, the *Llaneros*, win, there will be many plants to gather for food. Jicarilla boys jog all year in preparation for the race, which represents a time when their people relied on the bounties of nature to survive.

For information about the dates of various ceremonies and races, contact the Jicarilla Apache Tribal Museum (see "Places to Visit"). The museum displays and sells Apache arts and crafts, including beadwork, leather work, and basketry.

THE NAVAJOS

Although the Navajos are primarily located in northern Arizona and New Mexico today, they once also occupied the canyons of southwestern Colorado, the present location of the Southern Ute reservations. Navajo rock art on canyon walls and abandoned, crumbling hogans is a reminder of their stay in Colorado.

Spaniards called these people the *Apache de nabajo*, a twisted version of the Tewa Pueblo words for "strangers of the cultivated fields." Navajos call themselves the *Diné*, "the People," or "the Earth Surface People," referring to their gods' emergence from the world below to the present world, where they created the *Diné*.

Figure 60:
Pueblo influence was reflected in the mantas *(dresses) of Navajo women.*
Muslin pants and V-necked shirts, patterned after Mexican clothing,
were worn by men and boys.
Both sexes wore shoulder blankets and moccasins.
Photo courtesy of the Colorado Historical Society, 1872.

Beliefs

To Navajos, all things of nature are of equal importance to humankind. The gods are equal and rely on each other to succeed. Mother Earth cannot do her work without Father Sun and Father Sky; Changing Woman, who is responsible for the changing of the seasons, cannot succeed without all three of these deities. The *yeis* are the offspring of Father Sky and Mother Earth. These "Holy Ones" are neither good nor bad and are represented in various dances, and on rugs, baskets, and sandpaintings.

Elaborate ceremonies are conducted constantly to maintain a balance between humans and nature, a desired mental state known as *hozho*. Over fifty sacred chants are still used by singers, and countless songs are memorized exactly as they were passed down for generations to cure people of sickness, unbalanced emotional conditions, or estrangement from Navajo land and traditions. For example, many Navajos have the Enemy Way ceremony performed after serving in the military in foreign countries, being in a war, or living in a city.

Though today most Navajos live in houses or mobile homes, hogans (six-sided dwellings made of notched logs covered by dirt or shingles) are common in remote or rural settings, and many families maintain one specifically for ceremonial use. An elaborate sandpainting often is made on the hogan floor during a ceremony to help with the healing process. Colored sand is delicately poured

Figure 61:
Spaniards believed slavery was essential to the operation of their vast ranches in Mexico. Navajo children were captured more than any other Indians to work as servants or ranch hands. Photo courtesy of the Colorado Historical Society.

in intricate designs, including patterns depicting certain *yeis*. The patient sits on the painting and absorbs the powers of the *yeis*. After the ceremony, the sandpainting is destroyed so witches cannot undo the process.

Ritual sings such as the Nightway and Blessingway are also times of reunion and socializing, attended by hundreds of friends and relatives. In the past, the Navajos traveled on foot, horses, or in wagons; today families drive pickups to attend ceremonies of relatives who might live over two hundred miles away.

Clothing and Personal Adornment

Once the Navajo people were established in the Southwest, their clothing reflected the influences of their neighbors. Women wore wool dresses similar to the Pueblo *manta* made of two identical pieces sewn together at the sides and shoulders (that often left one shoulder exposed). A woven sash or later a concha belt, often made of silver dollars, was worn at the waist. In the late nineteenth century, women began to wear calico shirts and long calico or denim skirts as commercial cloth became available.

Men commonly wore white muslin pants slit up the sides of the legs, patterned after Spanish-Mexican trousers. V-necked shirts of muslin or, later, calico were worn. Both sexes wore shoulder blankets, buckskin leggings and moccasins, and lots of silver and turquoise jewelry. Men and women wore their hair tied in a long bun called a *chonga*. Men often tied colorful cotton headbands around their heads.

History and Culture

Along with the people who were to become the Apaches, the Navajos began their southern migrations from Canada perhaps as early as A.D. 1100. They may have arrived in southwestern Colorado and northwestern New Mexico about the time the Anasazi were abandoning their pueblos, and it is possible that Navajo raids of Anasazi food supplies or women were at least partly responsible for the Anasazi abandonment of the Four Corners region. The sandy canyons of northwestern New Mexico and southwestern Colorado where the

Navajos settled were called *Dinetah* (Deh-nay-TAH), the "Land of the People."

The Navajos grew corn, a practice learned from their Pueblo neighbors, and hunted and gathered to survive. They lived in log or stone houses (hogans), usually scattered over wide distances since Navajos moved according to seasons to be near resources or for ceremonial reasons. This seminomadic lifestyle rather than the more crowded, sedate village life worked well for smaller Navajo family groups.

Hogans originally were tipi-shaped dwellings of poles and sticks, covered with mud. In more recent times, notched logs were piled up to form six or eight walls with log roofs covered by dirt or shingles. Although hogans are houses, they are also sacred. Navajo ceremonies are still held in hogans, even if a family lives in a modern house or trailer.

The clan system was, and still is, one of the foundations of Navajo life. A child becomes a member of his/her mother's clan and is said to be "born to" her clan. He or she is "born for" his or her father's clan and considers anyone of the father's clan to be a sibling. A Navajo should not marry anybody from either clan. For example, if a woman was born to the Bitter Water Clan and born for the Salt Clan, she should marry a man who was not of either the Bitter Water or Salt clans. Evidence of the importance of clans in Navajo culture is the fact that when Navajos introduce themselves, they state where they are from and to what clan they belong.

Many Navajos adapted to a life of farming. However, crop growing all but ceased when Spaniards inadvertently brought sheep, goats, and horses into Navajos' lives. At that time many Navajos became horsemen and shepherds, leading their herds up to the grassy foothills of Colorado's San Juan Mountains in the summer and bringing the animals down to the high desert of the Four Corners area during the winter.

The Navajo population may have doubled in size when clans, families, and even entire villages of frightened Pueblo people came to live with them after the Spanish returned in 1692, after being ousted from the country for twelve years due to the Pueblo Revolt of 1680. The Pueblos, who for centuries had refined the art of weaving, may have taught the craft to their hosts. Navajo women spun yarn from sheep wool and wove handsome, warm blankets that soon became some of the most popular trade items in the Southwest.

The Navajos became wealthy through raids, particularly raids of the Pawnees and Utes from whom they captured many women and children

Figure 62:
Tipi-like houses of poles and mud originally sheltered Navajo families.
Later, settlers' cabins inspired horizontal log wall construction,
but a circular shape was retained because ceremonies and traditions
had always been carried out in houses with round floor plans.
Photo courtesy of the Colorado Historical Society.

for the slave trade. In turn, the Utes were also relentless in capturing and raiding Navajos and by 1775 had pushed all Navajos from southwestern Colorado. Both tribes traded their captives with the Spanish, and the Spanish also raided them for slaves.

It is estimated that there were three to six thousand Indian slaves in Spanish homes in New Mexico in the 1800s, and three out of four were Navajos. Although cruel, slavery was seen as the only possible way to run the vast ranches of New Mexico and to build the towns from which the Spanish hoped to expand their empire. Indians themselves had been taking captives for years; now they could trade them for horses, cattle, sheep, and produce.

It was during this time of tense relations between the various tribes and the Spanish that the Americans acquired Navajo land through the Mexican War. As more and more Mexican and American settlers

Figure 63:
Goats and sheep provide meat for Navajo meals as well as yarn for weaving.
Livestock are sold when money is needed.
Photo courtesy of the Colorado Historical Society.

moved into land claimed by the Navajos, treaties were made reducing the size of their landholdings. The Navajos were told to stop raiding New Mexican settlements, but New Mexicans were still capturing Navajo slaves. Confused and angry, some Navajos attacked Fort Defiance (just north of the present-day tribal headquarters of Window Rock, Arizona). Although the attack was not successful, it gave Americans an excuse to get rid of the Navajos forever.

In 1863, all Navajos were ordered to go to Fort Sumner, New Mexico, a place that reportedly had no wood, poor water, and soil unfit for farming. Few Navajos living in the thirty-thousand-square-mile area heard of the order, and Colonel Christopher (Kit) Carson was put in charge of rounding up the "hostile" Navajos who had not turned themselves in. Although he thought the Navajos could be pacified without war, he reluctantly followed his orders, pursuing a devastating "scorched earth" policy which involved the destruction of hogans, cornfields, peach trees, cattle, sheep, water holes, and people. Over 7,000 Navajos were captured or surrendered and were forced to walk over three hundred miles to the desolate wasteland of Fort Sumner. People were shot who were too sick or tired to keep up. When they arrived at the fort, hundreds died of starvation, dysentery, and other diseases.

Four years later the Navajos were allowed to return to their homeland because the government was embarrassed at the number of deaths occurring and could not afford to feed the thousands of miserable Navajos. After returning to their homeland, the Navajos began to regain strength; the population grew, and their reservation was expanded far to the west, although it did not include southwestern Colorado. To bolster the economy, women wove rugs for the tourist trade, while men perfected the art of silversmithing. Sheep herds increased, and crops were planted. Medical facilities were built, and children were sent to school, which unfortunately did not support Navajo traditions since children were not allowed to speak their language and their religion was discouraged.

The Navajos Today

The Navajo Nation occupies the largest reservation in the United States, which stretches across much of northeastern Arizona and the northwestern corner of New Mexico, as well as smaller reservations in Ramah, Alamo, and Cañoncito, New Mexico. The large reservation is divided into 110 chapters, with each chapter having a community center, called a chapter house, where local meetings and get-togethers are held. Each chapter elects one or two representatives to the Tribal Council, which is headed by an elected president. The council meets several times a year in the Navajo Nation capital of Window Rock, Arizona. Committees set up by the council deal with many issues, including natural resources, law, and community and economic development.

Despite the problems of having to deal with non-Indian cultures, the Navajos have preserved their traditions and maintained the importance of the family. Ancient ceremonies, such as the Blessingway Ceremony, are still practiced, and the sweat house plays an important role in the lives of many Navajos. When ill, Navajos may go to a clinic but may also seek the advice of a medicine man. Out of his medicine pouch he might pull bags of soil from the four sacred mountains which surround

Figure 64:
Navajo women have always enjoyed weaving blankets
and rugs outdoors. Large rugs require enormous looms,
weighted down with rocks to keep them stable.
Photo courtesy of the Colorado Historical Society.

the traditional homeland of the Navajos: Arizona's San Francisco Peaks and Navajo Mountain, Mount Taylor in New Mexico, and 13,000-foot-high Mount Hesperus in the lovely La Plata Mountains in the San Juan Range of southern Colorado.

The vast Navajo Reservation has few job opportunities. The Bureau of Indian Affairs and the tribal government offer employment to those living near Window Rock and Fort Defiance. Coal mining operations and the making of traditional arts and crafts also provide some employment, but sheep raising still supports many families in the rural areas. Sheep and goats provide food and wool for rug weaving; they are sold when money is needed or are used as payment to medicine men. Navajos who are educated off the reservation often return—the pull of the culture and the land is powerful.

PLACES TO VISIT

Arizona

CANYON DE CHELLY NATIONAL MONUMENT
P.O. Box 588
Chinle, AZ 86503
(520)674-5436

The monument includes outstanding ancient ruins and rock art in a red rock canyon owned and occupied by the Navajos. Sites can be viewed by driving along the rim of the canyon or by taking an authorized tour through the canyon. Audiovisual programs and interpretative talks are offered at the visitor center as well as a reconstructed hogan and an exhibit of Navajo culture.

HUBBELL TRADING POST NATIONAL HISTORIC SITE
P.O. Box 388
Ganado, AZ 86505
(602) 755-3254

The National Park Service offers a Navajo exhibit with weaving demonstrations.

NAVAJO COMMUNITY COLLEGE
Ned A. Hatathli Museum and Gallery
Tsaile, AZ 86556
(602) 724-3311

The museum offers an excellent exhibit of the Navajo Creation Myth with dioramas, as well as exhibits dealing with past and current history. Navajo rugs and sandpaintings are also on display.

NAVAJO NATIONAL MONUMENT
HC 71, Box 3
Tonalea, AZ 86044-9704
(520)672-2366

Cliff dwellings at the monument, located fifty-nine miles from Tuba City, can be seen on tours accompanied by a park ranger. Exhibits and slide programs at the visitor center describe the ways of the Anasazi and show examples of their arts and crafts. A Navajo Tribal Guild concession in the visitor center sells objects made by the Indians.

Colorado

COLORADO HISTORY MUSEUM
1300 Broadway
Denver, CO 80203
(303)866-4686

The museum has displays of Colorado Plains Indian cultures as well as exhibits on the life of early non-Indian settlers in the region.

New Mexico

JICARILLA APACHE TRIBAL MUSEUM
Jicarilla Apache Indian Reservation
Box 507
Dulce, NM 87528
(505)759-3242

The museum displays and sells Apache arts and crafts, including beadwork, leather work, and basketry.

Wyoming

SHOSHONE TRIBAL CULTURAL CENTER
P.O. Box 1008
Fort Washakie, WY 82514
(307)332-9106

The center offers traditional craft classes to tribal members, sponsors the annual Treaty Day Commemoration in June (which is open to the public), and has a museum with historic exhibits as well as Shoshone arts and crafts.

Suggestions for Further Reading

Kammer, Jerry. *The Second Long Walk: The Navajo-Hopi Land Dispute.* Albuquerque: University of New Mexico Press, 1980.

Kelly, Klara Bonsak, and Harris Francis. *Navajo Sacred Places.* Bloomington and Indianapolis: Indiana University Press, 1994.

Ortiz, Alfonso, ed. *Handbook of North American Indians.* Vol. 10, *Southwest.* Washington, D.C.: Smithsonian Institution, 1983.

Terrell, John. *The Navajos: The Past and Present of a Great People.* New York, London: Harper and Row, 1970.

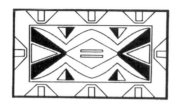

10

The Plains Indians

THE COMANCHES

The daring Comanche horsemen and their families, who at one time ruled the southern Plains with their neighbors the Kiowas, originally came to Colorado from far to the north. They were a Shoshonean group, hunters and gatherers probably living along the Snake River in southern Idaho. In sign language, a wavy motion with the right hand at the waist, indicating "snake," or the way they used to weave their house walls, represents the Shoshone as well as the Comanche tribes, whose languages are almost identical.

Figure 65:
Comanches, relatives of the Shoshones, came to Colorado from the mountainous country of
Wyoming. Although these Comanche women have long hair and wear clothing made of
fabric, their ancestors cut their hair short and wore buckskin blouses and skirts.
Photo courtesy of the Denver Public Library.

Around 1700, this Shoshonean group obtained horses, probably through trade with tribes to the south. At first the horses were used as food, but soon it was obvious that they were more useful as pack animals and as transportation to hunt larger animals and wage war. The people moved from their homeland to the southeast. Eastern Colorado served as their base of operations for almost seventy years. After pushing the Apaches south, they had the area to themselves. By 1705 they were raiding tribes as far away as Kansas, Oklahoma, New Mexico, and Texas. The Kiowas, probably better equipped with guns, finally pushed the Comanches south of the Arkansas River (Figure 33, page 98). By 1790, however, the two tribes were allies, and together they kept the Utes of western Colorado from spreading east onto the Plains.

The Utes, who lived primarily west of the Rockies, were enemies of these ferocious raiders and called them *Komantcia*, meaning "anyone who wants to fight me all the time." The Spaniards, who often felt the same way about them, called them Comanches.

Property frequently changed hands among the Comanches due to gambling and give-aways. Horses were gambled, but Comanches became so fond of their favorite horses, it was as if they lost children if they had to give them up. As a result of this fondness for their horses, the Comanches were very protective of them. During battle shields of rawhide were used to cover the front and sides of the best horses. A successful Comanche warrior might own from fifty to two hundred horses while a wealthy man of a northern Colorado tribe might only own thirty-five, being farther away from the Mexican ranches which involuntarily served as the sources of horses.

Beliefs

Comanche religion included the belief in a Great Spirit who created human bones from stones, blood from dew, eyes from water, strength from storms, and thoughts from waterfalls. The head of the first man touched the sky, but hard work shrunk the giant down to the size of a present-day human. Earth was the mother who fed the Comanches, while moon guarded raiders and was prayed to before horse-stealing ventures. Thunderbird caused thunder by flapping its wings and lightning by blinking its eyes. Clouds were its shadows, and rain came from a lake on its back. The Comanches feared Thunderbird and were quiet during a storm so they would not offend it. Spirits of the dead went beyond the setting sun to a place where there was no cold or pain, warriors did not age, and game and horses were abundant. However, at some point the souls were reborn on earth again, to ensure that there would be enough Comanches.

Clothing and Personal Adornment

Comanche women wore skirts and poncholike blouses, both made of buckskin. Their hair was short, and they painted dots and colorful lines on their faces. Men wore shirts and leggings with much fringe attached. They wore their hair in two long braids, which often touched the ground, and sometimes wove human or horse hair into the braids. As teenagers, Comanche males had eight holes pierced in the upper, curved parts of their ears. Their favorite earrings were long thin shells from Mexico, the weight of which bent their ears over at the top.

Figure 66:
Long fringe and long hair
typified Comanche male
adornment. Human or horse
hair was woven into braids to
lengthen them; sometimes they
touched the ground.
Photo courtesy of the
Denver Public Library.

History and Culture

Southeastern Colorado was the northwestern boundary of the realm known as Comancheria—an area roughly six hundred miles from north to south and four hundred miles from east to west. Comanches plundered food from the pueblos along the Rio Grande and thousands of horses from the ranches of northern Mexico. They became the major supplier of horses for most Plains tribes. Often the Comanches escaped to their homeland in Colorado or to the vast Staked Plains region of northwestern Texas. They were seldom pursued, since on the Staked Plains there were few water holes, and only people familiar with the area could survive.

Taos and other New Mexican Spanish villages were constantly raided by Comanches. In 1779, Juan Bautista de Anza, governor of New Mexico, led several hundred soldiers into southeastern Colorado and killed seventeen Comanches between today's Walsenburg and Pueblo. Among the dead were Green Horn (Cuerno Verde in Spanish), a Comanche chief, and his son. Today, Greenhorn Mountain rises high above the foothills where the chief of that name was killed.

During a period in which a truce was called, some Comanches traded with the New Mexico Spaniards in the late 1700s and early 1800s. The Spanish traders were known as "Comancheros." Other Comanches asked the Spanish to help build a village on the Arkansas River, several miles east of Pueblo, Colorado. Although it was deserted in four months, the little Comanche settlement was the first adobe town in Colorado. Although Comanches saw advantages in maintaining friendly relations with some Spaniards, they felt no desire to garner relationships with the newcomers from the eastern United States.

In 1849, cholera and smallpox were brought by California gold seekers traveling from Austin towards El Paso, Texas, and entire Comanche bands were wiped out. The gold seekers blazed trails through the forbidding Staked Plains and, after finding the few water holes, began to settle there. During the Civil War the Comanches regained strength and numbers due to the lack of troops, which were fighting back East. Soon, however, non-Indian hunters made food scarce, and the Comanches were forced to sign treaties to obtain rations.

These rations were distributed at Fort Sill, in southwestern Oklahoma near their new reservation with the Kiowas surrounding the Wichita Mountains. The Comanches were told to sell their horses and to farm, an impossible order for a people whose lives and honor centered

▲

around raiding, warfare, and hunting. The rations often included rancid meat and wormy flour, and many men illegally left the reservation to find food for their families. The most notorious of the raiders was a handsome man named Quanah Parker, son of a white woman taken captive at an early age who married a leader of one of the Comanche bands. Finally, the United States Army decided the only way to deal with the Comanches was to attack and destroy all villages off the reservation. Hundreds of Indians were killed, their tipis, food, and belongings burned. Thousands of horses were shot. The weakened survivors stumbled back to the reservation. The Comanches were a beaten people.

Quanah Parker, whose very name sent shivers down the spines of the bravest of settlers, became a man of peace and did all he could to make the Comanches "civilized" and educated. He refused to give up his several wives, however, arguing that a prominent leader played host to so many people he needed more than one wife just to keep everyone fed. (Poly-gamy was also common among Plains

Figure 67:
The son of Cynthia Ann Parker,
Quanah Parker was the famous
leader of the Comanche band
that was last to surrender to
the American army. After
surrendering, Parker urged
cooperation with his former
enemies and made friends with
his mother's relatives.
Photo courtesy of the
Denver Public Library.

Figure 68: Captured as a child, Cynthia Ann Parker grew up Comanche and married a prominent Comanche, Nacona. Well-meaning settlers recaptured her and her youngest child several decades later and returned her to relatives. After her baby died, she starved herself to death rather than live without her Comanche family. In this photo her hair is cut short, probably in mourning for Nacona, who was most likely killed when she was recaptured. Photo courtesy of the Denver Public Library.

tribes to ensure that widows of fallen warriors and other unattached women were provided for.) When asked to give up all but one wife, Parker replied that someone other than himself should tell the wives which should leave. He was not asked again, and the government built him a large house where he and all his wives could live with their many children.

Under the Allotment Act of 1887, each Comanche was given 160 acres of land, and the rest of their reservation was sold. In July of 1901, thirty thousand settlers moved onto the last of their old hunting grounds. The old reservation roads were soon packed with wagons full of settlers and supplies. Within weeks, fields were plowed and homes were built on the old reservation land. The towns of Hobart, Anadarko, and Lawton were created—the latter being the largest and a typical Wild West town, complete with saloon brawls and gambling.

Figure 69:
Impressed by Quanah Parker's peacekeeping skills, the federal government built him
a house large enough for his several wives and many children.
Photo courtesy of the Denver Public Library.

The Comanches Today

Many Comanches eventually intermarried with other tribes and non-Indians. Over nine thousand, however, are still official tribal members, and approximately fifty-five hundred reside in Oklahoma. Comanche communities include Lawton, Indiahoma, Cache, Apache, and Walters, all located in the southwestern part of Oklahoma, surrounding Fort Sill Military Reservation. The communities are still comprised of Comanche bands, the ones living north of Medicine Park, just north of Fort Sill, being the most traditional. Each area has a tribal community center, and benefit dances are held almost every weekend to assist those in need, including elders, servicemen, and women.

The Comanche Business Committee consists of seven members and is overseen by a tribal chairman and vice-chairman. Although the unemployment rate remains high, some jobs are provided by the army, oil fields, and the tribal government, which is headquartered in Medicine

Park. Also, some larger communities employ Comanches as teachers and other professional workers, and a Comanche-owned bingo operation in Lawton provides jobs for roughly seventy people. Despite these opportunities, the Comanches suffer from poverty and discrimination.

Tribal organizations, including the Comanche Indian Veterans Association and the Little Ponies (Vietnam veterans proud of their warrior heritage and intent on keeping Comanche traditions alive), sponsor various powwows and gatherings all year long. For the last three years an event called the Comanche Nation Fair, which was popular in the late 1930s and 1940s, has been revived. It is held the first weekend in October in Craterville Park on the Fort Sill Military Reservation. During the weekend, the Fort Sill soldiers, who help with the preparation of the grounds, vacate the area in the Wichita Mountains, and some twenty-five thousand Indians from all across the country assemble for dancing and celebration.

Comanches interact with various organizations in Texas, an area that constituted the major range of their ancestors in historic times. There, ceremonial dances are held in the town of Santa Ana. In the future tribal members plan to meet with the governor of Texas to discuss certain treaties made in the nineteenth century that were not upheld. Comanches are proud of their heritage, which includes possibly the most fierce and determined fighters of the southern Plains.

THE KIOWAS

The Kiowas were originally a mountain people who lived in cold and snowy western Montana along the Yellowstone River. The word *Kiowa* comes from their name for themselves, *Ga-i-gwu*, which may mean "face painted in different colors" (their faces were often painted in red). Kiowa elders also have interpreted the name to mean an assembly of intelligent people. In the mountains of Montana they hunted small game and gathered wild plants in the summertime. Tribal legend tells of a split of the tribe, brought on by an argument between two chiefs over how an antelope should be divided. One group moved northwest and was never heard of again. The other, the group now known as the Kiowas, moved southeast and settled east of the Black Hills in present-day South Dakota. Here the Kiowas lived the life of a typical Plains tribe, always moving in search of buffalo herds and raiding other tribes and Mexican ranches for horses. Their neighbors were the Crows, who became their friends and taught them the Sun Dance. The Crows were originally a forest people, coming to Montana from the East not much earlier than the Kiowas. The latter traded with their eastern neighbors, the Mandans and Arikaras, who obtained goods from the French along the Missouri River.

At some point, possibly during the 1600s, the Kiowas were joined by a group of Apaches, perhaps a band moving south from Canada. Although they spoke a different language, the Apaches merged with the Kiowas and adopted their lifestyle. They are called Kiowa-Apaches (hereafter referred to as the Kiowas).

The Kiowas left their Crow friends and moved to the South Platte River, part of which flows through northeastern Colorado. Then, around 1775, the Arapahoes and Cheyennes may have forced the Kiowas and their southern neighbors, the Comanches, south of the Arkansas River in southern Colorado. It is more likely, however, that the Kiowa and Comanche tribes merely wanted to live in a better climate with more plentiful game and to be closer to the source of Mexican horses.

The Kiowas then pushed the Comanches further south of the Arkansas. Soon, however, around 1790, they made peace. These two powerful allied tribes eventually controlled the southern Plains. They drove many neighboring tribes from their hunting grounds and ranged from Colorado far into Texas, New Mexico, Kansas, and Mexico.

Beliefs

The Kiowas believed they came from the underworld and that their ancestors emerged one at a time when the Creator tapped on a log— until a pregnant woman got stuck and no more could follow. Tahli, a child of the sun, did the Kiowas many favors. Then he divided himself up. The Ten Medicine Bundles, sacred medicine to the Kiowas, represent the body of Tahli. Saynday is a trickster, about whom many stories were told around Kiowa tipi fires late into the night.

The Sun Dance was very important to the Kiowas. When living up north near the Crows, they had acquired the *Tai-me*, a sacred doll representing the Sun Dance medicine. The *Tai-me* was always attached to the Sun Dance pole. Women were allowed to dance at the Sun Dance. Neither men nor women pierced their skin as did Indians of the northern Plains tribes.

Clothing and Personal Adornment

The men wore large ear pendants, exposed on one side by the tradition of cutting their hair short on the right. Traditionally, this was done to keep the hair from interfering with the bowstring in battle. The rest of the hair was long, braided, and often decorated with silver disks. Women often painted the parts of their hair red.

Both men and women wore moccasins decorated with long heel fringes. These trailed dramatically behind when riding and served to wipe out tracks on the ground. After trade goods were available, men's moccasins were decorated with narrow strips of silver or sheet-iron, which were attached to the fringes on top of the moccasins. These "tinklers" made a merry sound when people walked.

History and Culture

The Kiowas had more horses per person than any other Plains tribe. From 1740 to 1835, they reigned supreme on the southern Plains with their allies, the Comanches. Then the effects of the settlers and soldiers took hold. As with most Indian tribes, it was not killing by soldiers' guns that reduced their numbers drastically but foreign diseases that slaughtered their people.

With the opening of the Santa Fe Trail, which paralleled the Arkansas River through southeastern Colorado, merchants traveled from Independence, Missouri, to Santa Fe, New Mexico, carrying pots, pans, blankets, guns, and other goods the Plains Indians found useful. Although the Santa Fe Trail was a source of supplies for the Kiowas, travelers on the trail also brought smallpox, which killed more than half the Kiowas in 1849.

In 1853, after the United States had acquired Texas, New Mexico, and southern Colorado from Mexico, the depleted Kiowas and their Comanche allies signed the Fort Atkinson Treaty. In this treaty they promised not to attack travelers on the Santa Fe Trail, and to allow the government to build forts and roads. In return, the federal government was to provide military protection from angry settlers to the Indians as well as farming tools, food, and other provisions. None of the parties abided by the treaty. The military failed to protect the Indians from settlers' attacks, and what few provisions they sent were of little use to

Figure 70:
Kiowa leaders Satanta (shown in photo) and
Lone Wolf requested a peace conference with
General Custer, who held both men hostage until
all Kiowas had surrendered.
Photo courtesy of the Denver Public Library.

Indians. Kiowa and Comanche raids became infrequent along the Santa Fe Trail but continued in Texas. In 1858, the discovery of gold in Colorado brought thousands of miners into the area, and the lifestyle of the Kiowas, along with that of other Plains Indians, was threatened.

During the Civil War, however, soldiers were needed back East, and it was easier for the Kiowas to raid for food and horses. When Governor Evans of Colorado sent messages from Denver to the Plains tribes demanding them to report to military forts or be considered hostile, the Kiowas moved completely out of Colorado and Kansas and joined the Comanches in Texas. Upon hearing of the Sand Creek Massacre in Colorado, where United States troops slaughtered Cheyenne and Arapahoe women and children, the Kiowas, Comanches, and many other Plains tribes attacked settlers with a vengeance.

In November of 1864, Colonel Kit Carson attacked a village of Kiowas and Comanches in the Texas Panhandle. During what historians call the Battle of Adobe Walls, about 60 Indians were killed and 150 wounded. The army then burned all the tipis in the village, destroying all winter supplies. The tribes never fully recovered from the losses (Gerson 1964). The next year a treaty was signed. The Kiowas and Comanches agreed to give up their claims in Colorado, New Mexico, and Kansas and move to a reservation in parts of Texas and Oklahoma. Some of the Indians, however, continued to raid for food and supplies.

Figure 71:
Kiowas and other Indians tried to recapture some of the excitement of a
traditional buffalo hunt by chasing cattle on horseback on ration day.
Photo courtesy of the Colorado Historical Society.

When the transcontinental railroad pushed its way through Kansas in the early 1870s, it brought with it buffalo hunters who slaughtered the resources of the Plains tribes. Another treaty was made with the southern Plains Indians in the hope the railroads would not be raided; and because their food source was disappearing, the Indians signed, resigned to live on government rations.

However, the Kiowas found it difficult to remain on the reservation, and raiding resumed. Then General George Armstrong Custer's brutal attack on Black Kettle's Cheyenne village on the Washita River upset the Kiowas, who were camped nearby. Although two of their bravest chiefs, Lone Wolf and Satanta, met with Custer to talk peace, Custer held them hostage until the rest of the tribe surrendered.

Satanta and other Kiowas frustrated with reservation life still raided in Texas, which was a Confederate state all through the Civil War. By 1874 the government had been successful in exterminating the buffalo—the only policy that guaranteed destruction of the Plains Indian culture. The Kiowas' horses were then killed or auctioned off. With the

Figure 72:
In early July Kiowas
gather from all parts
of the United States for
the annual Sun Dance
and Gourd Clan
ceremonies in
southwestern
Oklahoma.
Photo courtesy of the
Denver Public Library.

disappearance of buffalo and horses, the spirit of the Kiowas, and other Plains Indians, was crushed. Malnutrition, measles, whooping cough, pneumonia, and tuberculosis reduced their numbers drastically. Their ceremonies were soon curtailed as well, and in 1889 the Kiowas were no longer allowed to hold their Sun Dance.

The ways of whites confused the Kiowas. For example, the Indians' practice of giving gifts to spread their wealth was not considered civilized by whites. Instead, the Indians were told to be selfish and keep what was theirs. Also, the men were encouraged to farm, work which was considered dishonorable for men in the Plains Indian culture. Some money was made by leasing reservation land to non-Indian ranchers. In 1892, under the Jerome Agreement, each Kiowa and Comanche was given 160 acres of land. The rest of the reservation land was sold, and soon settled by non-Indians.

*Figure 73:
A Kiowa father
and daughter.
Photo courtesy of the
Denver Public Library.*

The Kiowas Today

Roughly ten thousand people claim Kiowa heritage. Although some still own allotted land near the tribal headquarters in Carnegie, Oklahoma, and the Kiowa Agency in Anadarko, many live in cities such as Tulsa, Lawton, Dallas, Fort Worth, Albuquerque, Los Angeles, Phoenix, Wichita, and Denver. Vocations pursued include education, law, medicine, federal and state work, and arts and crafts. Kiowas take pride in stressing the importance of education to their young people.

Kiowas flock to southwestern Oklahoma in early July for the annual Sun Dance and Gourd Clan celebration. The towns of Carnegie and Anadarko host many reunions at this festive time of the year.

A revival of traditional arts and crafts has occurred, and many Kiowas take part in the American Indian Exposition held every year in

Anadarko. Many American Indian artists and writers are of Kiowa descent, among them N. Scott Momaday, author of *The Way to Rainy Mountain* and the Pulitzer Prize-winning *House Made of Dawn*. Experienced as well as young Kiowa artists display their work at the Kiowa Tribal Museum in Carnegie. Ten murals painted by Kiowa artists, said to be worth over a million dollars, grace the walls of the museum. The murals depict the history of the tribe as related through historical accounts and tribal legends.

THE ARAPAHOES

Arapahoe tradition as well as archaeological evidence places the Arapahoes originally in the Red River Valley of Minnesota near the western shore of Lake Superior. Here they lived in permanent dome-shaped bark houses, as did other tribes, farming corn, beans, and squash and paddling the clear lake waters in birch bark canoes. Gradually they moved west, as did their neighbors, the Blackfeet, perhaps due to over-population and pressure from hostile neighbors. The mother language of both tribes, as well as that of the Cheyennes, is Algonquin, the language of the Great Lakes.

By 1650 the Arapahoes were probably on the northern Plains, hunting buffalo and trading with the Comanches for horses. In the late 1700s, the tribe split. Arapahoe legend describes the tribe fording a wide river (perhaps the Missouri) on the ice. According to Northern Arapahoe storyteller Merle Haas, a child saw a hornlike object protruding from the ice and asked his grandmother to cut it off so he could play with it. When she tried to cut it off, the horn began to bleed. A huge water monster, to which the horn was attached, reared up out of the water and drowned those crossing on the ice (Haas 1994, personal communication). The people who had not yet crossed remained on the north side and became known as the Gros Ventres, meaning "big bellies" in French. The people who went south became known as the Arapahoes, a word similar to the Siouan Crow term meaning "tattooed people"; the word also may be derived from the Pawnee word *Tirapihu*, which means "he buys, or trades."

The Arapahoes, an outgoing and gregarious people, were known far and wide for their trading abilities. Arapahoes have no *r* sound in their language and refer to themselves in their language simply as "Our People."

Figure 74:
The number of elk teeth on the dress of this Arapahoe woman (Freckled Face) suggests her husband was a successful hunter and provider. Photo courtesy of the Denver Public Library.

An ancient Algonquin word for the Arapahoes (*Kananavich*, meaning the "Bison Path People") describes the lifestyle pursued after leaving the Great Lakes region. One Arapahoe legend describes how a culture hero invented the bow using a buffalo rib and how use of the bow and arrow replaced the hunting method of running buffalo over cliffs.

The Crow and Blackfoot sign for Northern Arapahoes is tapping the breast with the fingertips several times. To indicate themselves, Southern Arapahoes placed the right forefinger next to the nose, signifying the path to the sun. This sign led those unfamiliar with their culture to call them "rubbed nose Indians."

Beliefs

Although the Arapahoes changed their lifestyle from more sedentary farming to nomadic buffalo hunting, they still retained their ancient beliefs that revolved around the life-giving importance of the sun. Early observers mistakenly called them sun worshipers. They believed in a Great Spirit called Man-Above. According to Arapahoe elders, before missionaries arrived, Man-Above was called *Houu*; after Christianity was introduced he was called *Hihcebe'inen*. Arapahoes often worshiped Him near waterfalls and hot springs, especially before battling enemies such as the Utes.

The most important ceremonial item of the Arapahoes was (and is) the Flat-Pipe, or *Seicha*. The Flat Pipe played an important role in the Arapahoe creation story. The telling of the story is still considered sacred. Consequently, although it has been printed in other sources, it will not be told here, out of respect for Arapahoe traditions.

Clothing and Personal Adornment

The Arapahoes dressed as other Plains Indians did—leather leggings and shirts for the men and leather dresses for the women, decorated with porcupine quills, elk teeth, and, later, beads. Long ago Arapahoe men wore their hair in a bun over their foreheads, some think to provide shade, others say to look fierce. Later, the style changed to a braid over each ear with a scalp lock in the middle of the back of the head. Women's hair was worn loose at one time, then parted and braided on both sides. Young women wore face paint in streaks on their foreheads, cheeks, and noses to represent war while older women painted dots on cheekbones, foreheads, and between their eyes to express their desire for peace. Those in mourning did not paint their faces until a year after a loved one's death. According to Merle Haas, Arapahoes cut their hair as a sign of mourning; some still do today, burying it with their loved ones (Haas 1994, personal communication).

History and Culture

The Arapahoes probably arrived in Colorado in the later 1700s. By then the Kiowas and Comanches had moved to southeastern Colorado, and the Arapahoes were well supplied with horses, through trade and raiding. Favored winter camps were the sheltered canyons on the east side of the Rocky Mountains, such as the Cache la Poudre and Big Thompson in present-day Rocky Mountain National Park. With the melting of the snows, they rode east into the Plains to hunt buffalo as far as South Dakota and western Kansas and Nebraska. Evidence suggests they sometimes rode higher up into the mountains during the summer since tipi rings have been found in Rocky Mountain National Park. Large river boulders were hauled up to the top of Old Man Mountain, an Arapahoe vision quest site. According to elderly Arapahoes, an eagle trap was used on the top of Longs Peak. This mountain and adjacent Mt. Meeker were called Nesotaieux by the French, supposedly their version of an Indian word, probably Arapahoe, meaning "the two guides." The French name was Les Deux Oreilles—"the two ears."

On excursions northeast into the Black Hills, the Arapahoes encountered the Cheyennes, who also had relocated from the Great Lakes region. Recognizing a kinship, the two tribes became allies, although their languages were different enough to require use of sign language.

Enemies of the Arapahoes and Cheyennes included the Utes, Shoshones, Kiowas, and Comanches (at least after about 1825), as well as the Pawnees of Kansas and Nebraska. When the Delawares and Shawnees were forced onto a Kansas reservation, they also became immediate foes. Horse stealing and battles of revenge were common between these tribes, although battles were not as bitter as those against the Utes and Shoshones, the mountain tribes to the west. Battles with the mountain tribes on the Plains usually resulted in victory by the Arapahoes and Cheyennes, but these tribes were at a severe disadvantage when attacked in mountain territory. The Arapahoes believed that Man-Above had created the Rockies to separate them from the Utes and Shoshones. In 1840, the Southern Arapahoes and Cheyennes made peace with the Kiowas and Comanches, a peace which lasted until all the tribes were conquered by the United States Army.

Figure 75:
This Sun Dance camp attracted Arapahoes from all over the region
for the life renewal ceremony. Photo courtesy of the Denver Public Library.

The mountain men were usually treated kindly by the Arapahoes, although traders were occasionally the targets of horse raids. When the trading post known as Bent's Fort was built along the Arkansas River and the Santa Fe Trail around 1833, Arapahoes and their Cheyenne allies were attracted by the trade goods. At this time the tribes divided—the Northern Arapahoes and Cheyennes roamed primarily north of the South Platte River in northern Colorado while the southern tribes, which became known as the Southern Arapahoes and Cheyennes, moved along the Arkansas River in southeastern Colorado so they could take advantage of trading at Bent's Fort (although both tribes had hunted near the Arkansas River prior to construction of the post).

Kiowas and Comanches traded at Bent's Fort but were not allowed inside since there was mutual distrust between them and the traders. The Arapahoes traded horses for goods at the post, horses often stolen from other tribes that also traded there. Travelers on the Santa Fe Trail en route from Independence, Missouri, to Santa Fe, New Mexico, with wagon caravans full of trade goods, occasionally proved too tempting for Arapahoe warriors. When Arapahoe warriors were headed home

Figure 76:
Although posed with a gun, this Arapahoe boy belonged to a tribe that sought peaceful
relations with miners and settlers until the Sand Creek Massacre occurred in 1864.
Photo courtesy of the Denver Public Library.

after an unsuccessful raid on an enemy tribe, they might attack a wagon train to get horses they had not been able to steal from their enemies.

In 1858, the Colorado gold rush crushed any hopes of enforcing the Fort Laramie Treaty, which in 1851 had designated all of eastern Colorado north of the Arkansas River reservation land. The town sites

of Auraria, Denver, and Montana City were established without con-
sulting the Indians. And log buildings were rapidly constructed along
Cherry Creek, the favored hunting ground of the Arapahoes.

Chief Left Hand (Niwot in Arapahoe), the Arapahoe who had many
white friends in the Boulder region, said of the miners near Idaho
Springs, a sacred area to the tribe, "You come to get our gold, eat our
grass, burn our timber and kill and drive off our game" (Coel 1981,
65). Alarmed at the army invasion, some Cheyennes and Arapahoes
contemplated farming as a possible solution to the crisis. Left Hand
even drove his family in a wagon east along the Oregon Trail through
enemy Indian territory to see for himself how farming worked.
Although he worked on farms throughout Nebraska during the fall harvest, he finally came to the conclusion that farming would not suit his
people. Instead, he returned home to convince his tribe and federal
agents that cattle ranching might be the answer. Margaret Coel hints in
her book *Chief Left Hand, Southern Arapaho* that he might have had
raising buffalo in mind, instead of domesticated cattle, a logical course
of action that is being discussed today by environmental groups.

Shortly after Left Hand arrived back home to his village at the confluence of the South Platte River and Beaver Creek, the Arapahoes
moved to their traditional winter camp in Boulder Valley, near the cliffs
later called the Flatirons. They arrived to discover a group of gold seekers camped nearby. Against the will of several of his warriors, Left Hand
allowed the men to winter there but insisted they leave in the spring.
But they did not leave; and when a gang of drunken thugs from Denver
molested Arapahoe women in Left Hand's camp while the men were
out hunting, it was all the chief could do to keep the enraged men from
attacking the entire town. This disgraceful act was censored by most
Denver citizens, but the offenders were not severely punished.

Left Hand's brother Neva befriended George Jackson, a miner
who had discovered gold in Idaho Springs in the winter of 1858. Jackson was so impressed with Neva that he named a mountain after him.
Left Hand was later killed at the Sand Creek Massacre. Today, he is
remembered by place names in Colorado: Left Hand Canyon east of
Boulder, Niwot Mountain in the Indian Peaks, and the town of Niwot,
between Boulder and Longmont.

An Arapahoe leader named Friday was named by the famous trapper and trader Thomas Fitzpatrick, who, on a Friday in 1831, found
him as a child wandering the Plains after being accidentally left behind

when his band moved camp. Fitzpatrick grew fond of the boy and sent him to school for two years in St. Louis, where he learned English. While the two were trapping together seven years later, some Northern Arapahoes recognized Friday, and he returned to his people. His natural hunting abilities and bravery as a warrior earned him great respect, along with his interpretation skills. He was constantly urging peaceful relations with the settlers, with whose sheer numbers and power he was well acquainted.

Later, Marshall Cook, an associate of George Jackson, described the events leading up to the demise of most of Friday's band at the hands of the famous trading family, the St. Vrains. Cook's story is the only known account of this event. According to Cook, the St. Vrains had left their trading post, Fort St. Vrain, to transport their buffalo robes and hides to St. Louis. One of the brothers left his wife and child at the fort with other workers, who were entrusted with their care. When it was discovered that the woman and child happened to be from a tribe the Arapahoes considered bitter enemies, members of Friday's band killed the two to avenge the wrongs of their tribe. Not realizing the full implications of what they had done, they stayed near the post until the St. Vrains returned. When the husband discovered what had happened, he reportedly had Friday's band invited to the post for a feast. The cannon in the watchtower was loaded, and seventy-five armed men were stationed around the courtyard. When the unarmed Indians entered the courtyard, the cannon opened fire. Those not mowed down by the cannon fire were shot by the men surrounding them. Only a few escaped, and Friday was among the survivors. Cook reported that every year he painted his face black and sat on the crumbling walls of the abandoned fort, moaning and howling in agony for his dead family and friends (Trenholm 1986, 151–52).

By 1859 there were fifty thousand immigrants in Colorado, and the Arapahoes were beginning to starve. Miners slaughtered game for sport, and their noisy mining activities drove off the other animals. Not all the settlers were insensitive to the plight of the Indians, however. In January of that year, some miners hosted a feast for five hundred Arapahoe warriors and their families.

As was the case with other tribes, cholera and smallpox drastically reduced the population of the Arapahoes. The surviving children were so hungry that they were observed eating the corn that horses dropped from their mouths on Denver streets. Seeing this pathetic sight, some

Figure 77:
Sharp Nose, a
prominent Northern
Arapahoe leader,
traveled to Washington,
D.C., to convince
President Hayes to
allow the Northern
Arapahoes to go to
Wyoming instead of
Indian Territory
(Oklahoma).
Photo by N. Rose,
courtesy of the
Denver Public Library.

townsfolk tossed corn to the children, scattering it as if it were chicken feed. Even though the settlers were trespassing and building towns on Indian land, they complained bitterly when a cow or sheep was stolen to feed a starving Indian family.

In 1861, a small reservation was established between the Arkansas River and Sand Creek for the Arapahoes and Cheyennes. The Arapahoes were to live in the eastern half, the Cheyennes in the western part. An irrigation ditch was dug, and the Indian agent, Samuel Colley, although admitting the Indians were not ready to farm, said they could lease the land. However, no Indians wanted to move there because there were no buffalo and little other game to hunt.

Although rations were distributed, it was at distant posts; the bands of Left Hand, Little Raven, and a leader named Storm were living on army rations at Fort Larned, Kansas, located almost 170 miles to the east of the reservation. It was reported by an agent sent to investigate the situation at the fort, H. Y. Ketcham, that the commanding officer was usually drunk and often abusive towards the tribal leaders. In addition, the trader at the fort's store was trading bottles of whiskey to the Indians for their last buffalo robes. Smallpox was rampant, and Ketcham vaccinated everyone he could. He found the Arapahoes to be friendly and kind even though they were sick and starving.

Soon the Northern Arapahoes, also in a starving state, joined their southern relatives, upsetting the Cheyennes, who were competing for the rations. The Northern Arapahoes did not want to return to their homeland because the Sioux were trying to convince them to go to war with the settlers. Most Arapahoes felt that no matter how distasteful it was to live on rations, it was now the only way they could feed their families. Friday's band, reportedly greatly reduced after the massacre at Fort St. Vrain, was joined by two others, also Northern Arapahoes. This group pleaded for a treaty that would provide a reservation for them on the Cache la Poudre.

The Sioux continually put pressure on the Arapahoes to join them in a war against the settlers. The Arapahoe leader Little Raven and a Kiowa chief named Yellow Buffalo stated to Major Anthony at Fort Lyon (located on the Arkansas River in eastern Colorado) that the Sioux planned to attack the emigrant trails along the Arkansas and Platte rivers in the spring of 1864. The chiefs told Anthony the Arapahoes and Kiowas wanted no part of the plan. (Anthony was a key leader in keeping the peace with the tribes of the Platte River and Arkansas River regions.)

Soldiers who could not tell the difference between a hostile Comanche or a peaceful Arapahoe, shot at friendly Indians. The killing of approximately fifty non-warring Arapahoes, including Left Hand, and a greater number of Cheyennes at Sand Creek enraged all the Plains tribes (see Chapter 7, "General History of the Plains Tribes").

In 1867, after two years of raiding, hiding, and starving, the Arapahoes signed the Medicine Lodge Treaty, along with the Cheyenne, Kiowa, and Comanche tribes. This treaty established reservations in the Kansas and Oklahoma territories. The Arapahoes were forced out of Colorado. The Northern Arapahoes were determined not to live in Indian Territory (Oklahoma), where the Southern Arapahoes had to share a reservation with the Cheyennes.

Friday and two other respected Northern Arapahoe leaders, Sharp Nose and Black Coal, traveled to Washington, D.C., to talk with President

Hayes. The leaders convinced the president that their people would become sickly and many would die if they were forced to join the Southern Arapahoes in Indian Territory. The mission was successful, and the Northern Arapahoes did not have to go to Indian Territory. The leaders returned to their people in a wagon full of gifts, wearing medals and suits given them by the president. The wagon was painted black, indicating victory over an enemy.

The Northern Arapahoes in Wyoming

In 1878, the Northern Arapahoes were moved to the Shoshone Reservation near the Wind River Mountains in western Wyoming (the Shoshones had always been enemies and did not welcome their uninvited guests). There they raised livestock and tried to farm, but ranchers outside the reservation often rustled cattle, and the government did not provide the necessary equipment to harvest grain. Rations were reduced, given only to the disabled and elderly; sometimes the meager rations were stolen by dishonest agents and non-Indian neighbors. Wood cutting and freighting for the agency provided some work, but most families were in great debt to the agency from buying food. Children were sent to schools, where they were forced to cut their hair and were not allowed to speak their language or to practice Arapahoe traditions.

Finally, irrigation canals were dug by the government, but tribal members were charged for the water. When President Franklin Delano Roosevelt appointed John Collier commissioner of Indian affairs in 1934, the Northern Arapahoes, along with other tribes, formed their own governing bodies. A monetary award was given the Northern Arapahoes and Shoshones when the Shoshones filed suit for having the Arapahoes placed on their reservation in 1878. Part of the money was used to purchase back allotment land that had been sold to non-Indians. The Arapahoes also had to use the money to pay back the government for equipment, wagons, and gifts given them after being located on the reservation.

In July of 1914, two Arapahoes from the Wind River Reservation visited Rocky Mountain National Park. The trip was partly organized by Enos Mills, park naturalist and promoter. Gro Griswold, age seventy-three, and Sherman Sage, sixty-three, were accompanied by Tom Crispin, the official interpreter on the reservation. Griswold had been about twenty years old and Sage about thirteen when they had last been in the park, during the 1850s. When the Arapahoes got off the

Figure 78:
Respected Arapahoe leaders include (in the first row): left, Friday; third from left, Six
Feathers; fourth from left, Black Coal (note missing fingers, probably cut off in mourning);
and fifth from left, Sharp Nose. Photo courtesy of the Denver Public Library.

Figure 79:
Arapahoe children, as most Indian children confined to reservations, were forced to cut their
hair, wear non-Indian clothing, and were punished when they spoke their own language.
Photo courtesy of the Denver Public Library, circa 1880 to 1885.

Figure 80:
Northern Arapahoes Sherman Sage, left, and Gro
Griswold visited Rocky Mountain National Park in
1914. More than fifty years had passed since they had
been in their homeland, but they were able to identify
old trails, camping areas, and battlegrounds.
Photo courtesy of the Colorado Historical Society.

train in Loveland on July 14, they were deluged with crowds and questions. On horseback they followed old Indian trails from Estes Park to Grand Lake and back, visiting campsites and high vista points. Among information the Arapahoes gave regarding the history of the area was the fact that there was an eagle trap on Long's Peak. As the Arapahoes got further into the mountains, they noted many piles of rocks that had served as trail markers, including some which dated from the pre-horse era and were thus perhaps three hundred to four hundred years old. Their name for the original route of present-day Trail Ridge Road was the Child's Trail, or Children's Trail, so called because it was so steep that in the old days the Arapahoe children had been forced to dismount and walk the precipitous route. This trail was also called the Ute Trail. Griswold and Sage said the rock piles also marked locations where the first men had fallen in certain battles with other tribes. Place names often referred to where the fights had occurred or other significant events the tribe wanted to commemorate. Sage remembered a battle with an Apache group near Beaver Park that had taken place when he was about four years old. Both men told of separate fights with Ute and Shoshone warriors along Devil's Gulch.

The Arapahoes left the park on July 29, having been there close to two weeks. They were taken to Fort Collins, where they made two dictaphone records of the Arapahoe language before heading back to the Wind River Reservation.

The Northern Arapahoes Today

There are roughly four thousand Northern Arapahoes living on the Wind River Reservation in northwestern Wyoming. Most available jobs are with the tribal government and the Bureau of Indian Affairs, but some families manage to farm. Battles over water rights are on-going, and many Northern Arapahoes, along with the Shoshones, hope one day to allow much of the Wind River and its tributaries to function as wild streams again.

Settlements of extended families dot the beautiful landscape stretching east of the Wind River Range of the Rocky Mountains. As in the old days, children are cared for by parents, grandparents, and cousins and are famous throughout the state for their athletic prowess. Few non-Indians live on the reservation and are only encountered in the towns of Lander and Riverton, where the Indians do their shopping.

Partly due to this isolation, many traditional values have been maintained. However, most Arapahoes

Figure 81:
Sherman Sage was sixty-three when he visited Rocky Mountain National Park. He and Gro Griswold made two dictaphone records of the Arapahoe language before they returned to the Wind River Reservation.
Photo courtesy of the Colorado Historical Society.

under forty-five years of age do not speak the language. To reverse this trend, recently classes have been established for kindergarten students to teach them Arapahoe, and soon the Head Start classes will be teaching the language as well. Religious ceremonies are still conducted with great reverence. Southern Arapahoes from Oklahoma travel to Wyoming annually to attend ceremonies such as the Offerings Lodge (Sun Dance), the most important Northern Arapahoe ritual.

Northern Arapahoe tribal government is similar to that of the Shoshones. Decisions concerning issues pertinent to both tribes are made by the Joint Tribal Council, while those just dealing with the Northern Arapahoes are addressed by their own General Council and administered by the Business Council.

The Southern Arapahoes in Oklahoma

The Southern Arapahoes did not fare at all well when forced to live in Indian Territory (Oklahoma). In 1887, each Arapahoe was given 160 acres of land to farm. Three and a half out of 4 million acres of reservation land were opened to settlement. The Indians soon discovered that most of the land was useless for farming. For example, Big Mouth, a respected Arapahoe leader, planted eighty acres of corn, but grasshoppers, cattle, and drought killed the entire crop. The reservation also lacked medical care, and many children died of consumption.

Traders swapped illegal whiskey for buffalo robes—although buffalo had been exterminated north of the Arkansas River, there were still some left in Oklahoma. Wives of the Arapahoe hunters were furious with their husbands. For a single bottle of bad whiskey, a man would give away a buffalo robe his wife had spent days preparing in order to trade it for staples such as flour, coffee, and sugar. The Arapahoe wives rebelled and even reported the traders who were turning their husbands into alcoholics; eight men were arrested.

Many restrictions were placed on the Southern Arapahoes that undermined their traditions. In 1889, for example, they were told not to speak their language in school. One woman said she would go down to the school's furnace room to talk to herself so she would not forget it. Men were also told to cut their long hair, of which they were so proud. In addition, all ceremonies, dances, and feasts were banned.

In desperation, in the late 1880s many Arapahoes became followers of the Ghost Dance religion that was becoming popular with so many tribes. The dance was started by a Paiute Indian in Nevada named Wavoka, who had a vision instructing him to have the Indians dance in a circle holding hands. Certain shirts were worn that supposedly could not be penetrated with bullets. After dancing for hours, or even days, without food or water, many people would see visions of a new world—one without white people. All the buffalo would return, and all the Indians killed by whites would be there. It was believed that if the people danced the Ghost Dance long enough, the vision would become a reality. The Ghost Dance faded in popularity after the United States Army shot three hundred Sioux Ghost Dancers at Wounded Knee, South Dakota, in December 1890—their Ghost Dance shirts did not protect them.

A cult centered around the eating of the peyote cactus soon replaced the Ghost Dance. This cactus, which grows only in Mexico and along the Rio Grande in Texas, was eaten as an offering to God. Many Christian elements were incorporated into the ceremony, which stressed goodness and high morals. One result of this cult was that numerous Arapahoe alcoholics gave up drinking after joining it. The peyote ceremony was (and still is) often held in a tipi and lasted all night. Drums were beaten, songs were sung, and prayers were offered for troubled loved ones. The peyote ritual is becoming more popular today with many American Indians of all tribes and has become associated with the Native American Church.

In 1896, the Dutch Reformed Church built a mission near the Arapahoe and Cheyenne communities in Oklahoma. They started an industrial school and gave work to every Arapahoe and Cheyenne woman who wanted it. These women revived their old art of beadwork, which is some of the best in the world.

According to Southern Arapahoe elder Virgil Franklin, Sr., Quakers influenced Arapahoe culture in the early 1900s. Thinking it was in the best interest of the Indians, they bribed the Arapahoes with horses, wagons, and commodities to give up their traditional values and accept the Quaker religion. Franklin believes this was one of the reasons the Southern Arapahoes became less traditional than their northern relatives in Wyoming.

The Southern Arapahoes were given land allotments, and these were gradually sold off to pay bills. By 1928, only 37 percent of the allotted land was still owned by Southern Arapahoes. Even those who still owned their own land often moved to large camps of their kinsmen, where they lived in tipis and held traditional dances. At Christmas time, most Southern Arapahoes would assemble in one large village when their children came home from boarding schools for vacation.

Many children who attended eastern schools returned to Oklahoma with better educations but found there were few jobs available. Some returned to their traditional practices, such as the Offerings Lodge ceremony. Although most Southern Arapahoes had abandoned their tipis and lived in houses by the 1920s, poverty was rampant. Families survived by the traditional practice of sharing. Elders, who might still own allotted land, would donate to the rest of the family income gained from farming or leasing their land.

Arapahoe towns grew up around the areas where the old bands had originally settled. The town of Geary, Oklahoma, was the site of Left Hand's band, which remained together after his death at Sand Creek. Other Arapahoe communities included Canton, Calumet, and Colony, Oklahoma.

Clans remained important to the Arapahoes. Among them were the Tomahawk, Water Sprinkling, Star, and Crazy, or Dog Soup, Clan. According to Virgil Franklin, Sr., non-Indians often sought the healing herbs and powers of the Crazy Clan's medicine men (Franklin 1994, personal communication).

After World War II, many Southern Arapahoes moved to cities. By 1950, only one-third of the tribe still owned allotment land, and they could barely eke a living from it. People would return to the land, however, to participate in ceremonies involving the Medicine Wheel and Offerings Lodge.

In the 1940s, Southern Arapahoes began attending Offerings Lodge and other ceremonies of the Northern Arapahoes in Wyoming, as there were no Southern Arapahoe elders alive who knew how to conduct their own rituals. Many Southern Arapahoes also became active in the Native American Church.

The Southern Arapahoes Today

West-central Oklahoma is the home of many Arapahoes, an area once known as the Arapahoe-Cheyenne Reservation. Canton and Geary are predominantly Arapahoe communities. Calumet, which, according to Virgil Franklin, Sr., was named for the sacred Flat Pipe, is also home to Arapahoes (Virgil Franklin 1994, personal communication).

The tribe is closely allied with the Cheyennes, and both tribes often sponsor mutual powwows, benefit dances, and other social activities. A description of these events, the Cheyenne-Arapahoe Business Committee, and other concerns can be found in the section "Southern Cheyennes and Arapahoes Today."

THE CHEYENNES

Long ago, earth lodges housed the people later known as the Cheyennes. The lodges were spread along rivers in the Great Lakes region, where squash, beans, and corn were cultivated on the river terraces. These agriculturists spoke Algonquin, the same basic language as that spoken by the Arapahoes. Hostile tribes eventually forced the farmers south; they were first observed by non-Indians in 1650 in northern Illinois and later southern Minnesota. By 1700 they were ranging north and west from their home base of Nebraska and South Dakota. Roughly forty years later, the Chippewas massacred most of the Cheyennes; those who survived fled to the forests of the Black Hills in South Dakota.

After horses were obtained from the Comanches and Kiowas, the Cheyennes became natural horsemen and soon hunted buffalo almost exclusively. After a time the Sioux pushed the Cheyennes out of the Black Hills, and the Cheyenne men, tall and wiry, became the most feared of all the Plains warriors. The Sioux became their allies as did the Arapahoes. The Sioux, Arapahoes, and Cheyennes became known as the Platte River tribes.

The Cheyennes called themselves *Tsistsistas*, which means "The People." The name by which they are known today comes from the Sioux word *Shahiyena*, meaning "People of Strange Speech."

Beliefs

Like most tribes that moved from one area to another, the Cheyennes acquired new survival techniques but kept their old religion.

They believed in two main gods, the Wise One Above and the God of the Earth, who lived underground. Other spirits lived at the four cardinal points. When Cheyennes smoked, the pipes were always pointed first to the sky and earth, then to the east, south, west, and north, to honor their gods and spirits. Offerings were placed near springs, rivers, high bluffs, and hills—places where other powerful spirits lived.

Prayers offered to animals were not addressed specifically to them but to the powers they possessed. The Cheyennes prayed for the power of the buffalo to provide the people with food and tipi covers and to run on smooth ground so the horses and hunters would not be injured. The power of the mule deer helped medicine men cure the sick. Birds of prey—eagles, ravens, hawks, owls, and magpies—were strong war medicine because they captured their prey and ate their flesh. The feathers of gray eagles had much power; a man wearing a war bonnet of gray eagle feathers could not be harmed by arrows or bullets. Among many Cheyenne (and other) groups, owls were associated with bad luck. A cricket held in the hand would point its antennae in the direction where buffalo were located. If one antenna pointed in the opposite direction, a small herd was grazing where it pointed.

Hostile spirits lived in certain springs and might shoot arrows into people who carelessly jumped across them, causing sickness. They also inhabited strange-looking hills or bluffs. In the 1890s, a Cheyenne man exemplified how humans could be affected by such spirits. The man fell ill and could not be healed. Finally, someone noticed he had built his house between two peculiar-looking peaks and realized the spirits traveling from one to the other had to go over his house when they visited each other. When he moved his house away from the travel route of the spirits, his health immediately improved.

The most cherished and honored items of the Cheyennes were the four sacred Medicine Arrows, received by a man named Sweet Medicine, or Medicine Root, from a supernatural being. Two of the arrows, called Man Arrows, had black shafts and represented victory in war; the other two were painted red, symbolizing the gathering and hunting of food. As long as the Arrow Renewal Ceremony was performed properly, the tribe would have plenty of food and be safe from enemies. The Medicine Arrows were always kept by the arrow keeper, the office of which was passed down from the priest to his son or younger brother—or someone the priest designated if he had no sons. Before taking charge of the arrows, the priest sacrificed strips of skin from his

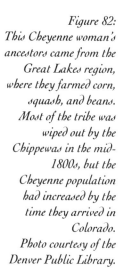

Figure 82:
This Cheyenne woman's
ancestors came from the
Great Lakes region,
where they farmed corn,
squash, and beans.
Most of the tribe was
wiped out by the
Chippewas in the mid-
1800s, but the
Cheyenne population
had increased by the
time they arrived in
Colorado.
Photo courtesy of the
Denver Public Library.

body. The Arrow Renewal Ceremony was so exacting that many did not care to participate in it since if a mistake were made, the entire tribe would suffer the consequences. However, everyone participated in the feast that occurred after the renewal ceremony.

In 1830, the Cheyenne Medicine Arrows were captured by the Pawnees during a battle. A Cheyenne charged at a Pawnee with a spear that had the sacred arrow bundle tied to it, and the Pawnee dodged the spear but managed to grab the bundle. The Cheyennes were horrified. Although substitute arrows were made, they did not have the same power. When peace was made with the Pawnees years later, the Cheyennes were able to repossess the original arrows, but it was too late since they had already endured misfortune. The Cheyennes blamed all their adversity of the next century on the loss of their Medicine Arrows—and the desecration of their sacred Buffalo Hat.

In addition to the Medicine Arrows, the sacred Buffalo Hat has always been extremely important to the tribe's welfare. Two painted buffalo horns were attached to the hat; the rest was covered with blue beads. It was closely guarded by a priest in his tipi, which was treated with great respect; people spoke in soft voices inside, and children were not allowed to play nearby. The tipi also served as a sanctuary since nobody, not even an enemy, could be harmed when inside.

The hat was shown only on three types of occasions—when many of the tribe were ill, when the Medicine Arrows were renewed, and when it was occasionally worn in battle. In 1869, the Buffalo Hat priest died, and the sacred hat was temporarily entrusted to a friend of his. When the dead priest's son returned four years later to claim the hat, the priest's friend refused to give it up until forced to do so by the Fox Soldiers. The son learned much later that one of the horns had been removed by a wife of the temporary custodian. The subsequent deaths of most of the members of the desecrator's family, and many of the devastating problems that the Cheyennes later suffered, were blamed on the loss of the horn. Today, the Buffalo Hat is reverently cared for by an honored individual on the Northern Cheyenne Reservation at Lame Deer, Montana.

The Sun Dance, or Medicine Lodge Ceremony, was one of the most important of the Cheyenne ceremonies. It was held in the spring when the dozen or so bands gathered together for the communal buffalo hunt (as close as possible to the summer solstice). The Sun Dance was performed to ensure food, heal the sick, and bring victory in war. It was usually arranged by someone who had promised to sponsor it if allowed to survive a specific battle or a serious wound or illness.

The Cheyenne Sun Dance was similar to that of the other Plains tribes. Men danced for four days without food or water, after which designs of nature's blessings were painted on the dancers' bodies, including the sun, moon, plants, and flowers. Skewers were thrust through the flesh of the back and chest and tied by rope to the center pole. Then the skewers were ripped out while the dancers blew whistles and jerked back from the pole. Although the Cheyennes reportedly practiced self-torture more than the other tribes, they did not do so to prove manhood or show off but as a sacrifice for the welfare of the tribe and renewal of all life on earth.

Figure 83:
Wolf Robe was elected
chief because of his
good sense, generosity,
and self-control
(equanimity), as were
all of the Cheyennes'
traditional
forty-four chiefs.
Photo by F. A.
Rinehart, courtesy of
the Denver Public
Library.

The Cheyenne warriors were organized in military societies, as were warriors of several other Plains tribes. There were usually four or five of these warrior societies, among them the Wolf, Elk, Bowstring, and Dog Soldiers. Each society had its own style of dress, dances, and sacred songs. The members called each other brother and protected each other in battle. Being a chief of a military society was one of the most prestigious roles one could attain as a warrior. The soldier chief took the lead in battle and had to rally his brothers even when disaster was inevitable. He was considered the bravest of all and was not expected to live long. Most men, but not all, belonged to a warrior society. When a notable Cheyenne leader told General Nelson A. Miles that he had never belonged to one, the general responded that he wasn't a West Point man himself.

The Dog Soldiers, many of them half-Sioux and sometimes referred to as the Cheyenne Sioux, were the most aggressive and feared of all Plains warriors during the 1800s. Headdresses of raven feathers were worn during dances, but the most honored item to be owned by a Dog Soldier was the dog rope. This was a long hide sash magnificently decorated with quillwork and feathers, with a small pointed wooden pin attached to it. During battle, the one wearing the rope over his shoulder might stick the pin in the ground and pledge not to leave the spot and to fight to his death—unless someone pulled the pin for him. Great ceremony accompanied the passing of the rope to another Dog Soldier.

The rear column of a moving camp consisted of the Dog Soldiers, who, unlike the other warrior societies, pitched their tipis separately from the rest of the group. Before the Battle of Summit Springs, where retreating Cheyennes were attacked by the United States Army in 1869, there were up to one hundred lodges of Dog Soldiers but afterwards only a handful, and the society never regained its membership after that.

Another important Cheyenne group, although not considered a warrior society, was the Contraries, men selected for their bravery, strength, and leadership abilities. Contraries painted their bodies red, wore red clothes, and did everything backwards. For example, on a cold winter day, a Contrary might exclaim how hot he was, tear off his buffalo robe, and rub snow on his body. Contraries lived alone and did not socialize. Their daring was shown in battle—if they shifted their spears to their right arms, they could not retreat until the enemy was gone. Contraries, like Dog Soldiers, rarely lived to be old men.

Cheyenne tribal authority was officially held by forty-four chiefs, each elected to serve ten years of office. The chiefs were chosen for their intelligence, good judgment, and even temperaments. One of the major responsibilities was the movement of the camp and the determination of the place and time of the communal buffalo hunt. Each band usually had four chiefs, and these men had to work closely with the warrior society chiefs who carried out their decisions.

Clothing and Personal Adornment

Men's braids were wrapped with strips of otter fur or, when available later through trade, with brass wire; their scalp locks were decorated with flattened silver coins. Necklaces were made with fish vertebrae, or elk and deer teeth, before glass beads were used.

Cheyenne clothing was similar to that of most Plains Indians. As soon as little boys learned to walk, they wore a string around their waists but did not attach a breechcloth until they were older. Then the breechcloth became a very important item of clothing. Cheyenne men felt a loss of manhood if they removed their breechcloths, and some continued to wear breechcloths even after trousers were introduced. Fringed leggings were tied to the waist string and reached to the ankle. Thigh-length deerskin shirts had fringed sleeves and were beaded or decorated with porcupine quills. Enemy hair or scalps trimmed the seams.

Women's dresses, made of the soft skin of deer, sheep, elk, or antelope, were long, with capelike sleeves. They were also beautifully decorated with elk teeth, quills, and, later, glass beads. Cheyenne women were noted for their high morals and wore chastity belts of rope (though only at night and when traveling) until married.

Both men and women wore moccasins. Each moccasin was made from one piece of deer hide with a tough sole of used parfleche (from rawhide carrying boxes) sewed inside. Before being attached to the

Figure 84:
A Cheyenne woman
offers a pipe to the earth
during a ceremony.
Photo by Edward S.
Curtis, courtesy of the
Denver Public Library.

sole, beading or porcupine quillwork was worked on the moccasin. Winter moccasins had leather drawstrings attached to the tops to keep snow out and were made of old buffalo robes with the hair inside.

History and Culture

Sometime after 1825 the Cheyennes moved from the Missouri River region due to pressure from the Sioux. The Pawnees, Comanches, and Kiowas were constant targets of Cheyenne horse raids. During a retaliatory raid by the Kiowas and Comanches, forty-eight Cheyenne Bowstring warriors were killed, a devastating loss to the tribe. The Cheyennes got even in 1837 by killing fifty-eight Kiowas and Comanches at the Battle of Wolf Creek in northwestern Oklahoma (see Chapter 7, "General History of the Plains Tribes"). The tribes involved soon recognized the danger in such mass killings and perhaps saw the advantages of forming an alliance against their common enemy, the Utes, who lived in the mountains to the west. Consequently, they called for a peace council in 1840.

Thousands of Cheyennes, Arapahoes, Comanches, Kiowas, and Jicarilla Apaches gathered a few miles from Bent's Fort (see Chapter 7, "General History of the Plains Tribes"). Tipis lined the Arkansas River for several miles. For days, gifts were exchanged between all of the tribes. The Kiowas and Comanches gave away so many horses that almost every person in the other tribes had a new horse; some had several. After the gift giving, a great feast was held. The peace made among these tribes that had once been enemies was lasting. Together they often rode east into Kansas and Nebraska to raid the Pawnees or west over the mountains to attack the Utes.

During the 1830s and 1840s trade was brisk at Bent's Fort. The Cheyennes traded buffalo robes and beaver pelts for such things as cloth, blankets, knives, kettles, coffee, flour, and sugar. The unintentional tradeoffs were measles, smallpox, whooping cough, cholera, and alcoholism. In 1849, cholera killed about half of the Cheyenne tribe. In an 1853 report, Thomas Fitzpatrick, the Indian agent for the Cheyenne and Arapahoe tribes, wrote that the people were "actually in a starving state. They are in abject want of food half the year. Their women are pinched with want and their children are constantly crying out with hunger" (Lavender 1954, 349). That same year fifteen thousand emigrants crossed the Platte Trail in northern Colorado, cutting trees, killing game, and bringing more diseases.

The Cheyennes suffered the same negative effects of the Colorado gold rush as their Arapahoe friends did. When many were told to move to the reservation north of Bent's Fort on Sand Creek, they found it unfit for farming. Both tribes suffered. Rations rarely arrived and were often not edible by the time they got there. Despite the circumstances and although their allies the Comanches and Kiowas were constantly raiding settlers, the Cheyennes (and Arapahoes) generally remained peaceful unless provoked. An exception was the July 1864 raid with warriors from other tribes on stage stations in Colorado and Kansas for stock to feed their starving families. The United States Cavalry then attacked several Cheyenne camps in northern Colorado. Chiefs who wanted peace could not hold back the angry warriors, and by August Cheyennes, Arapahoes, and Sioux were plundering stage stations and settlements all along the South Platte River.

A turning point in relationships between the Cheyennes and the United States government was Colonel Chivington's 1864 massacre of peaceable Cheyennes and Arapahoes at Sand Creek (see Chapter 7, "General History of the Plains Tribes"), which prompted most of the Cheyennes to engage in full-time raiding of the settlers. From 1864 to 1868 all their raiding, however, could not feed their starving bands, who were constantly fleeing from United States soldiers. Finally, one band, headed by Chief Black Kettle, who had survived the Sand Creek Massacre in 1864, asked for protection at Fort Cobb, Oklahoma. When he was refused, he led his band along the Washita River in northwestern Oklahoma to camp near several bands of Comanches, Kiowas, Arapahoes, and Jicarilla Apaches.

On November 29, 1868, four years after the Sand Creek Massacre, to the day, Black Kettle's camp was attacked at dawn, this time by General George Armstrong Custer. In this battle, known as the Battle of the Washita, Custer claimed he and his men killed 103 warriors, but reliable sources place the number between 9 and 20 men, and between 18 and 40 women and children. Custer scarcely mentioned the women and children killed, saying only that 53 were taken prisoner. One of the young women captives, Monahsetah, was kept through the winter and spring and bore Custer a son, Yellow Swallow, who later fled north with the Northern Cheyennes led by Little Wolf and Dull Knife.

Black Kettle and his wife were killed at Washita while trying to cross the river on one horse (see Chapter 7, "General History of the Plains Tribes"). There, Custer burned all the tipis, food, robes and other clothing, and shot all the horses. Most people familiar with the event agree that the Battle of the Washita in Oklahoma should be called the Washita Massacre.

In July 1869, Major E. A. Carr attacked Tall Bull's Cheyenne Dog Soldiers at Summit Springs, north of the South Platte River in northeastern Colorado (see Chapter 7, "General History of the Plains Tribes"). Fifty-two Cheyennes were killed, including Tall Bull, and the entire village was destroyed. Survivors fled to Sioux villages. The Battle of Summit Springs ended the Cheyenne occupation of eastern Colorado.

The Northern Cheyennes were escorted to Fort Keogh, an army post that later became Miles City, Montana (a reservation was later created at Lame Deer). Most Southern Cheyennes surrendered at Camp Supply, Oklahoma. The reservation was moved to Darlington near the Texas border in Oklahoma, just north of the Kiowa-Comanche Reservation.

The non-Indian buffalo hunters had exterminated the herds north of the Arkansas River, but the Cheyennes continued to hunt buffalo that remained south of the river. However, soon these buffalo were slaughtered as well. Surveyors seemed to be everywhere, marking the way for railroads which would bring more settlers to the area. White horse thieves sneaked onto the reservation and captured hundreds of Cheyenne horses. The most devastating problem, however, was the presence of whiskey traders. Cheyenne men gave away fine buffalo robes, horses, and even guns for a few bottles of liquor. Drunk, or with few horses or guns, many men could not hunt for food, and government rations rarely appeared. Soon the Cheyennes were starving again.

Young Cheyenne men were restless. They needed opportunities to count coup or they would never be considered warriors. Comanches and Kiowas hounded the young men, telling them to join them in raids. In June 1874, some Cheyennes finally gave in and participated in an attack on twenty-eight buffalo hunters at Adobe Walls in northwestern Oklahoma Territory. The combined Indian forces were defeated by the hated buffalo hunters, whose deadly guns could hit targets up to a mile away.

Soon other Cheyennes began raiding, taking their families with them. A group of Northern Cheyennes who had been forced onto the

Southern Cheyenne Reservation in Oklahoma Territory escaped to their home in Montana. An account of this incredible trip, led by the veteran leaders Dull Knife and Little Wolf, is vividly described in Mari Sandoz's book *Cheyenne Autumn*. The army pursued them and destroyed villages, horses, and supplies until the tired, starving Cheyennes were captured.

Several decades later, after the Allotment Act of 1887, the Cheyennes lost their reservation to land-hungry white settlers. Disease, depression, unemployment, and alcoholism took their toll, but the Cheyennes clung to their beliefs, even when their ceremonies were outlawed.

The Northern Cheyennes Today

Approximately fifteen thousand Cheyennes live in the United States. Over six thousand live in Montana, and over three thousand live on the Northern Cheyenne Reservation at Lame Deer southeast of Billings. The Northern Cheyennes are among the most traditional of the tribes. Roughly 35 percent of the Northern Cheyennes still speak their own language.

Health services, the Police Department, offices of the Bureau of Indian Affairs, and the tribal headquarters are all located at Lame Deer. Ranching is the primary occupation of most Northern Cheyennes, with the tribal government, the BIA, service industries, and seasonal fire fighting providing other employment. However, nearly 60 percent of the population remains unemployed. The tribe faces the controversial issue of economic development versus retention of tribal traditions; although the reservation contains billions of tons of low-sulfur coal under the ground, it would require strip mining, which many Northern Cheyennes see as tearing up Mother Earth.

A motel, restaurant, marina, R.V. park, and gambling facility are being proposed at the Ten River Dam Recreation Area. The state of Montana borrowed $11 million from the tribe to raise the lake level, but the dam is considered faulty and the project remains in limbo.

Ties remain strong with the Southern Cheyennes in Oklahoma. Many families travel yearly from Montana to Oklahoma to gather for sacred tribal ceremonies such as the renewal ceremonies for the Medicine Arrows and the sacred Buffalo Hat.

The Southern Cheyennes and Arapahoes Today

The Southern Cheyennes and Arapahoes were originally placed on a reservation in the west-central part of Indian Country (Oklahoma). Today, there is no reservation, and less than half of the Southern Arapahoes and Cheyennes live on land originally allotted to them. Many Arapahoes live in Canton or Geary, while Seiling and Kingfisher are known as primarily Cheyenne communities.

Unemployment ranges from 40 to 70 percent, compared with the national rate of 5 to 15 percent. Few jobs are locally available, and employment is difficult to find in distant non-Indian communities due to discrimination. Some elderly people receive royalties from oil and gas produced on their allotted land parcels, but these contributions to the extended families do not stretch very far. Young people with college degrees sometimes find jobs with the tribes or move to cities to seek work.

The two tribes are represented by elected members on the six-member Cheyenne-Arapahoe Business Committee. The Cheyennes have four members, the Arapahoes two. The group manages federal services and promotes Arapahoe and Cheyenne interests in relations with oil companies and local, state, and federal entities. A bingo operation in Concho and other tribally owned businesses have been fostered by the business committee. Each tribe also has twelve or more chiefs, who are chosen to be the watchdogs of the business committee. These people, who must have participated in the Sun Dance for at least seven years, also serve as financial advisors to tribal members.

Under a nineteenth-century treaty signed by the United States government and the two tribes, the tribes leased old Fort Reno to the government for as long as the funds to lease were available. Now, the government can no longer afford to lease the fort and wants to put a veterans' cemetery at the location. The Southern Cheyenne and Arapahoe tribes feel the land is legally theirs and have plans to renovate the old fort for a museum and gift shops with themes interpreting the history and traditions of the tribes.

Arapahoe and Cheyenne traditions are maintained during benefit dances, which occur almost every weekend in Geary, Canton, Concho, and Watonga. Much planning is required for the dances. The sponsor, who wants to raise money for a certain cause or for community pow-wows, buys or collects gifts and food to be given away. Seven people are chosen to staff the dance: a head singer, head male and female dancers, an arena director, and a master of ceremonies. The staff receives the gifts at the benefit dance, the dancers contribute to the sponsor, and the sponsor donates the contributions to the chosen cause. This redistribution of goods is a practice of many Indian tribes, a major reason their cultures have survived for so long under circumstances that would have destroyed the traditions of most cultures.

Every summer caravans of Southern Cheyenne and Arapahoe families head north to the Northern Cheyenne Reservation southeast of Billings, Montana, and the Wind River (Arapahoe/Shoshone) Reservation north of Lander, Wyoming. The annual trips are made to attend Sun Dances and other ceremonies as well as to participate in powwows and to visit relatives. Although over a thousand miles apart, family ties are still strong among the northern and southern tribes, even after more than a century of separation.

PLACES TO VISIT

Colorado

COLORADO HISTORY MUSEUM
1300 Broadway
Denver, CO 80203
(303)866-3682

The museum displays crafts, clothing, and artifacts from Plains tribes that inhabited Colorado. Dioramas depict the lifestyles of Plains Indians.

Oklahoma

AMERICAN INDIAN EXPOSITION
Box 705
Anadarko, OK 73005
(405) 247-6651

One of the finest Indian fairs in the country. It includes a parade and a pageant with traditional songs and dances presented by many tribes, including Comanches, Kiowas, Kiowa-Apaches, Cheyennes, and Arapahoes. There is also competitive powwow dancing as well as crafts demonstrations and food booths.

INDIAN CITY USA
Highway 8
3 miles east of Anadarko, OK
(405)247-5661

The site features eight reconstructed Indian villages, including Kiowa tipis and Apache wickiups. Crafts and arts are displayed at the museum and gift shop. Special Indian programs occur throughout the year.

KIOWA TRIBAL MUSEUM
Tribal Office Complex
Carnegie, OK 73015
(405)654-2300

The museum exhibits traditional clothing and tools of the Kiowas. In the fall the museum hosts a powwow at which there is traditional dancing as well as food. There is a Kiowa Gourd Dance and an arts and crafts show during the Fourth of July weekend.

SOUTHERN PLAINS INDIAN MUSEUM AND CRAFTS CENTER
Highway 62
East side of Anadarko, OK
(405)247-6221

This is a sales outlet for the Oklahoma Indian Arts and Crafts Cooperative; all arts and crafts are authentic and of excellent quality.

Suggestions for Further Reading

Cash, Joseph H., and Gerald W. Wolff. *The Comanche People*. Phoenix, Ariz.: Indian Tribal Series, 1974.

Fowler, Oretta. *The Arapaho*. New York and Philadelphia: Chelsea House Publishers, 1989.

Grinnell, George Bird. *The Cheyenne Indians: Their History and Ways of Life*. Vol. 2. Lincoln and London: University of Nebraska Press, 1972.

Hyde, George. *Life of George Bent, Written from His Letters*. Norman: University of Oklahoma Press, 1968. Reprint, 1987.

Iverson, Peter. *The Plains Indians of the Twentieth Century*. Norman: University of Oklahoma Press, 1985.

Sandoz, Mari. *Cheyenne Autumn*. New York: Hastings House, 1953.

Trenholm, Virginia Cole. *The Arapahoes: Our People*. Norman: University of Oklahoma Press, 1986.

Wallace, Ernest, and E. Adamson Hoebel. *The Comanches: Lords of the Plains*. Norman: University of Oklahoma Press, 1976.

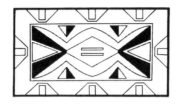

11

Rock Art of Prehistoric and Historic Indians

▲ ▲

*O*N CLIFFS OF RIVER CANYONS and in other locations throughout the western half of the state and in southeastern Colorado, the Indians left intriguing and beautiful symbols of their lives and spiritual worlds, now known as rock art.

Rock art consists of petroglyphs and dry or wet paintings, also called pictographs. Petroglyphs are carvings made with antlers or knives and chisels of hard stone ("petro" means rock; a glyph is a carving). Designs were pecked, ground, incised, or scratched onto usually vertical (though sometimes horizontal) walls. The Indians often chose smooth sandstone rock faces covered with a "desert varnish," or mineral stain on which to carve these panels. The carving exposed the lighter color underneath, making the imagery strikingly visible.

Rock paintings, or pictographs, were made of minerals and possibly fixatives, such as animal blood, plant saps, and whites from bird eggs. Local minerals provided a variety of colors: red from hematite, white from gypsum, yellow from limonite, and green-blue from azurite. The paint was applied to rock walls with the aid of brushes of animal hair or frayed yucca leaves, fingers, and sharpened sticks. Pictographs that have survived the centuries are mainly located in sheltered overhangs, where wind and rainfall have not obliterated them. Unfortunately, weathering has not been the only destructive force that has obliterated rock art. Since the arrival of non-Indians, rock art has been damaged and destroyed by bullets, saws, graffiti, jackhammers, bulldozers, and reservoirs. It is imperative never to touch or damage rock art in any way if it is encountered at sites—even oil from the hands will cause it to deteriorate.

Analysis of rock art in western Colorado and neighboring areas of the Colorado Plateau is presented in Sally J. Cole's book *Legacy on Stone.* Cole describes which cultures may have been responsible for certain styles and provides clues as to the possible meaning of some imagery. She avoids literal interpretation of the art, instead comparing certain designs to artifacts found at sites where the specific culture flourished or to pottery and basketry designs. She also uses information gathered from Indian descendants of the cultures to which the rock art is attributed to explain possible meanings. This is a refreshing and scholarly approach since it is impossible for twentieth-century non-Indians to understand complex spiritual and natural symbols from centuries ago.

The following rock art descriptions are based on Cole's Legacy on Stone.

GLEN CANYON STYLE 5 (6000 B.P.–A.D. 500)

Glen Canyon Style 5 rock art is the oldest recorded in Colorado and dates to the Archaic period. Named for a style identified in the Colorado River's Glen Canyon (some of it now covered by Lake Powell in Utah), this rock art form may have its origin up to six thousand years ago, although dates of three thousand to four thousand years ago are more accepted. Major river corridors, including the lower Dolores in west-central Colorado, were areas where Glen Canyon Style 5 petroglyphs were pecked. The similarity of this style with others as far away as Nevada, Wyoming, and California indicates Archaic peoples were using river corridors not only for hunting and gathering but as trade routes along which goods and ideas were exchanged.

In Colorado, the style includes anthropomorphs, or humanlike figures, with long bodies and horned headdresses and some head ornaments that look like floppy rabbit ears. Unlike many figures of this style in Utah, which lack appendages, the Colorado Glen Canyon Style 5 petroglyphs have arms, legs, and feet. Mountain sheep, deer, and elk with large rectangular bodies and small heads; round human heads (masks?) with large solid round eyes; and wavy lines and spirals are common motifs of this style.

Figure 85:
Headdresses, bulging eyes, and long bodies are attributes of Glen Canyon Style 5. Located on the lower Dolores River in west-central Colorado, this petroglyph represents the oldest rock art style in the state.

BARRIER CANYON STYLE (8000? B.P.–A.D. 500)

Ghostly painted and pecked humanlike figures with round hollow eyes stare out from canyon walls in Canyon Pintado and other places in northwestern Colorado. The likeness of the long, eerie forms (many without arms and legs) to horned figures of the Glen Canyon Style 5 suggests they were made during the same period and are associated with hunters and gathers of the plateau country.

When arms are present, Barrier Canyon Style figures may hold plants, sticks, or snakes. Often they are clustered close together and wear horned headdresses. Similar figures are sometimes associated with smaller humans or animals in such a way that they seem to be part of a

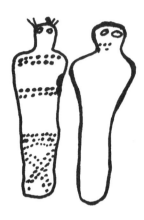

Figure 86:
Ghostly figures of the Archaic
Barrier Canyon Style similar to
these red pictographs in
Canyonlands National Park,
Utah, are also found in
some canyons of
northwestern Colorado.

story. It is speculated that these were gods or supernatural beings or shamans or priests or ancestors. Some Barrier Canyon Style panels appear to have had stone projectiles thrown or shot at them. Rather than vandalism, these mutilations could possibly be the result of symbolic attacks representing certain real or legendary events. Some Barrier Canyon Style pictographs have been completely mudded over, with newer images painted on top, indicating that perhaps the earlier symbolism was being deliberately hidden. As a parallel, Cole notes that the present-day Pueblo Indians of New Mexico and Arizona plaster over their kiva murals at the end of ceremonies, readying the walls for the next religious activity.

UNCOMPAHGRE STYLE
(3000 B.P.–A.D. 1000)

Uncompahgre Style rock art is pecked, drilled, stippled, and incised. Named after the Uncompahgre Plateau in west-central Colorado where most of it is found, this rock art differs dramatically from other Archaic forms in that few humanlike figures are represented. Instead, it consists mostly of animal images. Bears and bear paws are common

Figure 87:
Rock carvings of bears, mountain
sheep, and other animals typify Archaic
Uncompahgre Style petroglyphs such
as these on the Gunnison River in
west-central Colorado.

motifs. Other animal tracks such as those of deer, elk, bird, and possibly bison also were pecked on the rock walls. Mountain sheep, deer, and elk appear in groups, as if migrating or perhaps being driven by hunters. The few humans who are depicted often have upraised arms and stand near animals, perhaps representations of shamans invoking power to drive and hunt the animals.

INTERIOR LINE STYLE (PRE-A.D. 1–1000)

It is likely that hunters and gatherers of western Wyoming probably were in contact with Indians of eastern Utah and Colorado since some of their petroglyphs and pictographs are similar. Pecked and painted

designs known as the Interior Line Style are found on sandstone walls in Canyon Pintado, the Gunnison River drainage, and rocks north of the Yampa River in northwestern Colorado. The origin of the style, however, appears to be along the Wind River in Wyoming. Here, particularly around Dinwoody Lake, a unique style of painted or pecked humanlike forms with round heads sitting immediately atop broad shoulders predominates. Bodies are often bottle shaped, with round eyes similar to those of the ghostly Barrier Canyon figures. Incised or painted lines often fill in the body, with lines also possibly representing various articles of dress such as pouches, belts, sashes, and breast plates.

Figure 88: Artistic influence from Wyoming is seen in this red Interior Line Style pictograph in Routt County, northwestern Colorado.

Although the historic Shoshone tribe does not claim to have made the rock art, the tribe refers to the figures as Rock Ghost Beings or Water Ghost Beings, and their shamans visit the figures to gain power during vision quests. It is possible that ancient shamans also employed the figures in a similar manner, although the original artists may not have made the figures for such purposes.

ANASAZI ROCK ART (100? B.C.–A.D.1300)

The canyons and mesas of southwestern Colorado are full of rock art panels made by the Anasazi. Images are both painted and pecked, and styles changed as time passed. Animals and geometric designs abound; striking images are humanlike figures. Early styles show figures that wear necklaces, headdresses, and elaborate "hair bobs" and "hair whorls" similar to ones worn by unmarried Hopi women in historic times. Figures may have enormous hands and feet, and birds often sit atop their human heads. Historic Pueblos attach great significance to birds and feathers and use them in their ceremonies. Large shields appear to protect the bodies of some Anasazi figures of the later style. Cole suggests that masklike faces of the later style represent kachinas.

Figure 89:
Historic photos of Hopis show women wearing "hair bobs" similar to those depicted in Basketmaker III to Pueblo I Style petroglyphs along McElmo Creek in southwestern Colorado.

Rock shrines appear to be associated with some Anasazi rock art panels. Among the Hopi and Zuni Pueblo Indians, shrines and rock art panels are often controlled by certain clans or religious organizations.

FREMONT ROCK ART (A.D. 400–1500)

The petroglyphs and pictographs of the Fremont people are among the most elaborate in Colorado and the entire Southwest. Large, sometimes life-sized, broad-shouldered, and thin-waisted humanlike figures were pecked and painted. These often are shown wearing headdresses of horns or feathers. A flicker-feather headdress found in a cave in Dinosaur National Monument looks strikingly similar to head ornaments worn by Fremont rock art figures. Earrings, necklaces, kilts, and sashes also adorn forms. (One can only speculate as to whether these were pictures of supernaturals or shamans, or whether the Fremont dressed this lavishly.) Some figures carry staffs, or spears, and others are protected by large, round shields. What might be scalps or human heads are held by some figures. It is not known whether warfare was common at the time or whether these figures are part of mythological stories or ceremonies.

Although humanlike figures are the most striking Fremont images, spirals, circles, bighorn sheep, lizards, snakes, birds, moccasin tracks, paw prints, and other elements are common. Often figures are clustered together and seem to be illustrating a story, for example panels containing numerous bighorn sheep with hunters aiming at them with bows and arrows.

Cole notes that some earlier rock art of this style is solidly pecked while later designs are only outlined. Some more recent forms appear more abstract than earlier examples, with only eyes, mouths, headdresses, necklaces,

Figure 90:
Elaborate headdresses and broad shoulders on life-sized figures typify Fremont petroglyphs such as this staff-bearing anthropomorph in Glade Park, west-central Colorado.

and belts depicted. It is possible that the style changed through the years or that body outlines and other details were painted and the paint has since weathered away.

Examples of possible Fremont rock art show rounded humanlike figures with realistic noses as well as stick figures. These may be the most recent Fremont panels and suggest influence of the Utes or Shoshones, who probably entered the area prior to the demise of the Fremont culture. Today, numerous Fremont rock art panels can be visited at Fremont Indian State Park near Richfield, Utah.

HISTORIC ROCK ART

The Navajos, Utes, and Shoshones of western Colorado camped near elaborate panels of Fremont and Anasazi rock art and probably admired the skill and patience of the ancient artists who made them. As time passed these historic tribes added their own imagery. Such imagery is often easy to recognize since it usually includes tipis and horses, and, later, trains and cowboys, indicating cultures influenced by Europeans.

EASTERN SHOSHONE ROCK ART (A.D. 1300–1800 IN COLORADO)

Along the Yampa River drainage in the far northwestern part of the state and in Dinosaur National Monument, rock carvings and paintings may have been made by Eastern Shoshone groups, probably prior to the late 1700s before the Shoshones were pushed north by the Utes. A common motif is a painted human figure with a rectangular body and upraised arms, often carrying a shield or spear. Other humans also may carry a shield or spear. Often the shield is placed in front of the body, covering the entire torso, and thin or sticklike legs extend below. This rock art is presumed to be ceremonial in nature since it is found in isolated locations such as rock shelters, mountain slopes, and high ridgetops—some of which were perhaps vision quest sites.

Figure 91:
Shoshone-Style pictographs along the Yampa River substantiate the Shoshone presence in northwestern Colorado.

Later Shoshone rock art panels appear to represent specific stories, such as horse raids, ceremonies, or dances. Some panels are realistic and show lots of action, such as battle scenes with warriors on foot and mounted, carrying lances, guns, and shields, apparently fighting each other. Sometimes dead warriors appear to be lying on the ground, and, in one instance, an unmounted figure has been shot by an arrow and is falling backwards. Clusters of tipis are depicted in some panels. Cole cites a study of this imagery (also called Biographic Style rock art) which attempts to interpret the stories by identifying certain motifs such as tracks indicating direction of movement and even elements that might be symbolic of specific names of people.

UTE ROCK ART (A.D. 1600–1950)

Early Ute petroglyphs and pictographs depict elongated horses with small riders often portrayed as stick figures, illustrating hunting and warfare scenes. Later styles show more realistic human figures, some with elaborate, trailing headdresses, fringed leggings, and other details of clothing. Horses appear to be running, and details of bridles and saddles are depicted. Obvious battle scenes with riflemen and wounded warriors falling off their horses are also shown.

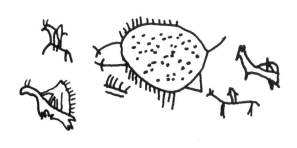

Figure 92:
A strange bug-like creature surrounded by mounted Utes is often interpreted as being a "plan view" of a buffalo. This historic petroglyph was carved on a boulder in a tributary canyon of the Gunnison River in west-central Colorado.

A Weenuche Ute leader named Jack House, who lived in a Navajo-style hogan in Mancos Canyon (now part of the Ute Tribal Park on Mesa Verde) in the first half of the twentieth century, may have made numerous images on boulders and cliff walls from about 1906 to 1950. One detailed image of a man wearing jeans, chaps, boots, and a cowboy hat has the words *J H Cowboy* carved above. Three horses and a cow are drawn nearby. The art of Jack House suggests how important ranching and cowboy culture came to be to the Utes.

NAVAJO ROCK ART (A.D. 1700–1950?)

Most Navajo rock art in Colorado is in the extreme southwestern part of the state. Many paintings are considered ceremonial in nature and probably depict supernatural beings known as *yeis* and possibly masked dancers known as *yeibichai*. These figures are usually elongated, with rectangular bodies, arms crooked at the elbows, and hands held up. Headdresses are often worn. Some forms resemble the supernaturals depicted in Navajo sandpaintings, representations of which are used in curing ceremonies.

Figure 93:
The style of this red rock painting along the Uncompahgre River in west-central Colorado may indicate the presence of a Navajo artist.

Sometimes painted crescents, stars, flowers, birds, and dragonflies are located high on the ceilings of rock overhangs, places impossible to reach. Since studies of the inaccessible art have revealed leaf impressions in the paint and dots in the center of the motifs it is thought that some designs may have been formed by yucca leaves, dipped in paint and shot with arrows to the rock ceiling. Navajo (or possibly Pueblo) stars are visible in Step House at Mesa Verde National Park.

Recent Navajo rock art depicts sheep, horses, hogans, trains, cars, cowboys, and pickup trucks. Because most Navajos in modern times have lived on the reservation south of the Colorado border, there are few such examples in Colorado.

ROCK ART OF SOUTHEASTERN COLORADO

Anthropomorphs, bear paws, squiggly lines that surround entire boulders, human footprints, doglike animals, snakes, deer, mountain sheep, mountain goats, and hoofprints are carved on some of the canyon walls in southeastern Colorado. These canyons, including four in the Comanche National Grasslands (managed by the United States Forest

Figure 94:
Bison and horses show
Plains influence in these
southeastern Colorado
petroglyphs while the
bison-horned headdress
with round eyes is a typical
Rio Grande Pueblo motif.

Service) and one owned by the United States Army, are southern tributaries of the Arkansas River. The oldest of this rock art is geometric in
appearance and resembles Archaic styles of the southern Plains and
Great Basin. Later petroglyphs and pictographs, including painted
handprints, carvings of round heads with round eyes and mouths, faces
with bison-horn headdresses, and figures similar to mudhead kachinas
and other Pueblo-like motifs in the canyons, suggest a southwestern
influence. Still other evidence, including adjacent Apishapa architecture,

indicates the presence of a people more influenced by those in the Oklahoma and Texas panhandles. A northwestern influence may be apparent as well in figures resembling Shoshone shield-bearing warriors.

Historic rock art of the area may be the work of Comanches and/or Kiowas as some of the designs are similar to those on Plains Indian tipis and shields.

PLACES TO VISIT

(Remember: never touch the rock art—even the oil from your hands can harm it.)

Colorado

CANYON PINTADO HISTORIC DISTRICT
Located along Colorado 139 between Douglas Pass and Rangely.

A sign at a rest area describes Fremont pictographs.

COMANCHE NATIONAL GRASSLANDS
27162 Highway 287
P.O. Box 127
Springfield, CO 81073
(719)523-6591

There are self-guided walking tours and occasionally guided tours in Picketwire and Vogel canyons, near La Junta, and Picture and Carrizo canyons near Springfield.

Utah

DINOSAUR NATIONAL MONUMENT
Jenson, UT 84035
(801)789-2115

Fremont rock art is visible in several locations. Ask for directions at the Visitor Center (in Colorado) or the quarry (Utah).

FREMONT INDIAN STATE PARK
11000 Clear Creek Canyon Road
Sevier, UT 84766
(801)527-4631

There are numerous magnificent Fremont rock art panels in the park as well as a museum. In addition, one of the most extensive Fremont villages ever discovered has been partially excavated and stabilized for public visitation.

Suggestions for Further Reading

Barnes, F. A. *Canyon Country Prehistoric Rock Art.* Salt Lake City, Utah: Wasatch Publishers, 1982.

Cole, Sally J. *Legacy on Stone: Rock Art of the Colorado Plateau and Four Corners Region.* Boulder, Colo.: Johnson Books, 1990.

Day, Jane S., Paul D. Friedman, Marcia J. Tate. *Rock Art of the Western Canyons.* Boulder, Colo.: Johnson Books, 1989.

Schaafsma, Polly. *Indian Rock Art of the Southwest.* Albuquerque: University of New Mexico Press, 1980.

Slifer, Dennis, and James Duffield. *Kokopelli: Fluteplayer Images in Rock Art.* Santa Fe, N.M.: Ancient City Press, 1994.

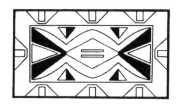

12

Non-Reservation
Indians Today

▲ ▲

*O*F ALL THE TRIBES THAT USED TO RANGE over the mountains, foothills, and Plains of Colorado, only the Southern and Ute Mountain Utes retain land in the state. However, according to J. Donald Hughes in his book *American Indians in Colorado* almost twenty-one thousand Indians live in the state today, the majority in Denver, Boulder, and Colorado Springs (although the Four Corners area has the highest percentage of the total population, due to the presence of the Ute Mountain and Southern Ute reservations).

Navajos and Sioux are the tribes most numerous in the cities. Many Navajos moved to Denver in the 1950s during a voluntary relocation program sponsored by the Bureau of Indian Affairs. Although the Navajos came with great expectations of training and employment, over half returned to the reservation. Navajo family ties are strong; life away from the reservation is lonely and alien. Jobs requiring the type of training the Navajos had were hard to find, many did not speak English well, and prejudice prevented many Navajos and other Indians from getting jobs.

EDUCATION AND ORGANIZATIONS

Common problems drew the Indians who remained in the cities together, and various social organizations were formed by Indians to help each other adjust to city life. In and surrounding the Denver area the White Buffalo Council, Lone Feather Council, and Pike's Peak Intertribal Indian Club sponsor dinners and powwows to raise money for Indians in need and to promote traditional values. The Denver Indian Center encourages the continuation of cultural traditions through educational programs and provides social services, employment assistance, health care for seniors, a preschool, and programs for drug and alcohol abuse.

Some Colorado schools and colleges promote Indian education. Fort Lewis College in Durango, originally an agricultural college for Indians, now educates students of all races, and Indians are given free tuition. Information about financial assistance for Indians is provided by the University of Colorado at Denver, which has an American Indian Education Program that caters to the needs of Indian students. Departments at the University of Colorado in Boulder pursue studies of American Indian cultures, history, and contemporary issues. Vine Deloria, Jr., a Sioux and author of several well-known books, including *Custer Died for Your Sins*, received his law degree from the University of Colorado.

Boulder is also the headquarters for a national organization called the Native American Rights Fund, which provides legal counsel to Indians. In addition, both Boulder and Denver are centers for activities of the American Indian Movement (AIM), an activist group intent on educating the public about contemporary Indian problems. Often AIM's methods are controversial, such as forcibly occupying the town of Wounded Knee in South Dakota and Alcatraz Island near San Francisco. Although the publicity of these events brought attention to many injustices, most Indians now try to work within the system.

TODAY'S POWWOWS

In the Algonquin language, the word *Pau Wau* referred to spiritual leaders and medicine men. Non-Indians mistakenly described entire ceremonies with the word, and it eventually became an accepted term by Indians. Today, powwows draw Indians from across the continent to share and reflect on their cultural traditions. Although outsiders might consider the singing, dancing, and colorful clothing to be entertainment, a powwow is a spiritual link to the past for Indian participants and should be treated with respect.

Originally, the powwow dances were held to benefit tribal members and were sponsored by elite warrior societies. Some tribes referred to the dances as Grass Dances. The Sioux referred to them as Omaha Dances, and the Shoshones and Arapahoes called them Wolf Dances. When confined to reservations, Indians were able to devote more time to dancing. The events served as a means of drawing communities together, and they eventually became contests with prizes awarded to the best performers.

Generally, a powwow commences on a Friday evening in an indoor or outdoor arena, which may be a gymnasium, football field, or an area perpetually designated as a powwow ground. The arena is considered sacred and is blessed prior to the powwow. No alcohol, drugs, profanity, or unfitting behavior are allowed in the dance arena. Elders, dancers, singers, and their families sit in lawn chairs immediately surrounding the arena; the rest of the audience sits further away in bleachers or chairs. As singers begin the first song accompanied by traditional drumming, everyone stands, and flag bearers lead the grand entry carrying the American flag, Eagle Staff, Canadian flag, and often the MIA-POW flag. To be chosen as a flag bearer is an honor bestowed on respected elders, traditional dancers, and war veterans. Following the flag bearers come the Indian royalty—tribal and organizational dignitaries and princesses. Finally, hundreds of entrants in traditional dress flood onto the dance arena, and the "Intertribal," a non-contest song, is danced. The excitement mounts as the arena gradually becomes packed with people of all ages, from many tribes.

Groups of drummers, called "drums," represent the different tribes. One group plays (sings and pounds drums) for a dance session; then another group plays for the next one. Various groups continue to play alternately for the different sessions.

Performances of the entrants are then judged according to age and style categories. Although dancing proficiency is important, especially the ability to stop on the last drum beat, it is just as critical to be wearing appropriate traditional clothing, or regalia. Tiny Tots comprise the first group five years old and under; children ages six to eleven are next; then children twelve to seventeen years old. Adults are divided into groups from eighteen to forty-nine years of age. Those over fifty belong in the Golden Age category.

Contests for men and boys include Traditional Dancing, Grass Dancing, and Fancy Dancing, which are often further subdivided into Northern Style and Straight Dancing (Southern Style). A Northern-Style Traditional Dancer represents a warrior scouting before battle. Regalia of such a dancer includes a roach (a narrow headdress of porcupine hair with an eagle feather), a bustle of feathers (usually eagle), a ribbon shirt, a choker and breastplate of bone, a breechcloth, leggings, anklets of sheep bells and angora goat hair, beaded cuffs, armbands, a belt, and moccasins. An eagle wing fan is usually carried. The audience stands for the Traditional Dancers out of respect for them and their eagle feathers. A Straight Dancer also wears a breechcloth, leggings, and porcupine roach, and carries an eagle feather fan. In addition, he wears a ribbon shirt, a choker of beads or silver, a wide beaded belt, and, most obviously, a trailer of otter skin decorated with ribbons, beads, and mirrors, which hangs down the dancer's back.

Contrasting with the older-style regalia of the Traditional Dancers is the apparel of the Grass Dancers. Long strands of brightly colored yarn drape down from yokes, breechcloths, and anklets, neon-orange being one of the favored colors. A porcupine roach or colorful bandanna covers the head of a Grass Dancer, who dances in sliding steps with graceful movements.

Athletic prowess is demonstrated by Fancy Dancers; their fast, original dance steps involve considerable agility and concentration. Their regalia includes anklets, a ribbon shirt, beaded cuffs, armbands, a belt, a yoke, a headband, a porcupine roach with feathers attached on a spinner that makes them whirl, and, most distinctively, a large double bustle of brightly colored feathers.

Female dancers compete in Traditional, Jingle Dress, and Shawl, or Fancy, Dancing. Traditional Dancing is often divided into Northern and Southern Styles and Buckskin and Cloth Dresses. Long fringe decorates the sleeves and bottoms of a buckskin dress, representing a waterfall, flowing constantly, as does the life and love from an Indian mother. Beads are sewn in beautiful patterns onto the yoke of a buckskin dress. The yoke of a cloth dress, usually made of calico, is also richly decorated—with coins, shells, or elk teeth sewn in rows. A buckskin or cloth dress is worn with a beaded belt or concho belt, leggings, moccasins, hair ties, and otter skin hair wraps. A woman wearing either dress style carries a beaded bag and a shawl folded over one arm. Northern-Style Traditional Dancing is danced in one place while those who dance the Southern Style move clockwise around the arena.

Dating from the 1920s to 1950s when it was popular among the Objibwa Nation, the Jingle Dance is noted for the traditional footwork and grace of the dancers. The "jingles," made of snuff can lids, make a loud yet gentle sound, imitating waves of water or thunder that scare away evil spirits. The regalia of a Jingle Dancer includes a beaded or concho belt, scarf, leggings, moccasins, and a fan made of an eagle's wing or tail.

The Shawl Dance represents the legend of a butterfly whose mate died in battle. The shawl symbolizes the cocoon which protected the grieving butterfly as she moved from stone to stone the world over, trying to find beauty so she could continue her life. Graceful movements and fancy footwork are executed by Shawl Dancers as they hold the shawls out from their shoulders and whirl about. Their dresses are made of shiny taffeta and are worn with beaded belts, barrettes, and hair ties.

Besides the "Intertribal," other non-contest events include the Blanket Dance and the Round Dance, in which all dancers as well as the audience can participate, dancing clockwise to the drumbeat. During the Blanket Dance, some of the Indian royalty hold a blanket between them and dance around the arena edge collecting money for people unable to pay their travel expenses to the powwow (Council Tree Powwow 1995).

One of the most popular powwows is held annually in Denver—the March Powwow, which draws hundreds of dancers from all over the United States. In addition to the dramatic events described above, the powwow also includes displays of crafts and jewelry sold in booths surrounding the arena. The public is welcome, and still photos are allowed with the permission of the dancers—but no video cameras should be used. The March Powwow is held in the Denver Coliseum (take Exit 275B off of Interstate 70). For further information, call (303)455-4575.

In addition to the annual March Powwow in Denver, a new event has been organized in western Colorado in the city of Delta—the Council Tree Powwow Dance Competition and Cultural Festival. Named after an old cottonwood tree where it is said that Utes held councils by the Gunnison River near Delta, this event will become an annual affair every September, the sponsors hope.

INDIANS TOMORROW

Today, the vast majority of Indians do not live on reservations. Vine Deloria, Jr., speaks of a future that involves urban Indians and reservation Indians forming "corporations" to explore ways of development that would help those in both areas. He stresses the importance of individual tribal identity along with the need for all tribes to work together. Although it is necessary for non-Indians to learn Indian history, it is equally important for non-Indians to realize that Indians are alive and well today and are more capable of solving their problems and creating their future than anyone else.

PLACES TO VISIT

Colorado

COUNCIL TREE POWWOW DANCE COMPETITION
AND CULTURAL FESTIVAL
360 Main Street
Delta, CO 81416
(800)436-4041

An annual powwow and cultural festival held in September featuring numerous dance competitions.

DENVER INDIAN CENTER
4407 Morrison Road
Denver, CO 80219
(303)936-2688

The center encourages the continuation of cultural traditions through educational programs and provides social services, employment assistance, and health care for seniors as well as a preschool and programs for drug and alcohol abuse.

MARCH POWWOW
Denver, CO
(303)455-4575

Hundreds of Indian dancers from all over the United States compete in various events; the powwow also includes displays of crafts and jewelry sold in booths surrounding the arena.

Oklahoma

INDIAN CITY USA
Highway 8
3 miles east of Anadarko, OK
(405)247-5661

The site features eight reconstructed Indian villages, including Kiowa tipis and Apache wickiups. Crafts and arts are displayed at the museum and gift shop. Special Indian programs occur throughout the year.

KIOWA TRIBAL MUSEUM
Tribal Office Complex
Carnegie, OK 73015
(405)654-2300

The museum exhibits traditional clothing and tools of the Kiowas. In the fall the museum hosts a powwow at which there is traditional dancing as well as food. There is a Kiowa Gourd Dance and an arts and crafts show during the Fourth of July weekend.

Suggestions for Further Reading

Crow Dog, Mary, with Richard Erdoes. *Lakota Woman*. New York: Grove Weidenfeld, 1990.
Deloria, Vine, Jr. *Custer Died for Your Sins*. London: Collier-Macmillan Limited, 1969.

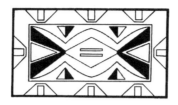

APPENDIX 1

The Process of Archaeological Excavation

▲ ▲

*E*VENTS THAT OCCURRED AND CULTURES THAT EXISTED in Colorado and elsewhere prior to the written word (in America before the arrival of the Spanish and English) are called "prehistoric." Such events and cultures are studied through the science of archaeology, which examines artifacts found on the surface of sites or during excavation. In Greek *archaeo* means "ancient"; *ology* means "the study of something." Any object used or altered by a human is considered an artifact that can provide clues about how people lived in the past. A site (a location with evidence of past human activity) might be a place where hunters butchered a mammoth, where farmers lived in a cliff dwelling, where horsemen camped by a river, or where historic settlers built a log cabin.

A site might answer questions such as how long people lived in a certain region, what kinds of resources (food, materials for making tools and clothes, and so forth) were available to them, or what types of animals they hunted. For example, a find of a large spear point with a groove in the center would tell an archaeologist that hunters of ancient bison or mammoths had possibly camped at a certain site. If artifacts made from materials foreign to a region are found, they could indicate that trade was going on with people from other areas. For example, the presence of shell beads would suggest trade with people from the coast; or finding obsidian, a glassy, volcanic rock preferred for stone tools but not widely available in Colorado, might indicate trade with an area near present-day Yellowstone National Park in Wyoming.

Unfortunately, vandalism of some sites has destroyed such evidence crucial to understanding the lifestyles of ancient cultures. Intrusive vandalism of archaeological sites, often referred to as "pothunting," is the illegal digging of artifacts with no regard for their potential cultural significance. Because burial offerings are sought by vandals to sell on the black market, graves are often destroyed. After a site has been vandalized it has usually lost most scientific value.

Archaeological sites and historic sites more than fifty years old are protected by various laws if they are located on public land—primarily lands held by the United States Forest Service, Bureau of Land Management, and National Park Service—and all burials are protected by state laws. The rampant digging of the Anasazi ruins at Mesa Verde National Park resulted in the Antiquities Act of 1906, which made it illegal to vandalize sites on public land. The more recent Archaeological Resources Protection Act requires that all sites of archaeological interest be protected if located on public lands.

When a project is proposed on public land, archaeologists are hired to systematically search the ground for signs of campfires, house remnants, or artifacts—an activity called archaeological surveying. When something cultural is located, it is plotted on a map and described. It might be a single flake or piece of pottery (called an isolated find), or it might be a village with rubble mounds and huge trash dumps (a site). If appropriate, a site map is then drawn. Because excavations are very expensive, whenever possible, projects that would involve disturbing the ground are avoided at sites eligible for the National Register of Historic Places list. The NRHP is a list of sites that have been declared valuable because of information they might contribute to the knowledge of prehistory or history. In Colorado, the list is kept by the State Historic Preservation Officer in Denver. If a site cannot be avoided, information is gathered from the site through excavation before it is destroyed by construction.

Regardless of whether a site is excavated by professional archaeologists or amateurs (such as private landowners or college students of archaeology), a research design outlining what questions might be answered by digging a site and how the excavation will proceed should be prepared prior to excavation. Such planning is necessary because excavation destroys a site as a source of future knowledge.

American Indians living today have concerns about excavations of sites of their ancestors, particularly those considered sacred and/or containing graves. Unless ancient graves are in danger of being destroyed, graves should not be disturbed at sites. A recent law called the Native American Graves Protection and Repatriation Act (NAGPRA) requires museums and other institutions to inventory their artifacts and human remains and return any considered sacred by American Indians to the groups associated with them. Consultation with local American Indian groups should occur prior to and during excavations. Many federal agencies now require Indian consultants to determine whether sites are sacred; and private archaeological companies often ask Indians to bless areas within their former lands that are proposed for disturbance.

When an area has been chosen for excavation, a grid is laid out according to a reference point called a datum, which can be anything permanent that can be relocated, such as a stake driven into the ground or a large rock. From the datum, strings running east, west, north, and south are extended outward to form squares a meter (thirty-nine inches) wide. Each grid square is then numbered according to its location relative to the datum.

Archaeologists usually excavate only a small portion of a site, selected according to which areas might produce important information. If there are obvious cultural layers that represent periods of occupation, the square is dug to expose those layers, usually in increments of ten centimeters (roughly four inches).

After digging, each shovelful of dirt is put in a screen and shaken to separate the earth from any artifacts that may have been missed such as flakes of stone; stone tools, such as knives or hide scrapers; spear and arrow points; animal bones; beads of shell, bone, or wood; or pieces of pottery. All artifacts are then bagged and labeled for future study.

In order to clarify how the various strata of a site may form, the following hypothetical description is given: Suppose a cave near a dry lake bed was occupied eight thousand years ago by a large family for several months. At this time, the nearby lake was full of water and provided waterfowl and fish for the family's consumption. Cooking hearths full of bird and fish bones were scattered throughout the cave. After the family left, dust blew over the hearths. Then a pack of wolves moved into the cave. Although the young puppies grew up and left the cave, the body of an older wolf that died there remained. The dryness of the cave preserved its bones, and winds covered them with dirt.

Later, another group of hunters sought shelter in the cave. While a young man was making several large spear points, rock flakes from his work fell in a pile at his feet, and one of his points was lost near a cooking hearth. Cattails cut from the lake shore were placed on the cave floor to sleep on. Although the people stayed only a month, they and their descendants returned to the cave every spring to hunt ducks and gather plants around the lake. Then the lake gradually dried up. A slab from the roof fell and covered the beds of cattails. After this, no humans visited the cave for a long time.

Several hundred years later, a family found the cave while hunting desert bighorn sheep. Though there were few sheep in the area, a young hunter managed to kill one with his bow and arrow. The women then butchered the sheep and cooked it in the cave. Because the hunt was not very successful, every bone was cracked to extract the edible marrow within. The women also collected seeds from Indian rice grass and ground them on a stone slab with a mano (a grinding stone). While reworking the end of an old arrowhead to make it dull to stun rabbits, an elderly man accidentally dropped the point into the fire.

Centuries later, archaeologists excavated the cave. In a rodent hole they noticed exposed layers of charcoal, with barren soil underneath and then more charcoal. They excavated according to these layers, or strata, knowing that the top layer was the most recent and that artifacts found below this layer would be increasingly older. In one unit the archaeologists found a reworked arrow point with a blunt end, probably fashioned to stun a small mammal. The small size of the point indicated that the last people to occupy the cave used the bow and arrow, probably no more than fifteen hundred years ago, at the time when arrows largely replaced spears. Then the archaeologists carefully excavated a mano, placing it in a bag with the dirt adhering to it. In the lab microscopic examination of the dirt revealed Indian rice grass pollen on the grinding surface. Bones of bighorn sheep were also discovered in the cooking hearths. The fact that the bones had been crushed to dig out the marrow was evidence that food might have been scarce at the time since the crushing of all bones for marrow extraction indicates stress.

The next layer excavated was full of animal bones and "sterile" soil—soil with no cultural or man-made materials. The archaeologists then came upon a layer of rock. With a pick axe they broke through it to see if part of the cave roof had fallen. Below the rock was an almost perfectly preserved bed of cattails—evidence that there was water in the lake during this group's stay. Several spear points, which are much larger than arrow points, indicated that this occupation must have occurred when spear throwers were used, long before bows and arrows were made. Further, knife-cut bird bones told the archaeologists that the people who lived in the cave ate birds.

Below this layer was another sterile layer. But dried droppings and the bones of a huge wolf provided information about animals that had lived there. Twenty centimeters lower lay a hearth with large chunks of charcoal and bird and fish bones—more evidence that humans had cooked here. The charcoal was removed and sent to a lab to be radio-carbon dated, resulting in the information that the firepit was almost eight thousand years old.

Radiocarbon dating (often called carbon-14 dating) is a commonly used dating method. All living things (trees, animals, people) absorb small amounts of radioactive carbon during their lives. When death occurs, the radioactive carbon decays at a measured rate. A piece of bone, wood, or charcoal can be mechanically processed to determine how much carbon is gone and to calculate the specimen's age. Sometimes, when rodents burrow into the layers and transport more recent dirt to older layers, false (more recent) dates are obtained. But this problem can be avoided by dating several charcoal samples.

Tree-ring dating, or dendrochronology, is used to determine the age of logs preserved in the roofs or walls of houses. (The air in the Southwest is so dry that wood can be preserved for hundreds of years.) As a tree grows, the rings grow wide during wet years and narrow during dry years. A chart of tree rings with known dates for the Southwest has been established. The ring pattern from a log is held up next to this chart, and the outermost ring coincides with the year the tree was cut (Figure 95, page 256). Studies of ancient tree rings have shown that

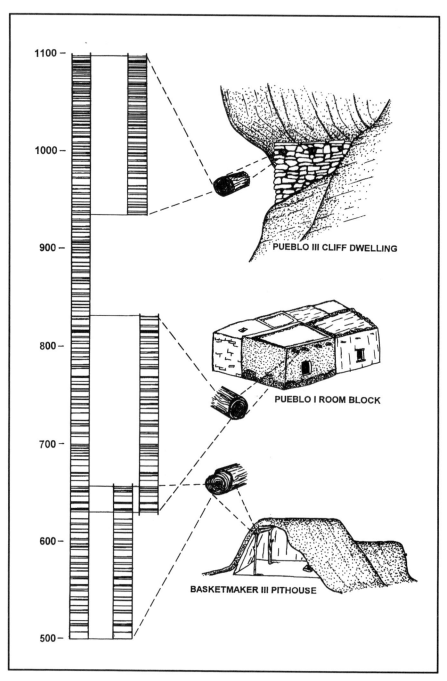

1100 —

1000 —

900 —

800 —

700 —

600 —

500 —

PUEBLO III CLIFF DWELLING

PUEBLO I ROOM BLOCK

BASKETMAKER III PITHOUSE

Figure 95:
Dendrochronology is the science of dating wood by comparing tree rings of a cut pole to a
standard chart of known ring width. Dry years produce narrow rings; moist years produce
wide rings. The outer ring coincides with the year the tree was cut.

there was a serious drought around seven hundred years ago—the same time that a large part of the Southwest was abandoned after having been farmed for over a thousand years. Archaeological research has shown that the area also was overpopulated, and its resources were depleted. Our present environmental problems are similar, and thus archaeological research can help us learn from prehistoric "mistakes."

Although spear points and arrowheads cannot be dated exactly, their approximate age is indicated by changes in style and by the fact that certain types of spear points were used to kill mammoths and giant bison which are now extinct—something we know from points found embedded in the bones of these animals. Because smaller projectile points are found in strata that lie above larger points, we know that projectile points became smaller as time passed. When projectile points are found in the same context as other artifacts whose age is known, they can be dated more precisely. For example, many points have been found in charcoal layers that are radiocarbon dated and are presumed to be the same age as the charcoal. Also, when archaeologists discover a point while excavating, they can usually find pictures of similar looking points that have been dated in other reports. Most early people living in the west-central and southwestern parts of North America made the same kinds of points and changed their styles about the same time (Figures 2, 8, 21, pages 7, 21, 58). For example, across most of the continent, smaller arrowheads replaced spear points when the bow and arrow came to be used about fifteen hundred years ago.

After a site is excavated, the artifacts collected are studied, and pollen and soil samples are analyzed. Tree-ring and radiocarbon dates are matched with artifacts so that the story of the people who lived there can be reconstructed. Finally, reports are written so that work from a single site augments our knowledge of ancient cultures as a whole.

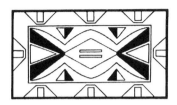

APPENDIX 2

Indian Place Names in Colorado

▲ ▲

(Based on William Bright, *Colorado Place Names*)

Mount Achonee: Indian Peaks Wilderness, Grand County. Cheyenne sub-chief, Ochanee ("One-Eye"), killed during Sand Creek Massacre.

Apishapa River: Southern tributary of Arkansas River, southeastern Colorado. Ute meaning "standing or stagnant water" (local slang is Fish Paw River).

Arapahoe: On U.S. 40, Cheyenne County. Tribe that ranged throughout eastern Colorado.

Arapaho Pass: Between Boulder and Grand counties.

North and South Arapaho Peaks: Between Boulder and Grand counties.

Arikaree: On U.S. 36 in Washington County. Tribe that occupied the Dakotas.

Arikaree Peak: In Boulder and Grand counties.

Arikaree River: In Yuma County.

Arkansas River: Plural of Arkansas, originally *aakansa*, Algonquin name for Sioux group.

Atchee: Railroad ghost town south of Baxter Pass, Mesa County. Northern Ute leader.

Camp Amache: Near Granada, Prowers County. World War II Japanese-American relocation camp. Amache, daughter of Ochinee (Lone Wolf), a Cheyenne leader; married John Wesley Powers.

Chattanooga: On U.S. 550, San Juan County. From Creek word meaning "rock rising to a point."

Chautauqua Park: A recreation center in Boulder. Iroquois word used to describe traveling cultural presentations of the late 1800s.

Chemung: In Cheyenne County. Named for New York town; Algonquin word for "big horn."

Cherokee Park: Named for Cherokee Indian who traveled through the area after trying to relocate on the Pacific Coast (he later established the Cherokee Nation in Oklahoma).

Cheyenne Wells: In Cheyenne County. Tribe that ranged throughout eastern Colorado.

Chief Hosa: On U.S. 40, Jefferson County. Named for Arapahoe leader, Ho'sa (Little Crow).

Chipeta: Wife of Uncompahgre Ute leader Ouray. From *chipit* ("water springing up").

Mount Chipeta: On Continental Divide, Chaffee County.

Chipeta Lakes: Montrose County.

Chipeta Park: On U.S. 24, El Paso County.

Cochetopa Pass: On Continental Divide, Saguache County. Ute *kuchupupan* ("buffalo passing"; *kuch* means "buffalo"). Pass connects Gunnison Valley to San Luis Valley; old buffalo and Indian trail.

Colorow Mountain: In Rio Blanco County. Named for Comanche adopted by the Northern Utes; well known in Colorado settlements in late 1800s.

Comanche: In Adams County. Tribe that ranged from southeastern Colorado into Oklahoma, Kansas, Texas, and New Mexico.

Comanche Peak: In Larimer County.

Cuerno Verde Park: South of Pueblo. Comanche leader killed by Spanish military leader De Anza in 1779, near this site. Means "greenhorn" in Spanish.

Greenhorn Mountain: West of Cuerno Verde Park.

Curecanti Pass: West of Gunnison, Gunnison County. Named for Curicata, an Uncompahgre Ute leader.

Curecanti Recreation Area: Morrow Point and Blue Mesa reservoirs.

Curecanti Needle: Rock feature near Blue Mesa Reservoir.

Mount Enentah: In Rocky Mountain National Park. From Arapahoe *enetahnotaiyah* ("man mountain"); pine trees at the peak appear as hair on a man's head.

Mount Guero: In Gunnison County. Named for Ute chief; Spanish meaning "fair in complexion."

Haiyaha Lake: In Rocky Mountain National Park. Arapahoe meaning "rock."

Haynach Lakes: In Rocky Mountain National Park. Arapahoe *hiiinech*, meaning "snow water."

Hiamovi Mountain: In Grand County. Name of Cheyenne who reportedly provided information for Natalie Curtis's 1908 work *The Indians' Book* (she claimed it meant "high chief").

Hiawatha: In Moffat County. Named after the Algonquin hero in the poem by Longfellow.

Hovenweep Canyon (National Monument): On Colorado-Utah border west of Cortez and the Ute Mountain Ute Reservation. From Ute *wii yap* meaning "canyon."

Ignacio: Southern Ute Reservation headquarters, La Plata County (southeast of Durango). Named for Ignacio, leader of the Weenuche band of Southern Utes.

Indian Peaks: Cluster of mountains straddling the Continental Divide in Grand and Boulder counties. Names from north to south are Paiute, Pawnee, Shoshone, Apache, Navajo, Kiowa, Arickaree, and Arapaho.

Kaibab: In Eagle County, probably from Ute *kaava'avich* meaning "mountain range."

Kannah Creek: On south side of Grand Mesa, southeast of Grand Junction. Possibly from Ute *kanav* meaning "willow," or *Kana wiya*, the "valley of willows."

Kawuneechee Valley: In Grand County. Named for an Arapahoe, Cawoonache (*koo'oh* meaning "wolf" or "coyote," *neechee* meaning "leader").

Kenosha Pass: In Park County. Named by a Wisconsin-born stage dri-
ver after a town in that state (Algonquin for "pike," the fish).

Kenosha Peak: Probably named after the pass.

Kinikinik: Along Colorado 14 in Larimer County. Delaware (Algonquin word for "tobacco."

Kiowa: Along Colorado 86 in Elbert County. Named for tribe that
ranged through southeastern Colorado, New Mexico, Kansas,
Oklahoma, and Texas.

Left Hand Creek: In the foothills of the Rocky Mountains, Boulder
County. Possibly named after Arapahoe leader Left Hand (Niwot),
or the left-handed fur trader and trapper Andrew Sublette.

Manitou Park: In Teller County. Named for Ute word referring to the
great Spirit.

Manitou Springs: On U.S. 24 in El Paso County.

Medicine Bow Mountains: Straddling Colorado-Wyoming border in
northeastern Colorado. Named for Medicine Bow River in
Wyoming. Thought to be from Indian phrase referring to a bow
that could capture medicine, or power.

Minnesota Creek: In Gunnison County. Named for the state, which
was named after the Dakota Sioux words *mni sota* meaning
"cloudy water."

Minnesota Pass: Named for the creek or vice versa.

Mishawaka: In Larimer County. Probably named for an Indiana town,
which was named for a Potawatomi phrase meaning "dead trees
place."

Missouri Mountain: In Chaffee County. Named for the tribe that lived
near the Missouri River (Algonquin).

Montezuma: On Snake River in Summit County. Named for Aztec emperor of Mexico (the Anasazi who lived in southwestern Colorado were originally thought to have been Aztecs).

Montezuma County: In southwestern Colorado.

Moqui Canyon: In Montezuma County. Named for the Hopis, a Pueblo group in northern Arizona (incorrect historic name).

Muckawanago Creek: In Pitkin County. Named for the Wisconsin tribe's word for "bear lair," *mukwanago.*

Nakai Peak: In Grand County. A Navajo word meaning "Mexican."

Nanita Lake: In Rocky Mountain National Park. Possibly a variation of a Navajo word referring to the Plains Indians.

Narraguinnep Canyon: In Dolores County. From a Ute word, *naragwinap*, meaning "battleground."

Navajo Peak: Part of Indian Peaks on Continental Divide in Grand and Boulder counties. Named for tribe that once occupied southwestern Colorado (and still occupies northeastern Arizona and northwestern New Mexico).

Neenoshe Reservoir: In Kiowa County. Osage *ni ozho* meaning "principal water."

Neeskah Reservoir: In Kiowa County. Osage *ni ska* meaning "white water."

Neesopah Reservoir: In Kiowa County. Osage *ni shupe* meaning "entrails water."

Mount Neota: On Continental Divide in Larimer and Grand counties. From Arapahoe *hoho'eniinote'hitee* meaning "mountain sheep's heart."

Mount Neva: On Continental Divide in Boulder and Grand counties. Named for Neva or Nevo, an Arapahoe leader and friend of Left Hand (Niwot).

Never Summer Mountains: In Jackson and Grand counties. A translation of the Arapahoe description of the range.

Mount Nisa: In Grand County. From Arapahoe *ni isso o* meaning "twin" (the mountain has two peaks).

Niwot: In Boulder County. Arapahoe for Left Hand, an Arapahoe leader. From *noowoothinoo* meaning "I am left-handed."

Niwot Mountain: Indian Peaks area, Boulder County.

Nokher Crags: In Never Summer Range, Jackson County. From Arapahoe *hoh'onookee* meaning "eagle rock."

Nokoni Lake: In Rocky Mountain National Park. Name of a Comanche band meaning "traveling in a circle."

Ogalalla Peak: On Continental Divide in Grand and Boulder counties. Band of Teton Sioux, *Oglala* meaning "they scatter their own."

Ogalalla Aquifer: Vast store of underground water spanning much of the Great Plains area, including eastern Colorado.

Ohio: In Gunnison County. Iroquois word meaning "beautiful river."

Ohio Peak: In San Juan County.

Olathe: On U.S. 50 in Montrose County between Delta and Montrose. Originally named Brown, then Colorow, after the Comanche adopted by the Northern Utes who used to frequent Colorado settlements, finally Olathe after a town in Kansas; Shawnee for "beautiful."

Ouray: Old mining town in Ouray County on U.S. 550. According to Ouray, the leader of the Uncompahgre band of Northern Utes, it was the first word he spoke as a baby. May be from *uri* meaning "main pole of a tipi" or *uur* meaning "arrow."

Ouray County.

Ouray Peak: In Chaffee County.

O-Wi-Yu-Kuts Plateau: In Moffat County. Possibly after an Indian leader, Awaiukut, or from Ute *uwaayakack* meaning "they're not coming."

Pahlone Peak: In Chaffee County. Possibly Ute *paru ni* meaning "thunder" or after Ouray's son, Peron.

Paiute Peak: On Continental Divide in Grand and Boulder counties. Named after a tribe in Nevada.

Parika Peak: In Jackson County. Pawnee *paariiku* meaning "horn" (possibly referring to shape of peak).

Pawnee Buttes: In Weld County, north of Raymer. Named for tribe that farmed in Kansas and Nebraska and hunted in Colorado.

Pawnee Peak: One of the Indian Peaks.

Pawnee Creek: Tributary of South Platte River.

Piceance Creek: In Rio Blanco County. Possibly *pice ance*, reportedly an Indian phrase (Ute?) meaning "tall grass" (also may have a crude non-Indian folk origin).

Poncha Mountain: In Chaffee County. Possibly from a Ute word meaning "tobacco."

Poncha Pass: In Chaffee and Saquache counties.

Poncha Springs: In Chaffee County at U.S. 50 and U.S. 285.

Punche Valley: In Conejos County. Possibly referring to *poncha*, a Ute word meaning "tobacco."

Rawah Peaks: In Larimer County. Ute *ura'wa* meaning "crest of a mountain ridge."

Saguache: On U.S. 285 in Saguache County. Ute *sagwach* meaning "the colors of blue or green."

Saguache County.

Santanta Peak: In Grand County. Possibly after Satank, from Kiowa *sei-tai-dei* meaning "white bear."

Satank: In Garfield County. Name of a Kiowa leader.

Sawatch Range: In Gunnison, Chaffee, and Saguache counties. Different spelling of Saguache.

Shawnee: On U.S. 285 in Park County. Named for tribe that originally inhabited Tennessee and South Carolina and was forced to go to a Kansas reservation.

Shoshone: On U.S. 6 in Garfield County. Named for tribe that ranged through Wyoming, northeastern Utah, and northwestern Colorado.

Shoshoni Peak: One of Indian Peaks in Grand County.

Sundance Mountain: In Rocky Mountain National Park, Larimer County. Named for one of the most important ceremonies of many Plains tribes.

Tabeguache Peak: In Chaffee County. Ute band *mogwatavungwants-ingwu* meaning "cedar bark sun-slope people."

Tabernash: On U.S. 40 in Grand County. Named for Ute killed by settler (possibly *tapo' n'ach* meaning "having a cramp").

Tachosa Valley: In Larimer and Boulder counties, east of Longs Peak. Possibly Kiowa word meaning "dwellers on the mountaintops" (once considered as a name for Colorado Territory).

Talahassee Creek: Tributary of Arkansas River in Fremont County, southeastern Colorado. From Florida city; Muskogee name for "old town."

Tennessee Pass: On Continental Divide in Eagle and Lake counties. Named after home state of Tennessee miners (originally named after Cherokee leader).

Teocalli Mountain: In Gunnison County. Aztec word meaning "temple."

Terra Tomah Mountain: In Rocky Mountain National Park. Named after words to a Cahuilla Indian song (southern California tribe), meaning unknown.

Tigiwon: In Eagle County (base camp for ascent of Mount of the Holy Cross). From Ute *Tugu'vun* meaning "friend."

Tioga: In Huerfano County. Named for town in Pennsylvania named for Iroquois word meaning "at the forks."

Toltec: In Huerfano County. Named for tribe in Mexico, *tolteca* meaning "people of the reeds."

Towaoc (TOY-yahk): Headquarters for Ute Mountain Utes, west of Cortez. From Ute *tu wayak* meaning "thank you" or "all right."

Uintah Range: In Moffat County (mostly in Utah). From Ute *yuvintu* meaning "pine canyon-mouth."

Unaweep Canyon: In Mesa County, southeast of Grand Junction. From Ute *kuna-wiiyap* meaning "fire canyon."

Uncompahgre Peak: In Hinsdale County, west of Lake City. From Ute *aka-paa-garur* meaning "red water source" from *aka-gar* ("red") and *paagarur* ("lake"), reportedly describing the source of the Uncompahgre River in the San Juan Mountains.

Uncompahgre River: Trends through San Juan, Montrose, and Delta counties, intersecting Gunnison River at Delta. (Chipeta and Ouray's farm was on the Uncompahgre River, south of Montrose.)

Uneva Peak: In Summit County. Possibly from Ute *yunav* meaning "mountainous country."

Ute Creek: Name of fourteen streams in Colorado.

Ute Peak: Three mountains.

Ute Mountain: In Boulder County.

Ute Pass: Five in the state (highest in Saguache County).

Wahatoya Creek: In Huerfano County; from Ute word meaning "twin mountains."

Wasatch Mountain: In Garfield County; Ute leader during early 1800s.

Watanga Mountain: In Garfield County; Arapahoe leader Wo'ataankoo, "Black Coyote."

Waunita Hot Springs: In Gunnison County; reportedly an Indian woman's name but possibly the Spanish name Juanita misspelled.

Mount Wuh: In Rocky Mountain National Park, Larimer County; Arapahoe *wox* meaning "bear."

Yampa: On Colorado 131 in Routt County; Ute band, after root *nanta, yanta,* or *yampa* in Ute (Shoshone is *wampa*).

Yarmony: In Eagle County; named for Ute Yaamani, "Quiet Man," who frequented the settlements of the area.

Yarmony Mountain: In Eagle County.

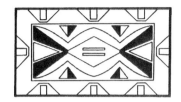

Bibliography

▲ ▲

Books and Articles

Aikens, C. Melvin. "Fremont Culture: Restatement of Some Problems." *American Antiquity* 37, no. 1 (1972): 61–66.

———."Plains Relationships of the Fremont Culture: A Hypothesis." *American Antiquity* 32, no. 2 (1967): 198–209.

Bains, Rae. *Indians of the Plains.* Nahwah, N.J.: Troll Associates, 1985.

Bakker, Elna, and Richard G. Lillard. *The Great Southwest.* Palo Alto, Calif.: American West, 1972.

Baldwin, Gordon C. *The Ancient Ones: Basketmakers and Cliff Dwellers of the Southwest.* New York: W. W. Norton and Company, 1963.

Bancroft-Hunt, Norman. *The Indians of the Great Plains.* Norman: University of Oklahoma Press, 1992.

Barnes, F. A. *Canyon Country Prehistoric Rock Art.* Salt Lake City, Utah: Wasatch Publishers, 1982.

Benedict, James B. "Footprints in the Snow: High-Altitude Cultural Ecology of the Colorado Front Range, USA." *Arctic and Alpine Research* 24, no. 1 (1992): 1–16.

Black, Kevin. "Mitigation Archaeological Excavations at Two Sites for the Cottonwood Pass Project, Chaffee and Gunnison Counties, Colorado," 1986. Manuscript on file at the Colorado Historical Society, Denver.

Bright, William. *Colorado Place Names.* Boulder, Colo.: Johnson Books, 1993.

Buckles, William G. "The Uncompahgre Complex: Historic Ute Archaeology and Prehistoric Archaeology on the Uncompahgre Plateau in West Central Colorado." Ph.D. diss., University of Colorado, 1971.

Cash, Joseph H., and Gerald W. Wolff. *The Comanche People.* Phoenix, Ariz.: Indian Tribal Series, 1974.

Cassells, E. Steve. *The Archaeology of Colorado.* Boulder, Colo.: Johnson Books, 1983.

———. "Hypothetical Sawtooth Game Drive Operation Scenario." Unpublished manuscript.

Coel, Margaret. *Chief Left Hand, Southern Arapaho.* Norman: University of Oklahoma Press, 1981.

Cole, Sally J. *Legacy on Stone: Rock Art of the Colorado Plateau and Four Corners Region.* Boulder, Colo.: Johnson Books, 1990.

———. *Rock Art of the Pinyon Canyon Archaeological Project and Southeast Colorado.* An unpublished report prepared for the University of Denver Archaeological Institute, Denver, Colorado.

Colorado Archaeological Society. Abstracts for CAS Annual Meeting. "High Altitude Archaeology: A Research Symposium," October 28–30, 1994.

Conner, Carl E., and Diana L. Langdon. "Battlement Mesa Community Project: Cultural Resources Study," 1983. Manuscript on file at the Colorado Historical Society, Denver.

Cordell, Linda S. *Prehistory of the Southwest.* Orlando, San Diego, New York, Austin, Boston, London, Sydney, Tokyo, Toronto: Academic Press/Harcourt, Brace, Jovanovich, 1984.

Council Tree Powwow Dance Competition and Cultural Festival. "Powwow General Information." Delta, Colo.: Council Tree Powwow Sponsors, 1995.

Crow Dog, Mary, with Richard Erdoes. *Lakota Woman.* New York: Grove Weidenfeld, 1990.

Day, Jane S., Paul D. Friedman, Marcia J. Tate. *Rock Art of the Western Canyons.* Boulder, Colo.: Johnson Books, 1989.

Deloria, Vine, Jr. *Custer Died for Your Sins.* London: Collier-Macmillan Limited, 1969.

Denver Art Museum. *Colorado's Native Heritage: A Handbook for Students and Teachers.* Denver, Colo.: Denver Art Museum, 1981.

Dozier, Edward P. *The Pueblo Indians of North America.* New York: Holt, Rinehart and Winston, 1970.

Drass, Richard R., and Peggy Flynn. "Temporal and Geographic Variations in Subsistence Practices for Plains Villagers in the Southern Plains." *Plains Anthropology, Journal of the Plains Anthropologist* 35, no. 128 (1990): 179–90.

Eastern Shoshone Cultural Resource Center. *The Eastern Shoshone.* Ft. Washakie, Wyo.: Eastern Shoshone Cultural Resource Center, n.d.

Ebeling, Walter. *Handbook of Indian Foods and Fibers in Arid America.* Berkeley and Los Angeles: University of California Press, 1986.

Elston, Robert G. "Prehistory of the Western Area." In *Great Basin,* edited by Warren L. D'Azevedo. *Handbook of North American Indians.* Vol. 11. Washington, D.C.: Smithsonian Institution/Government Printing Office, 1986.

Ferguson, William M., and Arthur H. Rohn. *Anasazi Ruins of the Southwest in Color.* Albuquerque: University of New Mexico Press, 1990.

Fowler, Oretta. *The Arapaho.* New York and Philadelphia: Chelsea House Publishers, 1989.

Frison, George C. "Experimental Use of Clovis Weaponry and Tools on African Elephants." *American Antiquity* 54, no. 4 (1989): 766–84.

———. *Prehistoric Hunters of the High Plains.* Laramie, Wyo.: Academic Press/Harcourt, Brace, Jovanovich, 1978.

Garner, Joe. "Gambling: Just Another Way to Survive." *Rocky Mountain News* (Denver, Colorado), November 25, 1990, 54.

Gerson, Noel B. *Kit Carson: Folk Hero and Man.* Garden City, N.Y.: Doubleday, 1964.

Gooding, John D., and William Lane Shields. *Sisyphus Shelter*. Colorado Cultural Resource Series No. 18. Denver, Colo.: Bureau of Land Management, 1985.

Gunnerson, James H. *The Fremont Culture: A Study in Culture Dynamics on the Northern Anasazi Frontier*. Papers of the Peabody Museum of American Archaeology and Ethnology 52, no.2. Cambridge, Mass.: Peabody Museum, 1969.

Grinnell, George Bird. *The Cheyenne Indians: Their History and Ways of Life*. Vol. 2. Lincoln and London: University of Nebraska Press, 1972.

Hauck, F. R. *Cultural Resource Evaluation in Central Utah, 1977*. Utah Bureau of Land Management, Cultural Resource Series No. 3. Salt Lake City, Utah: Bureau of Land Management, 1979.

Hoig, Stan. *The Cheyenne*. New York and Philadelphia: Chelsea House Publishers, 1989.

Houk, Rose. *Anasazi*. Tucson, Ariz.: Southwest Parks and Monuments Association, 1992.

Hubbard, Shirley. *Indians of Colorado: The Colorado Chronicles Volume 3*. Frederick, Colo.: Platte 'N Press, 1981.

Hughes, J. Donald. *American Indians in Colorado*. Boulder, Colo.: Pruett Publishing Company, 1987.

Hurst, C. T. "Completion of Tabeguache Cave II." *Southwestern Lore* 11, no. 1 (1945): 8–12.

Hyde, George. *Life of George Bent, Written from His Letters*. Norman: University of Oklahoma Press, 1968. Reprint, 1987.

Irk, Donald R. *Wild Edible Plants of the Western United States*. Happy Camp, Calif.: Naturegraph Publishers, 1975.

Iverson, Peter. *The Plains Indians of the Twentieth Century*. Norman: University of Oklahoma Press, 1985.

Jefferson, James, Robert W. Delaney, and Gregory C. Thompson. *The Southern Utes: A Tribal History*. Ignacio, Colo.: Southern Ute Tribe, 1972.

Jodry, Margaret A., and Dennis J. Stanford. "Stewarts' Cattle Guard Site." In *Ice Age Hunters of the Rockies*, edited by Dennis J. Stanford and Jane S. Day. Denver, Colo.: Denver Museum of Natural History and University Press of Colorado, 1992.

Kammer, Jerry. *The Second Long Walk: The Navajo-Hopi Land Dispute*. Albuquerque: University of New Mexico Press, 1980.

Kelly, Klara Bonsak, and Harris Francis. *Navajo Sacred Places*. Bloomington and Indianapolis: Indiana University Press, 1994.

"Kiowas Today." Carnegie, Okla.: Kiowa Tribe, n.d.

Koch, Ronald P. *Dress Clothing of the Plains Indians*. Norman: University of Oklahoma Press, 1977.

Lavender, David. *Bent's Fort*. Lincoln and London: University of Nebraska Press, 1954.

Lowie, Robert H. *Indians of the Plains*. Lincoln and London: University of Nebraska Press, 1982.

———. "The Northern Shoshone." In *Anthropological Papers of the American Museum of Natural History*. Vol. 2, part 2. New York: American Museum of Natural History, 1909.

Madsen, Brigham D. *The Northern Shoshoni*. Caldwell, Id.: Caxton Printers, 1980.

Mails, Thomas. *Mystic Warriors of the Plains*. New York: Marlowe and Company, 1995.

Marriott, Alice. *Indians of the Four Corners*. New York: Thomas Y. Crowell Company, 1952. Reprint, Santa Fe, N.M.: Ancient City Press, 1996.

Marsh, Charles. *People of the Shining Mountains*. Boulder, Colo.: Pruett Publishing Co., 1982.

Martorano, Marilyn. "Scarred Ponderosa Pine Trees, Reflecting Cultural Utilization of Bark." Master's thesis. Colorado State University, 1981.

Matlock, Gary. *Enemy Ancestors*. Flagstaff, Ariz.: Northland Publishing Co., 1988.

Matson, R. G. *The Origins of Southwestern Agriculture*. Tucson and London: University of Arizona Press, 1991.

Mayhall, Mildred P. *The Kiowas*. Norman: University of Oklahoma Press, 1975.

Metcalf, Michael D., and Kevin D. Black. *Archaeological Excavations at the Yarmony Pit House Site, Eagle County, Colorado*. Colorado Bureau of Land Management Cultural Resource Series No. 31. Denver, Colo.: Bureau of Land Management, 1991.

Moore, Michael. *Medicinal Plants of the Mountain West*. Santa Fe, N.M.: Museum of New Mexico Press, 1979.

Morss, Noel. *The Ancient Culture of the Fremont River in Utah*. Papers of the Peabody Museum of American Archaeology and Ethnology. Cambridge, Mass.: Peabody Museum, 1931.

Nabhan, Gary Paul. *Enduring Seeds: Native American Agriculture and Wild Plant Conservation*. San Francisco: North Point Press, 1989.

Noble, David Grant. *Ancient Ruins of the Southwest*. Flagstaff, Ariz.: Northland Publishing Co., 1991.

————, ed. *Understanding the Anasazi of Mesa Verde and Hovenweep*. Santa Fe, N.M.: Ancient City Press, 1991.

————, ed. *Houses Beneath the Rock: The Anasazi of Canyon de Chelly and Navajo National Monument*. Santa Fe, N.M.: Ancient City Press, 1991.

O'Neil, Brian. "The Archaeology of the Grand Junction Resource Area: Crossroads to the Colorado Plateau and the Southern Rocky Mountains—A Class I Overview." Unpublished manuscript.

Ortiz, Alfonso, ed. *Handbook of North American Indians*. Vol. 10. *Southwest*. Washington, D.C.: Smithsonian Institution, 1983.

Parker, Kathleen. *The Only True People: A History of the Native Americans of the Colorado Plateau*. Moab, Utah: Thunder Mesa Publishing, 1991.

Pettit, Jan. *Utes: The Mountain People*. Boulder, Colo.: Johnson Books, 1990.

Reed, Alan. *West Central Colorado Prehistoric Context*. Denver, Colo.: State Historical Society of Colorado, 1984.

Sandoz, Mari. *Cheyenne Autumn*. New York: Hastings House, 1953.

Schaafsma, Polly. *Indian Rock Art of the Southwest*. Albuquerque: University of New Mexico Press, 1980.

Shanks, Ralph, and Lisa Shanks. *North American Indian Travel Guide*. Petaluma, Calif.: Costano Books, 1986.

Shoshone Tribal Cultural Center. *Shoshone Tribal Cultural Center*. Ft. Washakie, Wyo.: Shoshone Tribal Cultural Center, n.d.

Slifer, Dennis, and James Duffield. *Kokopelli: Fluteplayer Images in Rock Art*. Santa Fe, N.M.: Ancient City Press, 1994.

Smith, Anne M. *Ethnography of the Northern Utes*. Santa Fe: Museum of New Mexico Press, 1974.

Smith, David P. *Ouray: Chief of the Utes*. Ouray, Colo.: Wayfinder Press, 1987.

Southern Ute Tribe. *Exploration in Southern Ute History*. Ignacio, Colo.: Piñon Press, 1989.

Sprague, Marshall. *Massacre: The Tragedy at White River*. Lincoln and London: University of Nebraska Press, 1957.

Stanford, Dennis J., and Jane S. Day, eds. *Ice Age Hunters of the Rockies.* Denver, Colo.: Denver Museum of Natural History and University Press of Colorado, 1992.

Terrell, John. *The Navajos: The Past and Present of a Great People.* New York, London: Harper and Row, 1970.

Titiev, Mischa. *Old Oraibi: A Study of the Hopi Indians of Third Mesa.* Albuquerque: University of New Mexico Press, 1992.

Trenholm, Virginia Cole. *The Arapahoes: Our People.* Norman: University of Oklahoma Press, 1986.

Trenholm, Virginia Cole, and Maurine Carley. *The Shoshonis: Sentinels of the Rockies.* Norman: University of Oklahoma Press, 1964.

Truesdale, James A. *Archaeological Investigations at Two Sites in Dinosaur National Monument: 42UN1724 and 5MF2645.* Division of Cultural Resources Selection Series No. 4. Denver, Colo.: National Park service, 1993.

Tyson, Carl N. *The Pawnee People.* Phoenix, Ariz.: Indian Tribal Series, 1974.

Wallace, Ernest, and E. Adamson Hoebel. *The Comanches: Lords of the Plains.* Norman: University of Oklahoma Press, 1976.

Wormington, H. M. *Ancient Man in North America.* Denver, Colo.: Denver Museum of Natural History, 1957.

———. *A Reappraisal of the Fremont Culture.* Denver, Colo.: Denver Museum of Natural History, 1955.

Wormington, H. M., and Robert H. Lister. *Archaeological Investigations on the Uncompahgre Plateau in West Central Colorado.* Denver, Colo.: Denver Museum of Natural History, 1956.

Wright, Muriel H. *A Guide to the Indian Tribes of Oklahoma.* Norman: University of Oklahoma Press, 1951.

Zier, Christain J., Stephen M. Kalasz, Margaret A. Van Ness, Anne H. Peebles, and Elaine Anderson. "The Avery Ranch Site Revisited." *Plains Anthropology, Journal of the Plains Anthropologist* 35, no. 128 (1990): 147–73.

Interviews and Correspondence

Ahtone, Deborah. Correspondence regarding the history, culture, and contemporary situation of the Kiowas, 1994.

Ahtone, Jacob. Correspondence regarding the history, culture, and contemporary situation of the Kiowas, 1994.

Brockman, Karen. Personal communication regarding excavations of Archaic pithouses near Maybell, 1994.

Chapoose, Betsy. Personal communication regarding clothing, personal adornment, and cradleboards of the Utes, 1994.

Cole, Sally J. Personal communication regarding the hunting methods of Archaic people.

Conner, Carl. Personal communication regarding excavation of the Kewclaw site, 1994.

Duncan, Clifford. Personal communication regarding bark procurement by the Northern Utes, 1994.

Franklin, Virgil, Sr. Personal communication regarding the history, culture, and contemporary situation of the Southern Arapahoes, 1994.

Haas, Merle. Personal communication and correspondence regarding the history, culture, and contemporary situation of the Northern Arapahoes, 1994.

Hartmann, Lynn. Personal communication regarding the Ute Mountain Ute tribal complex and the contemporary situation of the Ute Mountain Utes, 1994.

Hauck, Richard. Personal communication regarding possible Fremont lunar and solar alignments in Canyon Pintado, 1992.

Horn, Jonathan. Personal communication regarding tipi excavation on the Uncompahgre Plateau and game drive site near a Gunnison River canyon, 1992.

Moss, Alonzo, Sr. Personal communication via Merle Haas regarding legends and culture of the Northern Arapahoes.

Moss, Richard. Personal communication via Merle Haas regarding legends and culture of the Northern Arapahoes, 1994.

Nixon, Paul. Personal communication regarding the museum and site at the Cahokia Mound State Historic Site in Illinois, where he is the Assistant Site Manager, 1995.

Parker, Jennie. Personal communication regarding the history, culture, and contemporary situation of the Northern Cheyennes, 1994.

Sinkey, Ira. Personal communication regarding the contemporary situation of the Southern Arapahoes, 1994.

Small, Steve. Personal communication regarding the contemporary situation of the Northern Cheyennes, 1994.

Vigil, Charlotte. Personal communication regarding the traditional clothing of the Jicarilla Apaches, 1995.

Index

▲

More Titles About the American Indians
Available from Ancient City Press

Kokopelli: Fluteplayer Images in Rock Art
Dennis Slifer and James Duffield, ISBN 0-941270-80-7 paperback

A Cry from the Earth: Music of the North American Indians
John Bierhorst, ISBN 0-941270-53-X paperback

Pueblo Mothers and Children: Essays by Elsie Clews Parsons
Edited by Barbara Babcock, ISBN 0-941270-65-3 paperback

Indian Tales from Picuris Pueblo
Collected by John Harrington, ISBN 0-941270-50-5 paperback

Indian Running: Native American History and Tradition
Peter Nabokov, ISBN 0-941270-41-6 paperback

Life in the Pueblos
Ruth Underhill, ISBN 0-941270-68-8 paperback

Glimpses of the Ancient Southwest
David Stuart, ISBN 0-941270-21-1 paperback

Ancient City Press
P.O. Box 5401
Santa Fe, NM 87502
Telephone (505) 982-8195